Museum Membership Innovation

Museum Membership Innovation

Unlocking Ideas for Audience Engagement and Sustainable Revenue

Rosie Siemer

ROWMAN & LITTLEFIELD
Lanham • Boulder • New York • London

Published by Rowman & Littlefield
An imprint of The Rowman & Littlefield Publishing Group, Inc.
4501 Forbes Boulevard, Suite 200, Lanham, Maryland 20706
www.rowman.com

6 Tinworth Street, London SE11 5AL, United Kingdom

British Library Cataloguing in Publication Information Available

Library of Congress Cataloging-in-Publication Data Available

ISBN 978-1-5381-1472-8 (cloth: alk. paper)
ISBN 978-1-5381-1473-5 (pbk. : alk. paper)
ISBN 978-1-5381-1474-2 (electronic)

∞™ The paper used in this publication meets the minimum requirements of
American National Standard for Information Sciences—Permanence of Paper
for Printed Library Materials, ANSI/NISO Z39.48-1992.

For Ryan

Contents

List of Figures and Tables

FIGURES

LIST OF TABLES

Foreword

Museums are facing increasingly challenging times, times of financial change, changing culture trends, and changing societal and institutional needs. The historic shift in audience demographics, mindsets, and motivations are compounded by changes in government funding, endowment losses, and corporate support models.

Rosie Siemer outlines this new reality with expertise and grace, encouraging difficult conversations, the true necessity for experimentation, and offers thought leadership and case studies with practical application.

The title of the book refers to membership. But it's so much more than membership. This is the only book I'm aware of that touches on every part of the visitor journey at a museum; it's the most comprehensive audience engagement resource available. Every chapter made me more excited to work in this field than the last. Most of us in the sector know that membership is flat or declining. What does this mean for our audiences? Does this mean audiences are less loyal? Or that they just are looking for a different way to participate? Rosie does a great job adapting ideas from many different museums and other industries. It is well-researched and includes many thought leaders in the case studies, providing for practical and applicable examples.

I cannot underestimate the necessity of this book for anyone in the museum field. In addition to being forward-looking, it is also very thoughtful about the roles and opportunities for museums in this time. Using data, as well as her own experience in branding, marketing, business strategy, and nearly a decade of museum audience development leadership, Rosie addresses how museum leaders must hone their empathic skills in these challenging times. And what better place than museums for this empathy to happen.

I think Rosie is brave to not just accept the status quo for museums, and we should all be inspired by this opportunity. She addresses the "silos and sacred cows" that museums need to wake up to in order to address our own biases with metrics or changing cultures.

To remain viable, we have to adapt. Rosie makes the point that the average lifespan of a business model has fallen from 15 years to 5 years. What does this say about our 100 year plus business model in museums? Without adapting the practices in this book museums will be left behind.

Rosie doesn't claim to have all the answers. This is not a road map for what every museum leader should do. Rather, she sets the case for, and starts the dialog about, the future of museum audiences and membership. She challenges us all to begin to experiment. And not with low risk incremental change, but to try bold new ideas and develop cultures of innovation.

I know you, as a reader, will benefit from the insights of this book as much as I did.

Kristin Prestegaard
Chief Engagement Officer
Minneapolis Institute of Art

Preface

Once upon a time, there was a highly profitable company with millions of members. Through an incredibly successful and stable business model, the company became a leader in its category. In fact, it dominated the market. When customers thought of where to rent a movie, this was the company that was top of mind. Over the course of 15 years, the company established an enviable position as the number one movie rental company in the US. Yet, as it continued to enjoy seemingly effortless increases in market share and soaring profits, a quiet yet momentous shift was under way.

In 1999, while the company sat perched on its mountaintop, fat and happy, a newcomer competitor began nibbling away at its market share. Over the next seven years, consumers began to embrace a new way of renting movies—via the mail rather than through bricks-and-mortar retail locations. As word of mouth spread, more and more of the company's customers began to try this new movie-by-mail service. In a very short amount of time, a significant number of the company's customers had migrated to a small, upstart competitor. In 2007, seeking to adapt to consumers' rapidly changing preferences, the company launched its own rent-by-mail program. But it was too late. By the time the company adjusted its business model to respond to the evolving market, its customer base had eroded beyond repair. Three years later, the company filed for bankruptcy.

If you haven't guessed by now, I'm talking about the slow, agonizing death of the movie and video game rental giant, Blockbuster, and the rise of media titan Netflix. At the time of its bankruptcy filing in 2010, critics lamented that the demise of Blockbuster was a clear case of a company not seeing the technology trends that were disrupting its industry. In reality, technology wasn't at the root of Blockbuster's failure. Blockbuster succumbed to its own arrogance and refusal to listen to its audience. As columnist Jonathan Salem

Baskin remarked, "Blockbuster didn't lose its customers to Netflix or digital; they'd already long ago stopped belonging to the company in anything other than name. Membership meant nothing, or nothing good."[1] Blockbuster stopped innovating. The company was no longer listening to its customers and was ignoring critical pain points in the movie rental experience that Netflix was eager to solve.

With the benefit of looking back, we can see that Blockbuster's downfall did not result from customers deciding to stop renting from its bricks-and-mortar stores and start renting from Netflix via the mail. Instead, consumers were attracted to the new idea of unlimited, late fee–free movie rentals that Netflix's monthly subscription offered, and they began to move away from Blockbuster's pay-per-rental model. Netflix succeeded by solving an unmet need of Blockbuster's customers. For context, Netflix launched its live streaming service in 2007, the same year Blockbuster introduced its too-little-too-late DVD-by-mail program. That is, Netflix was already addressing the future needs of its growing customer base while Blockbuster was still reeling from the advent of the movie-by-mail concept Netflix introduced back in 1999.

While technology certainly played a role, the true cautionary lesson of the fateful tale of Blockbuster is that organizations that become complacent ultimately don't survive. In many ways, Blockbuster's failure was a result of its success. Because it was such a well-oiled machine with a strong customer base and an established business model, the company struggled to recognize that it was no longer meeting the needs of its customers. It became complacent and irrelevant.

THINKING DIFFERENTLY ABOUT MEMBERSHIP

In *The Innovator's Dilemma*—one of the most influential books ever written about innovation—author and Harvard Business School professor Clayton Christensen chronicles the unexpected, yet ultimately predictable, failure of several successful, well-managed companies. In his research, Christensen discovered that, as the marketplace shifts and the competitive landscape changes, good companies get increasingly better at serving the needs of current customers. Unfortunately, the practices that allow a company to become successful in the first place (e.g., listening to customers, establishing efficiencies, properly allocating resources, etc.) are, in fact, the very activities that risk self-annihilation by failing to be responsive to the needs of future customers. That is, the way decisions get made in successful organizations "sows the seeds of eventual failure," causing the innovator's dilemma.[2] Solving this perplexing problem requires a holistic rethink of the business model. While

Christensen's research focused primarily on disruptive technologies, the lesson of why well-established organizations become obsolete is one worth learning, as it has broader implications for why innovation is so important to long-term sustainability.

The first decade of the twenty-first century was a turbulent time for arts and culture organizations. While the economy has stabilized in recent years, the global financial crisis of 2008 left deep and lasting wounds that forced museums to adapt to a new normal. And, although many industries have slowly recovered from the Great Recession, the cultural sector is confronting increasingly worrisome financial distress. Declining attendance and stagnant (or, in many cases, decreasing) membership totals are widespread. Operating costs are rising, and funding sources are drying up. Overreliance on "block-busters" is creating an unsustainable cycle of boom and bust. In addition, museums are struggling to attract and retain new and different audiences. At the same time, massive shifts in demographics and lifestyles are bringing rapid changes in consumer behavior that threaten the survival of the museum business model—and these trends are particularly pronounced in membership.

Museums are part of a much larger leisure marketplace; however, their products, marketing strategies, and internal structures do not reflect this reality. Looking ahead, it is clear that we are entering a period of significant challenge for museums. Competition for leisure activities and culture-type experiences are growing exponentially in the mind of the consumer. From streaming video to food trucks, it is becoming increasingly difficult for museums to compete for time, attention, and dollars. Additionally, as consumers become more discriminating, they have a heightened expectation that products and services will be tailored to meet their individual needs. Yet museums continue to operate with a twentieth-century mindset of standardized, mass production—especially when it comes to membership.

The one-size-fits-all approach of the traditional membership model is out of step with the trends and expectations of today's consumer. The fundamental truths of the past no longer hold in this crowded marketplace. Change is required for museums to keep ahead of the curve and remain competitive. Thankfully, the time for taking steps to evolve has never been better. New research, bold experiments, and pioneering leaders have helped to usher in an era of fresh thinking that challenges the status quo of the traditional membership model.

A FRAMEWORK FOR INNOVATION

In my role as a strategic advisor and marketing partner to museums, I have encountered three persistent obstacles that I believe are holding cultural organizations back: First, old solutions are regularly prescribed to address new problems. Second, the marketing strategies employed are often wasteful and ineffective in achieving long-term results. Third, innovation is lagging when it comes to product development in membership. Despite the sincere intentions of museum professionals and their dedicated teams of advertising agencies, direct mail consultants, and market research partners, we have reached a critical juncture where business as usual will not serve us going forward. Regrettably, many well-meaning professionals have unknowingly been working under a set of assumptions that no longer hold true.

In writing this book, my aim is to provide an exploration of the ways in which the concept of membership is evolving in the museum space. Drawing from a wide range of research spanning the disciplines of behavioral economics and consumer psychology, this book offers insights into the trends shaping the future of museum membership. By exploring not only *how* organizations are adapting their membership programs but also *why*, the findings presented on the following pages affirm an urgent need for innovation in membership to more effectively engage with our current and future audiences. With an emphasis on the principles of design thinking and the lean startup methodology, the framework for innovation provided in this book serves as a guide to making thoughtful adjustments to existing membership programs and outlines a process for the creation of entirely new offerings to engage new and nontraditional audiences. Ultimately, my goal is to establish a preliminary thesis in which to begin a robust dialogue about the future of membership.

I intentionally take a broad view of membership innovation—from small experiments in messaging to large, full-scale program revamps. Importantly, the word *membership* is used throughout as a catchall term that encompasses the traditional model of membership (as described in chapter 3), as well as the many variations of the concept that reflect an expanding definition of membership. Building on the nine practices identified by The Wallace Foundation for successful audience-building programs (as shown in Figure 0.1), I advocate for development of an innovation practice that includes market research, experimentation, validated learning, organizational alignment, and preparing for growth.[3] Above all, I envision adoption of rapid prototyping, real-world testing, and continuous iteration that will allow museums to develop new audience-centric offerings.

The ideas presented in this book are not intended to be prescriptive. Rather, I seek to introduce practical principles and a methodology for innovation that have allowed organizations of all types to create, reinvent, and thrive. Armed with a framework for innovation, I hope to support museums in evolving their offering to attract and retain new audiences. By establishing a forward-looking, creative process for product development, I advocate for

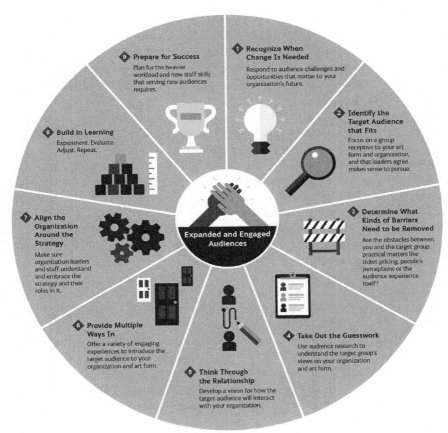

Figure 0.1. Nine Effective Practices of Audience-Building Programs

The Wallace Foundation, *The Road to Results: Effective Practices for Building Arts Audiences* available for free at www.wallacefoundation.org/knowledge-center/pages/the-road-to-results-effective-practices-for-building-arts-audiences.aspx.

an empathy-first approach that prioritizes the needs and desires of audiences. And through a discussion about creating a culture that fosters innovation, I promote the need for rethinking organizational structures, roles, systems, and metrics to encourage risk taking, collaboration, and agility.

LOOKING FOR THE BRIGHT SPOTS

In difficult times, our brains instinctively focus on the problem—fixating on what's wrong rather than looking for what's working well. In *Switch: How to Change Things When Change Is Hard*, authors Chip and Dan Heath describe how humans are hardwired to analyze problems, not success. While it feels a bit counterintuitive, identifying the things that are working today (no matter how small) and taking the time to understand why they are working is the first step in making progress. The Heath brothers refer to these glimmers of success as "bright spots." Bright spots are the early efforts that show promise and are worth emulating.

Encouraged by my colleagues from the field, I decided to go in search of examples and stories of bright spots in the museum sector. The bright spots featured in this book underscore the idea that big solutions can come from small steps. By selecting the particular case studies that I did, I am not suggesting that the programs or institutions profiled are the exemplar of successful innovation or that they are the *most* innovative ideas. Rather, I chose to share case studies that highlighted a range of approaches, as well as diversity in type of institution. My focus is on how and why the innovation happened to gain insight into practices that can be modeled by others. Importantly, innovation is not always about growing the fastest or achieving the biggest membership program possible. Every organization is unique, and each museum's goals are different. Finally, I also share stories from outside the museum sector to illustrate opportunities for creativity in engaging new audiences and to highlight broader consumer trends.

In addition, I've included sections labeled "sparks" throughout this book. The goal of a spark is to fuel conversation, ignite ideation, and serve as a catalyst for critical thinking about a particular topic. A spark may include a thought experiment or an exercise to encourage exploration of an idea. Many sparks are simply questions designed to foster open and curious dialogue.

WHO THIS BOOK IS FOR

I've structured this book with 12 chapters grouped into three parts. Part One provides an overview of the state of the industry and a review of trends shaping the future of museums. Part Two discusses opportunities for innovation and includes insights and examples from industry leaders, the behavioral and social sciences, and the fields of membership and marketing. Part Three covers how to get started building an innovation practice by putting the principles of design thinking and the lean startup methodology to work.

Presented as both a philosophy and a practical how-to, this book will help museum leaders to implement a continuous innovation practice at an institution-wide level, within a specific department, or in a team setting. Emphasis is placed on new audience development, marketing strategies, and bridging the gaps between non-visitor, visitor, donor, and member.

For Museum Directors, Organizational Leaders, and Board Members, this book offers insight into the opportunity and power of innovation in reaching and retaining new audiences. It will help you champion innovation at your institution and build a culture that encourages risk-taking, collaboration, and audience-centric thinking.

For Audience Development, Membership, Marketing, Advancement, and Visitor Services Professionals, this book is a call to action to think differently about your role and internal processes and how you define success. Within these pages you will find inspiration and ideas for where to begin experimenting, as well as guidance on how to push back on the status quo within your department and across the organization. Use this book as a resource to help you write the future of your museum.

For Foundations, Corporate Partners, and Philanthropists, your continued commitment to museums makes innovation possible. By funding initiatives that allow museums to take risks, you directly support the experimentation and learning necessary to build a sustainable future. This book offers you insight into the challenges facing today's museums and suggests areas of opportunity for driving innovation in the industry.

For Consultants and Agencies, through your talents and influence as trusted advisors to your clients, you will be at the forefront of the innovation movement. This book will help you better serve your clients by focusing on the right metrics, more effectively directing precious marketing dollars, and investing in long-term solutions. In partnership with your clients, this book will help you to participate in a new kind of conversation that creates a space for taking risks and asking difficult questions.

For Academics, Researchers, and Students, your importance in the museum field cannot be understated. Many of the topics explored in the following pages are limited by a lack of available research and published results. Your passion and thinking are needed to unlock the true potential of what is to come. There is a significant need for further research into the concepts presented in this book to fully understand the impact of innovation in the field of membership and museum audience development. This book is only a starting point for a much bigger discussion that you will help guide.

A NOTE ABOUT THE NUMBERS

Data referenced in this book are the most recent and authoritative available at the time of writing. Even so, much of the research cited is already out of date due to the investment of money and time required to fund large-scale studies. Where possible, I have included sources that offer more timely data or a different perspective. Importantly, my review found a significant gap in research regarding the motivations and perceptions of museum members. Further, much of the research publicly available is derived from self-reported data by museums or from audience surveys, neither of which are an ideal source for truly objective information. Finally, while the research presented here focuses primarily on the US and UK markets, many of the trends and takeaways are shared with museums worldwide.

LIMITATIONS AND ASSUMPTIONS

My perspective on innovation is shaped by my professional background as a researcher, consultant, and marketer. More specifically, my interest in innovation is expressly directed in the areas of membership and audience development. While I discuss key opportunities for collaborative product development and testing to better satisfy audience needs, my specific expertise is not in the areas of curatorial, interpretation, or program evaluation. Therefore, I do not attempt to address these aspects of the museum visitor experience. Instead, I aim to introduce a set of foundational principles and a framework that can be adapted and customized to spur continuous innovation across the museum. In particular, I advocate for a more dynamic and collaborative approach to strategic planning that invites a wide range of perspectives from across departments, as well as from external stakeholders.

Because there is a broad lexicon to describe various aspects and functions of the museum field, it will be helpful to review how I, personally, define the following terms. Of course, these are not definitive definitions but rather an attempt to create a shared language for engaging in the new conversations taking place in the museum field.

- *Museum:* As defined by the Institute of Museum and Library Services (IMLS), "Museums include, but are not limited to, aquariums, arboretums, art museums, botanical gardens, children's/youth museums, general museums (those having two or more significant disciplines), historic houses/ sites, history museums, natural history/anthropology museums, nature centers, planetariums, science/technology centers, specialized museums (limited to a single distinct subject), and zoological parks."[4]
- *Product:* In this book, I use the term *product* to describe anything a museum offers to its audiences, whether tangible or not. The programs, offerings, experiences, events, physical goods, and services that satisfy a need or desire are all considered products. Often, a product, such as membership, is comprised of a combination of both tangible goods and intangible services.

- *Membership:* At its core, when you strip away the decorative marketing and the obligatory protocol, membership is simply a product. And like any other product, it is designed to satisfy the needs of a particular audience. Throughout this book, I call out the need for something "other" than membership. In some cases, other refers to a marketing approach—a different word, pricing structure, or messaging framework to describe the existing features of the typical membership program. In other cases, the notion of other is an entirely different offering that allows audiences to engage with the organization in new and different ways. Because this is an emerging area of study, an industry-standard definition for these nascent concepts does not yet exist.
- *Member:* A person who has subscribed, donated, or purchased a membership (or similar product). In recent years, the definition of a member has expanded to include participants in something other than traditional membership, such as free membership, loyalty programs, affinity groups, giving programs, subscriptions, advocacy, and season passes.
- *Donor:* An individual who has contributed money without an expectation of receiving a product in exchange.
- *Visitor:* A person who has visited a museum in the past, currently visits museums, or will visit a museum in the future.
- *User:* A person who accesses the museum's website, mobile app, social media, or other digital property. In some cases, users may also be members who benefit from their membership through access to exclusive content or offerings available via a digital platform.
- *Consumer or Customer:* While some in the nonprofit field consider the term a dirty word, the fact is that we are all consumers. We all have needs, goals, and desires. Successful nonprofits are market driven and understand that they need to have a customer-centric mindset to create value and remain relevant. Throughout this book, I use the terms *consumer*, *customer*, *member*, *donor*, *visitor*, *user*, and *audience* interchangeably. They all pay their money (or give their money, or spend their time, or exchange something else of value, such as their attention, their data, or their voice) to an organization with the expectation that the museum will cocreate value with them to help solve their problems and realize their goals.
- *Audience Development:* As defined by the Arts Council of England, "Audiences can include visitors, readers, listeners, viewers, participants, learners, users of a product, and people who buy works of art and publications."[5] Therefore, the act of audience development is any "activity to help develop relationships with new and existing audiences. It can include aspects of marketing, commissioning, programming, involvement in decision making, education, customer care, and distribution."[6] Because audience development is very much an evolving term, museums are actively defining this concept by doing.

- *Audience Engagement:* A topic of much debate, engagement is a relative term that can mean many different things depending on whom you ask. One definition offered in the National Center for Arts Research (NCAR) report published by SMU DataArts at Southern Methodist University characterizes engagement as the aggregate number of "total touch points" of all stakeholder interactions, both in person and virtually.[7] Another definition of engagement offered by authors Anne Bergeron and Beth Tuttle is "the myriad ways that institutions build trust and loyalty, create meaningful experiences and learning, and invite, enable, and nurture relationships with and among people."[8] The International Audience Engagement Network (IAE) declares that "Audience engagement champions the emotional and social relationship between audiences and museums to sustain their future" and defines audience engagement as "any function or set of functions within museums whose core mandate is focused on the strategy, planning, delivery and evaluation of relationship-building with audiences, including the key points of interaction between visitors and a museum."[9] I use the term *engagement* to describe any valuable action taken by an individual, with the meaning of *valuable* to be defined by each organization. Thus, a new email subscriber may be considered as engagement to one museum, while donating may be tracked as engagement by another. Put another way, if audience development describes a specific activity designed to meet the needs of existing or potential audiences, audience engagement, then, is the desired outcome of a successful audience development strategy.

The concepts introduced in this book are not intended to be a substitute for a long-range institutional strategic plan or to serve as a stand-alone audience development plan. That said, I do expect that the ideas presented will and should challenge the efficacy of the conventional approach to marketing and membership planning.

GETTING STARTED

Few people have the good fortune to discover their life's passion, let alone build a career around it. I am extremely lucky to have the opportunity to blend my love of arts and culture, behavioral science, marketing, design, and technology into my work in audience development and membership. My goal in writing this book is to ignite new and necessary thinking among my colleagues in the museum field so that, together, we can answer one of our industry's most important questions: Are we actively designing our offerings to meet the needs of tomorrow's audiences?

As you dig into the concepts, methods, and questions presented throughout this book, I invite you to explore further research, musings, and idea sharing at membershipinnovation.com. Let's get started!

NOTES

1. Jonathan Salem Baskin, "The Internet Didn't Kill Blockbuster, the Company Did It to Itself," *Forbes*, November 8, 2013, https://www.forbes.com/sites/jonathan salembaskin/2013/11/08/the-internet-didnt-kill-blockbuster-the-company-did-it-to -itself/#6cb9f62b6488.

2. Clayton M. Christensen, *The Innovator's Dilemma: The Revolutionary Book That Will Change the Way You Do Business* (New York, NY: HarperCollins Publishers, 2011), xv.

3. Bob Harlow, "The Road to Results: Effective Practices for Building Arts Audiences," The Wallace Foundation (2014), 5, www.wallacefoundation.org/knowledge -center/pages/the-road-to-results-effective-practices-for-building-arts-audiences.aspx.

4. "Museums," Eligibility Criteria, Institute of Museum and Library Services, accessed September 25, 2019, https://www.imls.gov/grants/apply-grant/eligibility -criteria.

5. "Audience Development and Marketing," Arts Council National Lottery Project Grants Information Sheet, Arts Council England, published February 12, 2018, https://www.artscouncil.org.uk/sites/default/files/download-file/Information_sheets_ Audience_development_marketing_Project_grants.pdf, 3.

6. Ibid.

7. "Total Engagement and In-Person Engagement Index," Community Engagement, SMU DataArts, accessed September 25, 2019, http://mcs.smu.edu/artsre search2014/reports/community-engagement/what-reach-our-community-engage ment-first-looking-person-and-virtual#.

8. Anne Bergeron and Beth Tuttle, *Magnetic: The Art and Science of Engagement* (Washington, DC: The AAM Press, 2013), 60.

9. "International Audience Engagement Network, The Melbourne Group Meeting 15–16 March 2018 Melbourne, Australia," The IAE Melbourne Group, accessed September 25, 2019, https://www.ngv.vic.gov.au/wp-content/uploads/2018/07/2018_ IAE_Report.pdf, 4.

Acknowledgments

This book is the result of many inspired conversations, meaningful collaborations, and shared experiences over the past 10 years that are too numerous to list here. I am deeply grateful to my museum colleagues and the institutions who generously shared their time, their wisdom, and their stories. Listed in alphabetical order by organization, my warmest thanks to Spencer Jansen, Arkansas Arts Center; Cari Maslow, Carnegie Museums of Pittsburgh; Lisa Townsend and Erika Howse, Children's Museum of Indianapolis; Gabriel Mastin, Columbus Museum of Art; Tamara Wootton Forsyth and Ingrid Van Haastrecht, Dallas Museum of Art; Ashley Alexander, Denver Museum of Nature & Science; Sarah Owens, Exploratorium; Melissa Dietrich, Longwood Gardens; Kristin Prestegaard, Minneapolis Institute of Art; Brad Ingles, Museum of Contemporary Art Denver; Megan Bernard and Julia Propp, Museum of Fine Arts, Boston; Grace Meils and Mattie Wethington, Newfields; Jennifer Thomas, Saint Louis Art Museum; and William Harris, Kim Parker, and Amy Marks, Space Center Houston. Without their contribution and support this project would not have been possible.

I would like to express my deepest gratitude to Aidan Vega, Carrie Glassburn, Claire McKee, Jeff Spitko, John Lewis, Julie Aldridge, Lynn Swain, Meghan McCauley, and Rachel Broom, for their thoughtful input, constructive comments, and warm encouragement.

To the many individuals and organizations that invest in the museum industry and share their insights with the aim of raising all ships, thank you for your enduring support of the arts, culture, and conservation. In particular, I would like to thank the American Alliance of Museums; American Museum Membership Conference (AMMC); American Public Gardens Association; Association of Art Museum Directors; Association of Zoos & Aquariums; Colleen Dilenschneider, Chief Market Engagement Officer, IMPACTS

Research & Development; International Museum Membership Conference (IMMC); LaPlaca Cohen; SMU DataArts; and The Wallace Foundation.

I am indebted to Jon LaFloe, who diligently designed and formatted all of the graphics for this book. My deepest appreciation goes to Emily Boyle for her thorough review, invaluable comments, and attention to detail. And to the team at Rowman & Littlefield Publishers, thank you, Charles Harmon and Erinn Slanina, for your patience, support, and graciousness.

I would like to give special thanks to my family, whose love and encouragement are with me in whatever I pursue. To my husband and thought partner, Ryan, who dedicated countless hours of "Prime Ryan Time" to reviewing drafts and providing insightful feedback—you asked all the right questions, clarified my thinking, and challenged me to be courageous. I am forever grateful for your love and support.

PART ONE

Chapter One

New Realities

Today's museums are facing increasingly worrisome financial distress that threatens the survival of institutions that are unsure of how (or unwilling) to adapt. Over the past 25 years, the arts and culture sector has experienced a roller-coaster ride of inconsistent government funding, unprecedented endowment losses, unpredictable corporate support, and increased competition for philanthropic dollars.[1] While many sectors have recovered from the global financial crisis of 2008, the ripple effect of the Great Recession has left an indelible mark on the financial health of museums.

According to a 2018 special report commissioned by *Grantmakers in the Arts*, arts philanthropy researcher Steven Lawrence states that "support for the arts has fluctuated during the tumultuous period between 2000 and 2014. Unlike in prior economic downturns, where the arts showed consistency and resilience, an examination of recent arts and culture revenue and public and private funding suggests that the arts as they are traditionally perceived may represent a diminishing priority for foundation and corporate donors. While the nominal value of support for arts and culture in the United States remains impressive, relative to changes in support for other priorities, the arts have unquestionably lost ground."[2] Coupled with increasing operational costs, sharp declines in attendance, and shrinking membership numbers, this decline of philanthropic and public funding support means museum leaders are finding their institutions under greater financial pressure.

DOWNTREND IN CULTURAL ATTENDANCE

One of the most alarming trends facing the sector is the overall decline in cultural attendance. According to the National Endowment for the Arts

(NEA), attendance at art museums across the US has been steadily dropping over time. Participation in "benchmark" arts activities, including jazz
performances, classical music performances, operas, musical and nonmusical
plays, ballets, and visits to art museums or galleries, has been on a steady decline since 1992.[3] Analysis by the American Academy of Arts and Sciences'
Humanities Indicators supports this trend, showing that just 24 percent of
Americans report visiting a museum or art gallery in 2017.[4]

Importantly, while art museums comprise about only 5 percent of all
American museums, this downtrend in attendance is not isolated to art museums.[5] Indeed, the overall decline in cultural participation is bolstered by
SPPA data that indicate only 28 percent of US adults visited a historic site
in 2017, 8.9 percentage points lower than in 1982.[6] Further, findings from
a 2017 study by research firm IMPACTS suggest that museum attendance
is not keeping pace with US population growth. According to data collected from 224 museums and analyzed alongside results from the *National
Awareness, Attitudes, and Usage Study*, IMPACTS reports that traditional
visitors to cultural organizations are leaving the market at a faster rate than
they are being replaced. Colleen Dilenschneider, chief market engagement
officer at IMPACTS, refers to this phenomenon as "the negative substitution of the historic visitor," explaining that "for every one historic visitor
who leaves the US market (by way of death, relocation, or migration), they
are being replaced by only 0.948 of a person (by way of birth, relocation,
or immigration)."[7] Thus, museums in the US are suffering from a net loss
in attendance due to the effect of negative substitution.

Thankfully, the news isn't all bad. Many museums have bucked the trend
of declining visitation with strong growth in recent years. Worldwide, museum visits reached record levels in 2018 driven by the immense popularity
of temporary exhibitions and grand openings.[8] Additionally, many of the
UK's museums have seen an uptick in attendance. According to data from the
Department for Culture, Media and Sport, the number of visits to the UK's
major museums and galleries rose by 6 percent between April and October
2018 compared to the same period in 2017, reversing a previous downtrend in
visitation that occurred between 2015 and 2017.[9] However, this upward trend
did not apply to all sites. For instance, visitation at the British Museum was
down 5 percent from the prior year, and attendance declined by 29 percent
at Tate Modern and 26 percent at Tate Britain as both museums saw visitor
numbers normalizing after record visitation the previous year.[10] Overall, declines in museum attendance have remained persistent since 2014, despite the
short-term lift of so-called blockbuster exhibitions.[11]

THE BOTTOM LINE

Exacerbating the challenge of declining attendance, museums also are struggling with the increasing costs associated with day-to-day business. The Association of Art Museum Directors found that, to make ends meet, art museums overwhelmingly relied on contributions from donors and funders, public funding, and returns on endowments accounting for 63.5 percent of their revenue in 2017.[12] Troubling data from SMU DataArts and the National Center for Arts Research (NCAR) shows that it has become more difficult for arts and cultural organizations to break even because revenue has not kept pace with growing expenses.[13] Between 2010 and 2016, per capita revenues at cultural organizations increased by 17.3 percent while average per capita operating expenses increased by 27.1 percent.[14]

Analysis shows that, in 2016, the average cultural organization had a virtually breakeven operating surplus before depreciation equal to just 0.4 percent of total expenses, calculated by stripping away nonoperating funds that are often not available for regular day-to-day business, such as investment gains and capital campaign proceeds.[15] Another way to look at the financial health of a cultural organization is to examine operating surplus after depreciation, which includes depreciation, a noncash expense that estimates the annual loss in value of fixed assets. As shown in Figure 1.1, when including depreciation, the average cultural organization had an operating deficit equal to −4.2

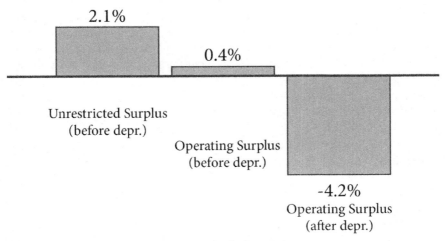

2.1%

0.4%

Unrestricted Surplus
(before depr.)

Operating Surplus
(before depr.)

-4.2%
Operating Surplus
(after depr.)

Figure 1.1. 3 Ways to Evaluate the Financial Bottom Line

SMU DataArts | the National Center for Arts Research exists to empower arts and cultural leaders with high-quality data and evidence-based resources and insights that help them to overcome challenges and increase impact. Visit www.culturaldata.org.

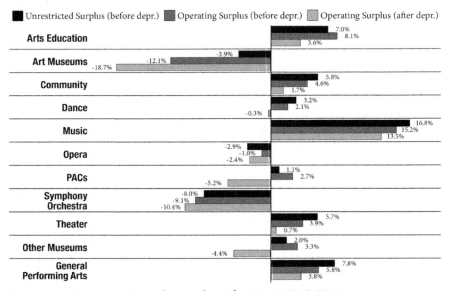

■ Unrestricted Surplus (before depr.)   ■ Operating Surplus (before depr.)   ☐ Operating Surplus (after depr.)

Arts Education	7.0% 8.1% 3.6%
Art Museums	-3.9% -12.1% -18.7%
Community	5.8% 4.6% 1.7%
Dance	3.2% 2.1% -0.3%
Music	16.8% 15.2% 13.5%
Opera	-2.9% -1.0% -2.4%
PACs	1.1% 2.7% -5.2%
Symphony Orchestra	-8.0% -9.1% -10.4%
Theater	5.7% 3.9% 0.7%
Other Museums	2.0% 3.3% -4.4%
General Performing Arts	7.8% 5.8% 3.8%

Figure 1.2.   By Sector, Operating Surplus (After Depr) 2013–2016

SMU DataArts | the National Center for Arts Research exists to empower arts and cultural leaders with high-quality data and evidence-based resources and insights that help them to overcome challenges and increase impact. Visit www.culturaldata.org.

percent of expenses, indicating that organizations are not currently bringing in the surplus funds needed to replace fixed assets as they wear out.[16]

SMU DataArts notes that the trend in deteriorating operating surplus within the cultural sector is a result of revenue growth not keeping pace with increasing expenses over time. Art museums, symphony orchestras, operas, and other museums showed the most severe operating deficits among all sectors (Figure 1.2).[17]

Another troubling fact is that museums tend to invest more per visitor than they charge for admission and amenities. According to data reported in *Art Museums by the Numbers*, in 2017 the amount spent by visitors per museum visit (including the cost of admissions and purchases at museum stores and restaurants) was only $8, while museums invested an average of $55 per visitor (Figure 1.3).[18]

With few exceptions, the news is littered with doom-and-gloom reports of undercapitalized expansions, empty galleries, and museums in financial distress. Many museums are doing what they can to cut costs, including hiring freezes, layoffs, and offering fewer programs. In 2018, the *Evening Standard* reported that 24 staff members at the National Portrait Gallery agreed to con-

Figure 1.3. Revenue vs. Expense per Visitor
Courtesy of the Association of Art Museum Directors.

tract buyouts, equating to a 7 percent reduction in staff, "to make sure that we are as efficient as possible, to streamline our core costs and ensure we are in the best possible shape for the future."[19]

In extreme cases, museums are shuttering operations or auctioning off artwork to stay afloat. The *New York Times* reported that auto museums across the country are closing at a rapid pace as their benefactors "get bored, tire of losing money or die."[20] Under intense criticism, the Berkshire Museum in Pittsfield, Massachusetts, began auctioning off part of its collection in 2018 to address the fiscal crisis caused by decades of financial losses that, according to news reports, amounted to annual budget shortfalls averaging $1.15 million for the past 10 years.[21] In the UK, more than 64 museums have closed since 2010—15 in 2016 alone—largely due to decreases in public funding.[22] Many publicly funded UK museums are facing a substantial funding crisis with government spending declining 31 percent between 2010 and 2016.[23] Expressing an unsettling viewpoint that reflects the general state of the sector, Van Shields, executive director of the troubled Berkshire Museum, agonized about the decision to deaccession part of its collection, asserting, "We can't care for our collection if we don't exist."[24]

This bleak new economic reality is taking a toll on the museum sector. Without a drastic and immediate intervention, more and more institutions are at risk of stumbling into a financial tailspin. Strategizing ways to engage new and diverse audiences is one path that will allow museums to thrive in uncertain times.

NOTES

1. Steven Lawrence, "Arts Funding at Twenty-Five: What Data and Analysis Continue to Tell Funders about the Field," Grantmakers in the Arts, Special Report, *GIA Reader* 29, no. 1 (Winter 2018): 8.

2. Ibid.

3. National Endowment for the Arts et al., "A Decade of Arts Engagement: Findings from the Survey of Public Participation in the Arts, 2002–2012," *NEA Research Report* 58 (January 2015): 3.

4. "Art Museum Attendance," Other Humanities Programs and Institutions for the Public, Humanities Indicators, updated August 2019, https://www.humanities indicators.org/content/indicatordoc.aspx?i=102#fig417.

5. "Museum Universe Data File FY 2014 Q3," Institute of Museum and Library Services, accessed September 25, 2019, https://www.imls.gov/assets/1/AssetMan ager/MUDF_TypeDist_2014q3.pdf.

6. "Historic Site Visits," Other Humanities Programs and Institutions for the Public, Humanities Indicators, updated August 2019, https://humanitiesindicators .org/content/indicatordoc.aspx?i=101.

7. Colleen Dilenschneider, "Negative Substitution: Why Cultural Organizations Must Better Engage New Audiences FAST (DATA)," *Know Your Own Bone*, January 25, 2017, https://www.colleendilen.com/2017/01/25/negative-substitution-why -cultural-organizations-must-better-engage-new-audiences-fast-data/.

8. Emily Sharpe and José Da Silva, "Art's Most Popular: Here Are 2018's Most Visited Shows and Museums," *The Art Newspaper*, March 24, 2019, https://www .theartnewspaper.com/analysis/fashion-provides-winning-formula.

9. Jessica Browne-Swinburne, "Visitor Numbers Boom at Nationals in North of England," *The Museums Association*, September 1, 2019, https://www.museums association.org/museums-journal/news/09012019-visitor-figures-dcms-2018.

10. Ibid.

11. Martin Bailey, "Is the UK Museum Boom Over?," *The Art Newspaper*, March 26, 2018, https://www.theartnewspaper.com/news/is-the-uk-museum-boom-over.

12. Association of Art Museum Directors, *Art Museums by the Numbers 2018*, 6, https://aamd.org/sites/default/files/document/Art%20Museums%20by%20the%20 Numbers%202018.pdf.

13. "Unrestricted and Operating Bottom Line," The Bottom Line Report, SMU DataArts, accessed September 25, 2019, http://mcs.smu.edu/artsresearch2014/re ports/bottom-line/Bottom-Line#.

14. Colleen Dilenschneider, "The Increasing Costs of Running Cultural Organizations (DATA)," *Know Your Own Bone*, March 28, 2018, https://www.colleendilen .com/2018/03/28/increasing-costs-running-cultural-organizations-data/.

15. "Unrestricted and Operating Bottom Line," The Bottom Line Report, SMU DataArts, accessed September 25, 2019, http://mcs.smu.edu/artsresearch2014/ reports/bottom-line/Bottom-Line#.

16. Ibid.

17. Ibid.

18. Association of Art Museum Directors, *Art Museums by the Numbers 2018*, 9, https://aamd.org/sites/default/files/document/Art%20Museums%20by%20the%20Numbers%202018.pdf.

19. Robert Dex, "National Portrait Gallery Axes 7% of Its Staff as Visits Fall by a Third," *Evening Standard*, April 18, 2018, https://www.standard.co.uk/go/london/arts/national-portrait-gallery-axes-7-of-its-staff-as-visits-fall-by-a-third-a3816806.html.

20. Steve Friess, "In the Car Museum Race, Some Drop Out," *New York Times*, May 10, 2018, https://www.nytimes.com/2018/05/10/business/car-museums-closing.html.

21. Carrie Saldo, "Two Rockwells Headed to Auction to Fund New Vision for The Berkshire Museum," *The Berkshire Eagle*, July 12, 2017, http://www.berkshireeagle.com/stories/two-rockwells-headed-to-auction-to-fund-new-vision-for-the-berkshire-museum,513284.

22. Museums Association, *Museums in the UK 2017 Report*, 5, https://www.museumsassociation.org/download?id=1219029.

23. Ibid.

24. Colin Moynihan, "Berkshire Museum's Planned Sale of Art Draws Opposition," *New York Times,* July 25, 2017, https://www.nytimes.com/2017/07/25/arts/design/berkshire-museum-art-auction-criticized.html.

Chapter Two

Microtrends and Major Shifts

Museums are at the precipice of a historic shift in audience demographics, mindset, and motivations. Myriad changes are culminating seemingly all at once: rapid technology emergence and adoption, cultural promiscuity, misconceptions and negative perceptions about cultural nonprofits, and the arrival of the most racially and ethnically diverse generation in US history.[1] A fundamental transformation is under way that will undeniably disrupt all aspects of the museum business—especially in the areas of marketing and membership.

THE NEXT GREAT GENERATION

According to projections by the US Census Bureau, the US population is projected to increase to 404 million by 2060, with adults aged 65 years and older on track to outnumber children for the first time by 2035.[2] Moreover, the US will become a "minority white" nation by 2045 at which point whites will comprise 49.7 percent of the population in contrast to 24.6 percent for Hispanics, 13.1 percent for blacks, 7.9 percent for Asians, and 3.8 percent for multiracial populations.[3] Much of this shift is being driven by the emergence of the millennial generation—defined as those born between 1981 and 1996.[4]

Millennials, over 75 million strong and representing nearly a quarter of the US population, have eclipsed the baby boomer generation in both size and influence. Comprised of a 44 percent minority demographic,[5] millennials are poised to become a potent force in the American social, economic, and political landscape with a spending power estimated at a staggering $1.4 trillion by 2020.[6] However, cultural institutions across the US have been challenged with reaching and engaging younger audiences. Data from the *National Awareness, Attitudes, and Usage Study* show that, while millennials are the most likely to become repeat museum visitors (they represent 30.9 percent of US cultural attendance), this demographic segment is underserved by museums by nearly 24 percent compared to the overall US population.[7] Only 21.9 percent of adult millennials visited a cultural organization in 2015.[8] It is no exaggeration that the future livelihood of the cultural sector depends on museums' ability to engage this critical audience.

They've never licked a postage stamp, and they've always been able to "Google it" if they didn't know the answer.[9] Meet the graduating class of 2019, the starting point for the first generation of post-millennials. Born after 1996, Generation Z, also known as Gen Zs or *Pivotals*, will soon account for 40 percent of the consumer market, and they are already flexing their influence as they take their first steps into adulthood.[10] The first generation to grow up completely digital, Gen Zs are truly mobile first, often feel overwhelmed by the amount of advertising they see, and are more likely than older generations to have installed some form of ad blocking technology.[11]

Gen Z represents a generation that is passionate about music, addicted to social media, and attracted to interactive marketing that allows them to cocreate or make decisions.[12] They are also a generation of social activists, with 60 percent expecting brands to take a stand on issues such as human rights, race, and sexual orientation.[13] Undeniably, the attitudes and behaviors of Gen Z will impact how the marketing landscape and museum business model develop in the coming years. If museums are to remain solvent in the decades to come, they will need to ensure that their content, experience, marketing, and offerings are desirable to future generations.

At the same time, museums are struggling to attract traditionally underrepresented audiences, including Hispanics and African Americans. According to the National Endowment for the Arts (NEA), although Hispanics and African Americans represent 14.9 percent and 11.4 percent of the US population, respectively, they comprise only 9.4 percent and 8.5 percent of all visitors to art museums.[14] While there are many theories and studies under way to explain *why* these differences in racial and ethnic patterns in museum attendance exist, the indisputable fact is that they are real. It is encouraging to note that, overall, museums are seeing an uptick in participation from diverse audiences. Take the Metropolitan Museum of Art, which increased its participation among nonwhite American visitors from 21 percent in 2007 to 27 percent in 2017.[15]

The NEA reported that African Americans, aged 18 to 24 and 35 to 44, and adults who received only "some college" education contributed to an increase in art museum attendance between 2012 and 2017.[16] Further, growth in visitation to places with historic or design value was boosted by women; African Americans and non-Hispanic whites, aged 35 to 44; and those whose formal education stopped with a high school diploma or a college degree.[17] However, this positive trend is muted when compared to total population figures. Museums should be striving to attract diverse audiences at a representative rate relative to the population. Without a substantial and immediate intervention to correct the disparity, the museums of tomorrow may well find their galleries (and coffers) empty.

THE MISSING AUDIENCE

The ways in which audiences perceive and participate in culture are also changing. Contrary to the common fiction that cost is a chief barrier to cultural participation, several landmark studies have firmly debunked this myth. Findings from the 2017 Culture Track study reveal that the primary barrier of cultural participation is a feeling that cultural activities are "not for someone like me."[18] Data from IMPACTS substantiate this claim, finding that approximately 4 in 10 people don't feel that they belong at an art, science, or history museum.[19] These negative perceptions are troubling as museums seek to attract new audiences.

Commissioned by the NEA, the groundbreaking report *When Going Gets Tough: Barriers and Motivations Affecting Arts Attendance* provides insight into the crucial "missing audience"—a not-so-trivial 31 million Americans who have expressed an interest in the arts but, for one reason or another, have not participated. While cost was certainly a factor (38.3 percent), the NEA found that lack of time was the number one barrier to participation (47.3 percent).[20] This was particularly true for parents, of whom nearly 60 percent said lack of time was the greatest single barrier to attendance.[21] Thus, museums are competing not only for share of wallet but also for *attention*—arguably the most finite resource in today's fast-paced, always-on, time-strapped world.

Inaccessibility (described as difficulty in getting to the museum) also was cited by many as a significant barrier to participation. Others stated not having a companion to go with was a strong barrier to attending a museum. Of particular interest, the NEA found that among interested nonattendees, "Mexican-Americans and non-Hispanic Blacks and African Americans more often said not having someone to go with prevented their attendance." Results from the Culture Track study reinforce these findings, identifying top-of-mind awareness, inconvenience, and not having anyone to go with as the greatest barriers to cultural participation.[22] Moreover, people of color were 82 percent more likely than non-Hispanic whites to state that cultural activities often do not "reflect people of all backgrounds" and that this lack of diversity is a barrier to participation.[23] Consequently, there are significant perception, logistic, and emotional factors affecting the decision to participate in the arts that need to be addressed in order to engage new audiences. These findings come at a critical time as racial and ethnic disparities in museum participation move to the forefront.

MINDSET AND MICRO-MOMENTS

Against a backdrop of historic demographic transformation, museums are grappling with a shift in consumer mindset. The cultural landscape is struggling to adapt amid emerging technologies, evolving social norms, and intensifying consumer expectations. In particular, museums have been caught off guard by rapid changes in lifestyle dynamics, family structure, technology adoption, and consumer behavior. Millennials (and post-millennials beginning with the rise of Gen Z) have very different attitudes, interests, and motivations than generations before them. Depending on which study you reference, millennials are either too lazy or too resourceful, too narcissistic or too globally minded, too optimistic or too cynical.

While it is unfair to shoehorn an entire generation into a neatly packaged archetype, there are unique markers, collective characteristics, and formative events that come together to create a shared generational mindset. Although generational study is more art than science, consensus among researchers has found the millennial mindset to be well defined when it comes to a desire for experiences that are interactive, immersive, seamless, and participatory. For better or worse, millennials' expectations and attitudes have deeply influenced a future that is already taking shape. This is an important must-not-ignore fact for museum leaders as they consider the needs and expectations of next-generation audiences.

Aside from the much-discussed nuances associated with millennials and their proclivities, there also are several emerging trends in consumer behavior, technology, and marketing that will have a universal impact across generations. Among these are personalization, data protection, customer centricity, and "micro-moments"—a term coined by Google to describe the growing number of potential brand touchpoints consumers experience on a daily basis. Key to them all are digital experiences. As the global research firm Forrester warned in its 2018 trends report, "Digital transformation is not elective surgery. It is the critical response needed to meet rising customer expectations, deliver individualized experiences at scale, and operate at the speed of the market."[24] Unfortunately, many museums and other nonprofits are falling behind in digital infrastructure and lagging in technology adoption.[25]

Other major trends affecting museums include household composition and attitudes related to marriage, sexuality, parenthood, and relationships. As attitudes have moved away from the old-fashioned concepts of the traditional family unit, life-stage milestones, and gender roles, many museum membership programs have failed to keep pace in reflecting these changes. For example, millennials are likely to live in multigenerational households (32 percent), and there is a growing trend toward co-living, or "doubled-up households," consisting of two or more working-aged adults living together who are not married or in a romantic relationship.[26] Millennials also are more than twice as likely as older Americans to identify as LGBTQ and much more likely (63 percent) to be allies of the LGBTQ community.[27] Additionally, the ageing of the baby boomer generation will generate a surge in the proportion of elderly Americans requiring museums to think differently about their offering and experience. As the majority of the global population begins to age, the number of people aged 65 years and older is projected to increase more than 60 percent by 2030 while youth populations will remain nearly flat.[28] These fundamental changes in lifestyles, interests, and needs require museums to adopt new approaches to content delivery, accessibility, membership benefits, pricing, and programming.

MEET THEM WHERE THEY ARE

At a time of unprecedented demographic and attitudinal change, museums must look toward intentional and thoughtful strategies for developing new audiences. If the current patterns in arts participation remain unchanged, museums risk irrelevancy and, ultimately, financial collapse.

The culmination of these momentous microtrends and tectonic demographic shifts illuminates the clear need for immediate investment in cultivating new audiences, as well as a radical transformation of the traditional membership model. If museums are going to remain viable in the future, adaptation is not an optional business strategy. Increasing engagement among new audiences requires that museums be prepared to meet audiences *where they are*, as opposed to waiting for new audiences to simply come around to becoming participants. Lastly, while some cultural organizations are enjoying strong attendance and ever-higher membership numbers, this is no time for complacency. Investing in developing alternative offerings to attract new audiences and better serve current members will be critical to ensuring the long-term sustainability of all institutions.

NOTES

1. Jillian Steinhauer, "Study Finds US Cultural Consumers Are Social and Promiscuous," *Hyperallergic*, April 28, 2014, https://hyperallergic.com/123030/study-finds-us-cultural-consumers-are-social-and-promiscuous/.

2. "Older People Projected to Outnumber Children for First Time in U.S. History," Newsroom, US Census Bureau, last updated September 6, 2018, https://www.census.gov/newsroom/press-releases/2018/cb18-41-population-projections.html.

3. William H. Frey, "The US Will Become 'Minority White' in 2045, Census Projects," The Brookings Institution, March 14, 2018, https://www.brookings.edu/blog/the-avenue/2018/03/14/the-us-will-become-minority-white-in-2045-census-projects/.

4. Michael Dimock, "Defining Generations: Where Millennials End and Generation Z begins," Pew Research Center, January 17, 2019, http://www.pewresearch.org/fact-tank/2018/03/01/defining-generations-where-millennials-end-and-post-millennials-begin/.

5. William H. Frey, "The Millennial Generation: A Demographic Bridge to America's Diverse Future," The Brookings Institution, January 2018, https://www.brookings.edu/research/millennials/.

6. Christopher Donnelly and Renato Scaff, "Who Are the Millennial Shoppers? And What Do They Really Want?," Accenture, accessed September 25, 2019, https://www.accenture.com/us-en/insight-outlook-who-are-millennial-shoppers-what-do-they-really-want-retail.

7. Colleen Dilenschneider, "Real Talk: Why Cultural Organizations Must Better Engage Millennials (DATA)," *Know Your Own Bone*, January 13, 2016, https://www.colleendilen.com/2016/01/13/real-talk-why-cultural-organizations-must-better-engage-millennials-data/.

8. Ibid.

9. Tom McBride, "The Beloit College Mindset List: Class of 2019 (Born 1997!)," *The Mindset Lists*, August 17, 2015, http://themindsetlist.com/2015/08/the-beloit-college-mindset-list-class-of-2019-born-1997/.

10. Nicolas Cole, "Is Marketing to Millennials Confusing? Just Wait. Generation Z Is Right around the Corner," *Inc.*, July 6, 2017, https://www.inc.com/nicolas-cole/is-marketing-to-millennials-confusing-just-wait-ge.html.

11. Lucy Handley, "Generation Z Likely to Avoid Advertising, Use Ad Blockers and Skip Content: Study," *CNBC*, January 11, 2017, https://www.cnbc.com/2017/01/11/generation-z-avoids-advertising-uses-ad-blockers-and-skips-content.html.

12. Kantar Millward Brown, *AdReaction: Engaging Gen X, Y and Z*, 2017, 9.

13. Barkley, Inc et al., "Getting to Know Gen Z: How the Pivotal Generation Is Different from Millennials," 19, http://www.millennialmarketing.com/2017/01/show-me-says-gen-z-pivotals-want-proof/.

14. National Endowment for the Arts et al., "A Decade of Arts Engagement: Findings from the Survey of Public Participation in the Arts, 2002–2012," *NEA Research Report* 58 (January 2015), 4, https://www.arts.gov/sites/default/files/2012-sppa-jan2015-rev.pdf.

15. Colleen Dilenschneider, "Why Some Cultural Organizations Overestimate Success in Welcoming Diverse Visitors," *Know Your Own Bone*, February 14, 2018, https://www.colleendilen.com/2018/02/14/cultural-organizations-overestimate-success-welcoming-diverse-visitors/.

16. National Endowment for the Arts et al., "US Trends in Arts Attendance and Literary Reading: 2002–2017," September 2018, 8, https://www.arts.gov/sites/default/files/2017-sppapreviewREV-sept2018.pdf.

17. Ibid.

18. LaPlaca Cohen, *Culture Track '17* (New York, NY 2017), 13, https://culturetrack.com/wp-content/uploads/2017/02/CT2017-Top-Line-Report.pdf.

19. Colleen Dilenschneider, "Cultural Organizations Are Still Not Reaching New Audiences (DATA)," *Know Your Own Bone*, November 8, 2017, https://www.colleendilen.com/2017/11/08/cultural-organizations-still-not-reaching-new-audiences-data/.

20. National Endowment for the Arts et al., "When Going Gets Tough: Barriers and Motivations Affecting Arts Attendance," *NEA Research Report* 59 (January 2015), 15, https://www.arts.gov/sites/default/files/when-going-gets-tough-revised2.pdf.

21. Ibid., 2.

22. LaPlaca Cohen, 13.

23. Ibid., 15.

24. Forrester, *Predictions 2018: A Year of Reckoning*, 2, https://go.forrester.com/wp-content/uploads/Forrester-2018-Predictions.pdf.

25. Zoe Amar, "Charities Could Lose a Third of Staff If They Don't Get a Grip on Digital Skills," *The Guardian*, March 23, 2017, https://www.theguardian.com/voluntary-sector-network/2017/mar/23/charities-lose-third-staff-digital-skills.

26. Richard Fry, "For First Time in Modern Era, Living with Parents Edges Out Other Living Arrangements for 18- to 34-Year-Olds," Pew Research Center, May 24, 2016, http://www.pewsocialtrends.org/2016/05/24/for-first-time-in-modern-era-living-with-parents-edges-out-other-living-arrangements-for-18-to-34-year-olds/; and "Share of Adults Living with Roommates Higher than Ever Before," Press Releases, Zillow, December 14, 2017, http://zillow.mediaroom.com/2017-12-14-Share-of-Adults-Living-with-Roommates-Higher-than-Ever-Before.

27. GLAAD, *Accelerating Acceptance 2017*, 5, http://www.glaad.org/files/aa/2017_GLAAD_Accelerating_Acceptance.pdf.

28. Wan He, Daniel Goodkind, and Paul Kowal, US Census Bureau, International Population Reports, P95/16-1, *An Aging World: 2015*, US Government Publishing Office, Washington, DC, 2016, https://census.gov/content/dam/Census/library/publications/2016/demo/p95-16-1.pdf.

Chapter Three

The Writing on the Wall

Cracks are beginning to form in the foundation of the traditional membership model at cultural organizations. This anxiety-inducing reality is a frequent topic of industry conferences and candid conversations because many in the field are questioning whether membership, as it exists today, will be viable in the future.

A TIPPING POINT

The consensus from several studies indicates that across the cultural sector, membership is in decline. Over the past several years, there has been a flat or downward trend in membership with "less than a quarter of cultural audiences holding either a membership or a subscription to a visual or performing arts organization" in 2017.[1] This trend indicates that cultural organizations have "reached a tipping point, where new models for cultural loyalty must be developed in order to forge meaningful relationships with audiences."[2] An analysis of more than 3,000 organizations supports this trend, finding that growth in membership and subscriptions has not kept pace with inflation. As shown in Table 3.1, earned revenue from subscriptions and memberships increased just 4.4 percent in absolute terms between 2010 and 2013, equating to a −2.4 percent drop when adjusted for inflation.[3]

Memberships and admissions combined account for approximately 13 percent of museum revenue.[4] However, individual and family memberships as a percentage of total contributions have been trending downward over the past several years—decreasing from 21 percent in 2014 to 19 percent in 2016, as shown in Table 3.2.[5]

Table 3.1. Relational Earned Revenue Index Trend

(3,115 Organizations)	2010	2011	2012	2013	2010–2013 Change	2010–2013 Change, adjusted for inflation
Arts Education	**1.4%**	**1.3%**	**1.3%**	**1.2%**	**-0.2%**	
Ave. Membership/Subsc. Revenue	$19,348	$18,706	$19,380	$18,469	-4.5%	-10.8%
Ave. Total Expenses (before depreciation)	$1,389,226	$1,479,036	$1,511,703	$1,582,560	13.9%	6.5%
Art Museums	**5.8%**	**6.3%**	**6.0%**	**6.2%**	**0.4%**	
Ave. Membership/Subsc. Revenue	$739,261	$860,298	$861,835	$865,699	17.1%	9.4%
Ave. Total Expenses (before depreciation)	$12,789,186	$13,617,852	$14,273,021	$13,895,897	8.7%	1.5%
Community	**2.4%**	**3.0%**	**3.0%**	**2.9%**	**0.6%**	
Ave. Membership/Subsc. Revenue	$21,027	$27,054	$27,383	$29,090	38.3%	29.3%
Ave. Total Expenses (before depreciation)	$883,783	$898,801	$925,318	$988,347	11.8%	4.5%
Dance	**6.9%**	**6.8%**	**6.3%**	**6.2%**	**-0.7%**	
Ave. Membership/Subsc. Revenue	$87,553	$87,008	$88,260	$87,697	0.2%	-6.4%
Ave. Total Expenses (before depreciation)	$1,267,290	$1,287,699	$1,397,573	$1,422,807	12.3%	4.9%
Music	**6.3%**	**5.7%**	**5.6%**	**5.4%**	**-0.9%**	
Ave. Membership/Subsc. Revenue	$20,312	$19,140	$19,590	$19,673	-3.1%	-9.5%
Ave. Total Expenses (before depreciation)	$320,977	$335,829	$352,248	$363,797	13.3%	5.9%

Opera	**14.4%**	**12.7%**	**12.4%**	**13.4%**	**-1.0%**	
Ave. Membership/Subsc. Revenue	$1,388,102	$1,225,281	$1,301,161	$1,212,418	-12.7%	-18.4%
Ave. Total Expenses (before depreciation)	$9,637,663	$9,640,987	$10,531,511	$9,078,102	-5.8%	-12.0%
PACs	**3.3%**	**3.3%**	**4.0%**	**4.0%**	**0.7%**	
Ave. Membership/Subsc. Revenue	$254,443	$268,942	$308,470	$304,709	19.8%	11.9%
Ave. Total Expenses (before depreciation)	$7,824,715	$8,089,120	$7,693,278	$7,699,548	-1.6%	-8.0%
Symphony Orchestras	**14.4%**	**13.6%**	**12.3%**	**13.3%**	**-1.1%**	
Ave. Membership/Subsc. Revenue	$593,357	$557,595	$578,476	$576,778	-2.8%	-9.2%
Ave. Total Expenses (before depreciation)	$4,117,262	$4,085,690	$4,700,323	$4,334,026	5.3%	-1.6%
Theatre	**15.5%**	**15.0%**	**14.6%**	**15.0%**	**-0.5%**	
Ave. Membership/Subsc. Revenue	$278,910	$280,805	$289,733	$299,421	7.4%	0.3%
Ave. Total Expenses (before depreciation)	$1,799,762	$1,870,473	$1,982,102	$1,991,686	10.7%	3.4%
Other Museums	**5.5%**	**5.4%**	**5.5%**	**5.6%**	**0.1%**	
Ave. Membership/Subsc. Revenue	$285,580	$297,301	$315,564	$319,987	12.0%	4.7%
Ave. Total Expenses (before depreciation)	$5,214,927	$5,474,561	$5,720,199	$5,707,648	9.4%	2.3%
General Performing Arts	**6.3%**	**6.1%**	**7.8%**	**6.1%**	**-0.2%**	
Ave. Membership/Subsc. Revenue	$74,435	$69,999	$97,575	$74,062	-0.5%	-7.0%
Ave. Total Expenses (before depreciation)	$1,173,661	$1,142,814	$1,253,659	$1,207,317	2.9%	-3.9%

SMU DataArts | the National Arts Center for Arts Research exists to empower arts and cultural leaders with high-quality data and evidence-based resources and insights that help them to overcome challenges and increase impact. Visit www.culturaldata.org.

Table 3.2.   Contributions to Art Museums

Source	2014	2015	2016
Individual and family memberships	21%	20%	19%
Corporate memberships	2%	2%	2%
Individual and family contributions	33%	32%	33%
Corporate contributions	11%	11%	12%
Foundations and trusts	21%	23%	21%
Benefit events	13%	13%	12%

Courtesy of the Association of Art Museum Directors.

TO JOIN OR NOT TO JOIN

What about the reasons for becoming a museum member? Research indicates that traditional members value six key benefits: free admission, belonging, supporting the organization, contributing to mission impact, exclusive access to events, and member discounts.[6] Of note, younger audiences express different motivations for joining. While free admission is still ranked as the number one benefit across audience segments, the primary benefits of membership for millennials are less transaction based, emphasizing instead more mission-oriented concepts, such as belonging, supporting, and impact.[7]

Compounding the complexity of membership trends is the industry's growing reliance on big-ticket temporary exhibitions, or so-called blockbusters. Mounting evidence suggests that the short-term success of attracting new members and recapturing lapsed members is largely based on the fleeting popularity of temporary exhibitions, rather than on long-term relationships and enduring value. A blockbuster-centric approach often creates a negative cycle of boom and bust. That is, heavy visitation and a spike in membership numbers during a special exhibition often drop off sharply the following year. Unfortunately, reliance on blockbusters to prop up attendance and membership numbers is a risky business proposition, leading to extremely expensive exhibitions and investment in marketing campaigns that are not a reliable or sustainable source of revenue for the institution.

In 2018, James Bradburne, director of Milan's Pinacoteca di Brera, told the *Financial Times*, "We lost our way in the '80s when directors were forced to use blockbusters to drive a museum's economy by increasing visitor numbers. Now they have become a drug because without them a museum won't be able to survive, but that betrays the very nature of our stewardship of the collections."[8] Museums are using blockbuster and special exhibitions as a hook to market membership, thereby creating an artificial lift in new member acquisition, renewals, and rejoins that are driven solely by the allure of novelty. Data show that 60.8 percent of lapsed members will postpone rejoining "until there is a new exhibit."[9] Thus, museums are inadvertently training members and prospective members to respond only when there is the lure of a new exhibition.

Notably, new research reveals a disconnect between the concepts of membership, loyalty, and philanthropy. Membership often is viewed by those in the museum field as an indicator of loyalty and philanthropic propensity. However, data indicate that approximately 50 percent of US museum attendees considered membership a consumer transaction—not charitable giving.[10] Yet audiences also seek relationship-focused values in a membership, including trustworthiness, quality, and a high level of customer service above the more transactional aspects of membership, such as discounts and product-related benefits.[11] Research also finds that parents, in particular, are more interested in joining membership programs that simplify their planning, offer on-site services such as childcare, and provide access to other organizations.[12]

BRIGHT SPOT: DMA FRIENDS AT THE DALLAS MUSEUM OF ART

Free membership is a topic of much debate in the industry. In 2013, the pioneering Dallas Museum of Art launched with much fanfare "the nation's first free museum membership program" with a goal of activating engagement and building long-term relationships with its visitors.[1] In a refreshing example of creativity, the Dallas Museum of Art (DMA) team dreamed up a bold and innovative idea aimed at broadening interest and encouraging repeat visitation to the museum.

The program, labeled DMA Friends, used a model similar to a frequent-flier program with an accrued point system that allowed members to earn credits that could be redeemed for rewards, such as dining discounts, access to special programs, and free event tickets. Funded by a multiyear grant, DMA Friends required only an email address to enroll. Introduced simultaneously with DMA Friends, the museum's DMA Partners program offered a philanthropic structure designed to garner support from individuals, corporations, and foundations. Two years after launching the DMA Friends program, the DMA announced that it had enrolled an astounding 100,000 visitors in the program with 96.8 percent of DMA Friends self-identifying as new members at the museum.[2] However, the total number of paid memberships decreased by 15 percent from 15,119 households in 2014 to 12,869 households in 2015.[3] On December 31, 2017, the DMA quietly ended its DMA Friends program and returned to a traditional paid membership model.[4]

There are many lessons to be learned from the DMA's bold experiment in audience engagement. First, museums must embrace the risk of failure.

Without trying new approaches to engage new audiences, the industry will surely suffer the fate of all who fail to innovate. Second, while the program was well funded, the metrics to gauge success may not have been the right measures. That is, an increase in attendance alone is not necessarily a marker of long-term engagement. Finally, due to the scale of the experiment, there was no room for iterative improvement. The museum went all in on an idea that was not grounded in demonstrable evidence. In the future, museums must devise a better way to capture data that will prove out the potential of an idea without putting the existing revenue model in peril.

The rise of free admission is another strategy that is exposing broader underlying troubles for museums. According to the Association of Art Museum Directors, 59 percent of museums surveyed charge a set admission fee, 34 percent offer free admission, and 7 percent ask for a suggested donation.[5] Many museums that introduce free admission do so in the hopes that removing the barrier of cost will jump-start attendance and draw new audiences through their doors.

Museums offering free admission often cite a goal of attracting a more diverse audience through this mechanism. After doing away with its $10 admission fee, the DMA saw annual attendance swell by 23 percent, representing a 35 percent increase in first-time visitors and a 29 percent increase in minority visitors since 2008.[6] However, such a result has not been the case for most museums, as researchers have yet to find a strong correlation between museum attendance and admission fees. For example, data suggest that not only does free admission fail to drive increased attendance by underserved or affordable access audiences, but it directly cannibalizes prospective members by attracting people with a higher household income who are likely to be returning visitors.[7] Further, as study after study affirms, cost is not a primary barrier to visitation. Indeed, cost is not the primary barrier for 30 percent of interested nonattendees who prefer to spend time engaging in some other leisure activity.[8]

It is important to note that there is serious risk in wrongly associating low income with diversity. Museums must be cautious to clearly define goals for engaging new audiences to ensure that inaccurate assumptions and stereotypes don't creep into strategy decisions. Further, eliminating admission fees creates a conflict with the established value proposition of the traditional membership model by negating a core benefit of joining, namely, free admission. Clearly, free admission is not a panacea for the challenge of declining visitation and may in fact exacerbate the downtrend in membership rates.

Looking ahead, the DMA plans to continue exploring ideas for how to attract a new generation of supporters with a focus on improving diversity and inclusion. Through the DMA Friends program, the DMA found that it is possible to reach new audiences and draw them in with novelty; however, the museum learned that curiosity alone is not a sustainable engagement strategy. The museum is now taking a deeper look at how to make audience interactions more meaningful. A key initiative in this area is formalizing the visitor experience and enhancing audience engagement to build a stronger, more intentional relationship with its community. Above all, the legacy of the DMA Friends program is that it served as a catalyst for the industry, inspiring experiments in new membership models and encouraging museum leaders to embrace the discomfort of uncertainty that comes from innovation.

NOTES

1. "First-Year Enrollments in Friends & Partners Membership Programs Soar at Dallas Museum of Art," Press, Dallas Museum of Art, accessed September 26, 2019, https://www.dma.org/press-release/first-year-enrollments-friends-partners-membership-programs-soar-dallas-museum-art.

2. "Dallas Museum of Art's DMA Friends Program Home to 100,000 Members," Press, Dallas Museum of Art, accessed September 26, 2019, https://www.dma.org/press-release/dallas-museum-art-s-dma-friends-program-home-100000-members.

3. Ibid.

4. "DMA Friends," Visit, Dallas Museum of Art, accessed September 26, 2019, https://www.dma.org/visit/dma-friends.

5. Association of Art Museum Directors, *Art Museums by the Numbers 2016*, 6, https://aamd.org/sites/default/files/document/Art%20Museums%20By%20the%20Numbers%202016.pdf.

6. "Dallas Museum of Art's DMA Friends Program Home to 100,000 Members."

7. Colleen Dilenschneider, "Free Admission Days Do Not Actually Attract Underserved Visitors to Cultural Organizations (DATA)," *Know Your Own Bone*, November 4, 2015, https://www.colleendilen.com/2015/11/04/free-admission-days-do-not-actually-attract-underserved-visitors-to-cultural-organizations-data/.

8. Colleen Dilenschneider, "Breaking Down Data-Informed Barriers to Visitation for Cultural Organizations (DATA)," *Know Your Own Bone*, March 29, 2017, https://www.colleendilen.com/2017/03/29/breaking-down-data-informed-barriers-to-visitation-for-cultural-organizations-data/.

Courtesy of the Dallas Museum of Art.

GIVING AND OWNING

Adding fuel to the fire are evolving perceptions of loyalty and philanthropy. While private contributions to the arts have increased slightly since 2000, there is growing concern among those in the field that there is an impending "generational shift away from supporting the types of institutions traditionally thought of as embodying the arts in the United States."[13] Younger audiences in particular have different motivations and expectations for giving. For example, millennials expect transparency, results, recognition, and technical savvy from nonprofit organizations. And despite a strong inclination to give, research finds that millennials tend to favor causes related to education, social-need charities, animal welfare, civil rights, and the environment above arts and culture.[14]

Shaped by the aftermath of the Great Recession, millennials are described as "an emerging generation of super savers."[15] Strapped with high levels of debt, increasing housing costs, and an unstable job market, 23 percent of millennials say financial anxiety makes them physically ill on a weekly or monthly basis.[16] Thus, while millennials express positive philanthropic intentions, the reality of their circumstance may be prohibitive to giving. And while the baby boomer generation has sustained cultural organizations through donations and membership dues for decades, their money will soon be funneled toward needs such as rising healthcare costs and long-term care. Many will leave the vast majority of their assets to children and grandchildren, placing their wealth in the hands of family who do not necessarily share their passion for a particular cause or join at the same rates. Consequently, museums must focus their efforts on cultivating new bases of support from younger and nontraditional audiences.

In recent years, the idea of owning something in the traditional sense has undergone a profound evolution in what has been dubbed the "ownership shift." Driven by a widespread transformation in attitudes prizing value over possession, the ownership shift has disrupted everything from the music industry (think, Spotify and Apple Music) to the auto market. Take for example the slew of start-ups propelling the growth in car sharing—a market that is projected to surge from 5.8 million users in 2015 to 35 million in 2021.[17] Even traditional automakers, such as Ford, BMW, and Porsche, are getting in on the ownership shift by testing flexible, subscription-style car-on-demand programs to entice commitment-phobic drivers into signing up for a monthly rental plan rather than buying or leasing their next vehicle.

In the age of Netflix, Amazon, Blue Apron, and Uber, is the traditional museum membership model still viable? While there are many contributing factors at play, staying the course is not a practical strategy for reviving sluggish membership programs. Consider the following insight from a study commissioned by the League of American Orchestras: Research found that patrons are dissatisfied with subscription products as they currently exist, concluding that orchestras will need to adapt to the changing demands of consumers in order to revitalize the subscription model. Recommendations for how to combat the rapid slide in subscriptions include everything from introducing smaller curated subscriptions; offering larger customized packages; developing entirely new types of membership; and doing more to attract millennials, such as "bring-a-friend" programs, monthly installment plans, and "buy now, choose later" options for performances.[18]

ANY COLOR YOU WANT

Henry Ford proclaimed that he would "build a motor car for the great multitude." To make this goal a reality, the Model T needed to be mass-produced and affordable. As Ford perfected the assembly line, it was observed that black paint dried the fastest allowing cars to be moved out of the factory more quickly. In 1909, Ford announced to his management team that "Any customer can have a car painted any colour that he wants so long as it is black."[19] A hallmark of the Industrial Age, one-size-fits-all standardization was central to meeting the demands of mass production. With few exceptions, museums are facing a future with a slowly eroding membership base. As museums move into a customer-centric era, it will be necessary to evolve the twentieth-century model of membership toward a more personalized offering.

NOTES

1. LaPlaca Cohen, *Culture Track '17* (New York, NY, 2017), 28, https://culture track.com/wp-content/uploads/2017/02/CT2017-Top-Line-Report.pdf.

2. Ibid., 31.

3. "What Is the Relationship of Earned Relational Revenue to Expenses (before Depreciation)?," Earned Relational Revenue, SMU DataArts, accessed September 25, 2019, http://mcs.smu.edu/artsresearch2014/reports/earned-revenue/what-relation ship-earned-relational-revenue-expenses-depreciation#/averages/arts-sector.

4. Association of Art Museum Directors, *Art Museums by the Numbers 2018*, 6, https://aamd.org/sites/default/files/document/Art%20Museums%20by%20the%20 Numbers%202018.pdf.

5. Association of Art Museum Directors, 9.

6. Colleen Dilenschneider, "Mission Motivated vs. Transaction Motivated Members: What Your Cultural Organization Needs to Know (DATA)," *Know Your Own Bone*, July 6, 2016, https://www.colleendilen.com/2016/07/06/mission-motivated-vs -transaction-motivated-members-what-your-cultural-organization-needs-to-know-data/.

7. Colleen Dilenschneider, "The Membership Benefits That Millennials Want from Cultural Organizations (DATA)," *Know Your Own Bone*, December 21, 2015, https:// www.colleendilen.com/2015/12/21/the-membership-benefits-that-millennials-want -from-cultural-organizations-data/.

8. Richard Holledge, "Down with Blockbusters! James Bradburne on the Art of Running a Museum," *Financial Times*, January 22, 2018, https://www.ft.com/content/ dc3e411c-f20b-11e7-bb7d-c3edfe974e9f.

9. Colleen Dilenschneider, "Death by Curation: The Exhibit Strategy That Threatens Visitation and Cultural Center Survival (DATA)," *Know Your Own Bone*, June 17, 2015, https://www.colleendilen.com/2015/06/17/death-by-curation-the-exhibit -strategy-that-threatens-visitation-and-cultural-center-survival-data/.

10. Mike Faulk, "Falling Membership Forces Missouri History Museum to Adapt," *St. Louis Post-Dispatch*, August 19, 2016, https://www.stltoday.com/news/local/metro/falling-membership-forces-missouri-history-museum-to-adapt/article_48cc7f7e-ff4d-5b58-97d0-b78a1ee96d78.html.

11. LaPlaca Cohen, 30.

12. Ibid., 32.

13. Steven Lawrence, "Arts Funding at Twenty-Five: What Data and Analysis Continue to Tell Funders about the Field," Grantmakers in the Arts, Special Report, *GIA Reader*, 29, no. 1 (Winter 2018): 13.

14. Caitlin Reilly, "The Kids Are Alright: Millennials Reluctant to Give, But Donate Generously When They Do," *Inside Philanthropy*, May 30, 2019, https://www.insidephilanthropy.com/home/2019/5/30/the-kids-are-alright-millennials-reluctant-to-give-but-donate-generously-when-they-do.

15. Catherine Collinson, "Millennial Workers: An Emerging Generation of Super Savers," *15th Annual Transamerica Retirement Survey* (July 2014), 9, https://www.transamericacenter.org/docs/default-source/resources/center-research/tcrs2014_sr_millennials.pdf.

16. "Millennials: Conflict between Instinct to Save and Urge to Spend Is Elevating Anxiety," News Releases, Northwestern Mutual, August 10, 2017, https://news.northwesternmutual.com/2017-08-10-Millennials-Conflict-between-Instinct-to-Save-and-Urge-to-Spend-is-Elevating-Anxiety.

17. Caitlin Harrington, "Automakers Are Making Car Ownership Optional," *Wired*, May 27, 2018, https://www.wired.com/story/automakers-subscription-car-ownership-optional.

18. Oliver Wyman et al., *Reimagining the Orchestra Subscription Model*, 2015, 5, http://www.oliverwyman.com/content/dam/oliver-wyman/global/en/2015/nov/Reimagining-the-Orchestra-Subscription-Model-Fall-2015.pdf.

19. William A. Levinson, Henry Ford, and Samuel Crowther, *The Expanded and Annotated My Life and Work: Henry Ford's Universal Code for World-Class Success* (Boca Raton, FL: CRC Press Taylor & Francis Group, 2013), 54.

Chapter Four

Silos, Sacred Cows, and Spaghetti Sauce

In his popular TED Talk, best-selling author Malcolm Gladwell shares one of the greatest stories about how experimentation revealed a previously hidden market worth $600 million.[1] The story begins in the early 1980s when Campbell Soup Company, owner of the popular brand of pasta sauces known as Prego, hired experimental psychologist and psychophysicist Howard Moskowitz to help the company find "the perfect spaghetti sauce" for its customers. Recognizing there was no such thing as the perfect spaghetti sauce, Moskowitz developed 45 different types of sauce for testing.[2]

Through a process of experimentation, Moskowitz discovered that Americans fell into three distinct groups: (1) those who like plain spaghetti sauce, (2) those who like spicy spaghetti sauce, and (3) those who like extra-chunky spaghetti sauce. This was a critical insight for Campbell's because, at the time, no company offered a chunky spaghetti sauce. In other words, a full one-third of the American market was unserved.[3] Following the results of this ground-breaking research, Campbell's introduced a new line of Prego sauces featuring an extra-chunky recipe, which quickly became the best-selling brand of sauce in the country. Today, there are more than 30 formulations of Prego pasta sauce, including several varieties of Garden Harvest Chunky.

The story of Prego spaghetti sauce demonstrates the importance of testing new ideas with real customers. By allowing customers to *taste* the different sauces, Campbell's made it easy for customers to react to the various formulations and provide their feedback in real time. Now imagine if Moskowitz had instead asked customers to *read* a description of the different types of sauces and then select the one they *thought* they would like best. It would be very difficult for customers to articulate their preferences without the opportunity to experience the flavor and texture of the sauces.

In his research with Campbell's, Moskowitz found that consumers did not necessarily know they wanted chunky spaghetti sauce—until they did. As Moskowitz is fond of saying, "the mind knows not what the tongue wants."[4] Before Moskowitz came along with his innovative research techniques, the standard practice in the food industry would have been to ask people what they wanted in a spaghetti sauce. However, obtaining insight into decision-making through traditional market research methods is limited due to the difficulty of explaining the driving forces behind an individual's preferences. As an insightful Steve Jobs once said, "A lot of times, people don't know what they want until you show it to them."[5] This is why museums must be more intentional about building competency in *showing* audiences what it is they don't yet know they want.

TALK IS CHEAP

As museums look to transition to a more customer-centric business model, one of the first conventions to be upended will be market research. For decades, the standard procedure for obtaining insights into audience motivations and attitudes has been surveys, interviews, and focus groups. Unfortunately, when it comes to our preferences, we are terrible at describing what we like and why. Moreover, these methods often are unreliable and vulnerable to a variety of bias, including social desirability bias, acquiescence bias, and the halo effect. Social desirability bias occurs when respondents answer questions in a way that presents themselves in the best possible light.[6] This bias can skew results about everything, from how much individuals really care about philanthropy to what they like to do in their free time. Acquiescence response bias involves respondents' tendency to agree with anything they happen to be asked. Often referred to as "yea-saying," acquiescence bias results in respondents politely liking every idea with which they are presented. This type of bias results in ambiguous scoring and can lead to invalid conclusions about true preferences. Finally, a pesky phenomenon known as the halo effect occurs when respondents rate something positively overall due to a single, positive attribute, resulting in a systemic response error and misleading data. For instance, a recent positive experience at the museum café may influence how a member rates their overall satisfaction with their membership.

Researcher biases also can creep into a study. For example, one of the most pervasive forms of bias in market research is confirmation bias. Confirmation bias occurs when researchers form hypotheses and then use respondents' feedback to affirm that belief. Researchers also can unintentionally put words into respondents' mouths or present concepts in a way that leads to bias. Asking survey questions in a particular order may skew results due to the influence of priming respondents with words and ideas that impact their attitudes, thoughts, and feelings on subsequent topics. While researchers can minimize bias by modifying phrasing, using indirect questioning, and adjusting the order of questions, it is impossible to entirely eliminate bias in qualitative market research.

The questions researchers tend to ask are often not the questions that need to be answered. Museums need to understand the *why* behind decisions. However, because focus groups and surveys are not analogous to real-life decision-making, it is difficult for consumers to communicate why they make the choices they do. For example, asking users to explain their thought process for clicking on a digital ad will not reveal the hidden motivations that influenced their decision. We base the majority of our decisions on a number of deep emotional and instinctual factors that traditional methods of market research are not conducive to sussing out.

Museum leaders also need to be aware of the potential negative impact of asking people to explain their reasons for making a certain choice. In a fascinating study about choice satisfaction, researchers designed an experiment in which subjects chose between two types of posters, fine art and humorous kittens, to see whether people would make different choices if they were asked to describe why they liked or disliked each poster.[7] In the experiment, subjects chose the fine art posters 95 percent of the time when they did not have to explain why, but this number fell to 64 percent when they were asked to analyze their choice. Summarizing the results of the study, the researchers concluded that the findings "add to the mounting body of evidence that thinking about the reasons for one's preferences can alter decision making in nonoptimal ways." In other words, asking people to describe *why* they made a certain choice creates an artificial mental process that can actually decrease satisfaction with their decision.

TRUE BUT USELESS

One of the biggest areas of opportunity for improvement in marketing and membership is measurement. As organizations build competency in agility, museum leaders will need to become more sophisticated in articulating goals and evaluating performance. Due to a complex combination of decades-old ingrained conventional wisdom and a flood of newly accessible data, museums are inadvertently investing significant resources in measuring the wrong metrics. These "true but useless" (TBU) measures often fall into the category of "vanity metrics" because they do not demonstrate a clear cause and effect.[8] Vanity metrics make us feel good, but they don't help us to make decisions.

Because they are easy to measure, vanity metrics permeate campaign reports and infiltrate planning meetings. For instance, in the realm of digital marketing, there are myriad vanity metrics that can be used to tell a good story without providing any real guidance on what action to take next. These frequently rose-colored vanity metrics include results like number of impressions, reach, website traffic, email opt-ins, open rate, click-through rate, Facebook page likes or Twitter followers, post-engagement rate, and unsubscribe rate (to name a few). In the business of membership, there are numerous vanity metrics that masquerade as meaningful measures, such as macro-level renewal rates, generic direct mail response rates, average gift, frequency of visits, on-site conversion rate, and nearly every indicator that comes out of a member survey.

When organizations rely on vanity metrics to guide their actions, they are at risk for making bad decisions. As Eric Ries explains in *The Lean Startup*, vanity metrics tempt managers into resorting to "the usual bag of success theater tricks . . . in a desperate attempt to make the gross numbers look better."[9] For museums, the proverbial bag of success theater tricks includes a long list of tactics used by membership and marketing managers (and their agencies) to show positive, if fleeting, results. Think back to the last time your museum scrambled to push out a last-minute Facebook ad campaign to boost sales, relied on a Hail Mary direct mail campaign to meet year-end membership numbers, offered a free tote bag to convert on-site visitors to members, or discounted dues to increase renewal rates. These tactics work in the short term to pump up topline vanity metrics, but they lack the value of informing strategic decision-making and generating long-term results. Moreover, such tactics require a never-ending cycle of cash infusions because this type of promotion-driven marketing often generates unsustainable windfall sales spikes.

As you think about the things you are measuring today, ask yourself why you're tracking those specific metrics. Is it because they truly help you make strategic decisions? It's worth noting that, just because something *can* be measured, doesn't mean it *should* be measured. The only metrics museum leaders should invest time in measuring are those that help them make decisions and create long-term value—everything else is a waste of energy.

GETTING UNSTUCK

Today's museums operate in a highly unstable and rapidly changing marketplace. This uncertainty poses a significant challenge when conducting strategic planning because the traditional approach to strategy making assumes that the marketplace is relatively predictable. That is, conventional membership planning relies heavily on assumptions based on the past performance of prior marketing efforts to forecast revenue projections. This overreliance on historical performance to guide future strategy can lead an organization to "achieve failure"—a phrase Ries defines as "successfully, faithfully, and rigorously executing a plan that turned out to have been utterly flawed."[10] To combat the risks associated with traditional strategic planning, museums must pivot toward a more dynamic, customer-oriented approach in which new ideas are constantly tested and evaluated in real time. This transition toward an experimental planning process requires that museums adopt an entrepreneurial mindset to enable the organization to innovate and respond quickly to new opportunities. Doing so can be a challenge for an organization that is deeply set in its ways, but museum leaders can take small steps that will lead to big impact over time.

Silos present yet another challenge to museum innovation. As museum leaders seek to reinvent their business model, they must begin with deep customer empathy and open communication across all divisions of the organization. Unfortunately, when it comes to stifling innovation, silos happen to be insidiously effective—creating blind spots that impede customer service, suppress product development, and spoil marketing opportunities. Too often, a museum's organizational systems, people, and processes unintentionally reinforce departmental competitiveness and actively work against collaboration.

Whether consciously or not, museum leaders encourage the formation of silos by not aligning departmental priorities and addressing conflict. This lack of esprit de corps across departments fosters a culture that breeds resentment, team rivalry, and infighting. In particular, "silo mentality," or the act of deliberately withholding information from other departments, is especially detrimental to innovation.[11] Manifesting in the form of turf wars, sabotage, and a lack of transparency between departments, a silo mentality results in a breakdown of trust among teams. Examples of silo mentality in museums are vast: the email list that is "owned" by the marketing department, the website that overwhelms users with a flood of departmentally focused content, the admissions associate who doesn't talk to visitors about membership, the accounting philosophy that won't accommodate monthly memberships, the membership campaign that sidesteps the marketing department, arbitrary rules regarding on-site signage—the list goes on. To thrive in tomorrow's marketplace, museum leaders need to work to foster a culture of innovation—one that encourages risk-taking, champions shared goals, and promotes genuine collaboration.

Looking ahead, museums face challenges in attempting to reach new audiences. Chief among these obstacles is the declining efficacy of advertising and an increased scrutiny of privacy controls. It is estimated that the average consumer is bombarded with marketing messages—up to 10,000 a day—leading to frustration with advertising that is irrelevant, intrusive, and annoying.[12] As advertisers compete for attention, consumers are getting better at tuning out the noise. Ad blockers, "banner blindness," and a general mistrust of advertisers is making it more difficult (and more expensive) to be effective. Moreover, growing concerns about privacy and new legislation aimed at curtailing advertising techniques such as behavioral data tracking are stamping out the utility of countless marketing tactics.

At a time when adaptation should be paramount, many in the museum profession remain trapped in the comfort of the familiar using and reusing the same approaches with the hope that what works today will keep working tomorrow. Indeed, the comfort of entrenched thinking can lead us to ignore information that contradicts our deeply held beliefs. As Roger Craver, co-editor of the influential fundraising blog *The Agitator*, astutely observes, nonprofit leaders are at risk of falling victim to "learning traps" that stand in the way of new thinking. Craver postulates that this causes many nonprofits to get "stuck in a flat or declining cycle because their fundraisers never change the business model because they are unable—or unwilling—to see information that does not conform to their perspective."[13]

Organizational muscle memory makes it difficult to unlearn old habits. Yet, as author Saul Kaplan describes in *The Business Model Innovation Factory*, "the half-life of a business model is declining," requiring more frequent reinventions for any business to remain viable.[14] Museums are not immune to this reality. To keep ahead of changing market conditions, museums will need to develop their capabilities to innovate, building new departmental interdependencies and organizational competencies, as well as actively focusing on diversity, equity, accessibility, and inclusion. In particular, as museums become more representative of the communities they serve, new voices will help shape the direction of audience engagement initiatives. Moreover, as more millennials join the workforce, their perspective will offer museums a unique opportunity to embrace a new mindset.

Ultimately, the remedy for getting unstuck and positioned to engage new audiences is the ability to embrace the discomfort that comes with letting go of old ideas, practices, and perspectives—even those that have worked well and contributed to our success in the past. As museums seek to reach new audiences, marketing and membership professionals must evolve from the outdated role of "product pushers" into a consultative, cocreator of meaningful experiences that satisfy audience needs. To succeed, every aspect of the membership program must be on the table for evaluation—from the value proposition and benefits to pricing and how we measure success. Innovation requires a hearty mix of curiosity, humility, and adaptability and necessitates a willingness to challenge sacred cows—to push back on those precedents and assumptions that no longer hold true. By challenging the status quo, Howard Moskowitz not only helped Campbell's identify an immense untapped market; he introduced the company to an innovation mindset.

NOTES

1. Malcolm Gladwell, "Choice, Happiness, and Spaghetti Sauce," TED, February 2004, https://www.ted.com/talks/malcolm_gladwell_on_spaghetti_sauce.

2. Malcolm Gladwell, "The Ketchup Conundrum," *The New Yorker*, August 29, 2004, https://www.newyorker.com/magazine/2004/09/06/the-ketchup-conundrum.

3. mike@mymedialabs.com, "Mind Genomics Explained: What's in the Secret Sauce?," Howard Moskowitz, July 23, 2014, http://howardmoskowitz.com/mind-genomics-explained-whats-in-the-secret-sauce/.

4. Gladwell, "The Ketchup Conundrum."

5. "Steve Jobs: 'There's Sanity Returning," *Business Week*, May 24, 1998, https://www.bloomberg.com/news/articles/1998-05-25/steve-jobs-theres-sanity-returning.

6. Olena Kaminska and Tom Foulsham, "Understanding Sources of Social Desirability Bias in Different Modes: Evidence from Eye-Tracking," Institute for Social & Economic Research Working Paper Series, no. 2013-04 (March 2013), 1, https://www.iser.essex.ac.uk/research/publications/working-papers/iser/2013-04.pdf.

7. Timothy D. Wilson, Douglas J. Lisle, Jonathan W. Schooler, Sara D. Hodges, Kristen J. Klaaren, and Suzanne J. LaFleur, "Introspecting about Reasons Can Reduce Post Choice Satisfaction," *Personality and Social Psychology Bulletin* 19, no. 3 (June 1993): 331–33.

8. In their best-selling book *Switch: How to Change Things When Change Is Hard*, authors Chip and Dan Heath recount the story of Jerry Sternin with Save the Children, who arrived in Vietnam in 1990 to fight malnutrition and was told "You have six months to make a difference." It was known that malnutrition was the result of a complex set of issues, including poor sanitation, poverty, a lack of clean water, and ignorance about nutrition. However, in Sternin's view, these facts were TBU—true but useless in the fight against childhood starvation.

9. Eric Ries, *The Lean Startup* (New York: Crown Business, 2011), 128.

10. Ibid., 22.

11. Will Kenton, "Silo Mentality," Business Essentials, Investopedia, updated June 25, 2019, https://www.investopedia.com/terms/s/silo-mentality.asp.

12. Jon Simpson, "Finding Brand Success in the Digital World," *Forbes*, August 25, 2017, https://www.forbes.com/sites/forbesagencycouncil/2017/08/25/finding-brand-success-in-the-digital-world/#3b2eaed7626e.

13. Roger Craver, "The Fundraisers I Fear," *The Agitator*, September 10, 2018, http://agitator.thedonorvoice.com/fundraisers-to-fear/.

14. Saul Kaplan, *The Business Model Innovation Factory: How to Stay Relevant When the World Is Changing* (Hoboken, NJ: John Wiley & Sons, Inc., 2012), 4.

PART TWO

Chapter Five

Making the Future

McDonald's sells a lot of milkshakes. Curiously, about half of these milk-shakes are sold before 8:30 in the morning. Researchers observed that the people who purchased a morning milkshake from McDonald's all exhibited the same characteristics and behaviors—they were always alone, the milk-shake was the only thing they bought, and they always got into their car and drove away with the milkshake.[1] This got researchers wondering, why do these particular customers choose to buy a milkshake in the morning? And, if McDonald's wants to increase sales of milkshakes, what would be the best strategy to accomplish this goal?

MILKSHAKES AND MOTIVATIONS

It is a very common practice for organizations to segment their market by customer demographics, product characteristics, and other criteria such as psychographics and past behavior. Yet there is more going on behind the buying decision-making process that these simplistic data points don't reveal. As renowned scholar and founder of modern marketing Theodore Levitt declared, "People don't want to buy a quarter-inch drill. They want a quarter-inch hole!"[2] This profound concept is at the heart of the Jobs to Be Done (JTBD) theory, and it's one of the most overlooked aspects of audience development among museum professionals.

The JTBD theory refers to a consumer's decision to buy something as "hiring" a particular product or service to do a specific job. This unique way of describing consumer behavior shifts the focus of product development away from shallow customer descriptors (like age, income level, or family structure) toward more meaningful motives that influence behavior. Thus, the introduction of a new vocabulary to describe consumer behavior serves to help marketers home in on the underlying motivations behind purchase decisions. As Harvard Business School professor Clayton Christensen explains, "every job people need or want to do has a social, a functional, and an emotional dimension. If marketers understand each of these dimensions, then they can design a product that's precisely targeted to the job."[3]

As it turns out, the people "hiring" a McDonald's milkshake in the morning were all commuters who needed something to eat that would fill them up while keeping them awake on their long, boring drive into work. With this broader context of the "job" needing to be done, we can quickly see that McDonald's competition for morning customers is not just other milkshakes or even other fast food restaurants that serve breakfast. Instead, McDonald's is competing against all other options that satisfy the job of providing an energy boost that lasts the duration of the morning commute. For these customers, the milkshake could just as easily have been substituted for some other snack, such as a bagel, a breakfast sandwich, or even a bowl of oatmeal (albeit a bit more difficult to eat with one hand while driving!). In the end, morning commuters who chose a milkshake preferred it over other options for a number of reasons: It was sugary, it lasted through the entire drive time, it was easy to drink in the car, and it was cheap and convenient to buy. It did the job.

It's worth noting that, if McDonald's had gone about its product development process in the conventional way, holding focus groups and asking people what would make a better milkshake, the company would have missed a key insight that revealed the hidden needs of these particular customers. By observing its morning customers in the real world and taking time to understand the *why* behind their behavior, McDonald's was able to learn about the job needing to be done.

BRIGHT SPOT: NEWFIELDS AND
THE EIGHT JOBS OF LEISURE

In the iconic 1989 film, *Field of Dreams,* Kevin Costner plays an Iowa corn farmer named Ray Kinsella who hears a mysterious voice telling him "If you build it, he will come." While Ray interpreted this statement as an instruction to build a baseball field, museum leaders should be heeding the call to build a customer-first business model.

An example of a museum heeding the call to become more audience centric by utilizing the JTBD theory is Newfields, the new name for the Indianapolis Museum of Art's (IMA) expansive campus in Indianapolis, Indiana.[1] The story of how Newfields came to be begins in 2012. The IMA is a world-class art museum home to more than 50,000 works, including one of the earliest known self-portraits by Rembrandt, the largest US collection of works by Paul Gaugin and the School of Pont-Aven, and an internationally renowned collection of Japanese paintings. Yet, at the time, the museum was over $120 million in debt with over 70 percent of its operating budget being funded from its endowment.[2] Perhaps most alarming was the fact that the museum was facing projections that showed 30 years of near static attendance. As Gary Stoppelman, former deputy director for Marketing and External Affairs at Newfields, lamented, "if the Museum continued its course, it would have to close its doors in a generation."[3]

In 2015, after seven years of offering free general admission, the museum implemented an $18 admission fee, approved a new strategic plan, and embraced a more active mission statement, "To enrich lives through exceptional experiences with art and nature."[4] And, in 2017, the IMA announced it would name its expansive campus Newfields, the home for the Indianapolis Museum of Art, Fairbanks Park, The Garden, Lilly House, the Madeline F. Elder Greenhouse, and the Miller House and Garden in Columbus, Indiana.[5] The decision to rebrand the IMA's 152-acre campus as Newfields was predicated on an extensive market segmentation study that intentionally broadened the IMA's competitive set, looking beyond demographics to understand the motivations and needs of visitors.

Whereas many museums look only to other cultural institutions for benchmarking and market competition, the IMA recognized that its competitive set was much larger—encompassing virtually all leisure activities in the area. To reach new audiences, the IMA would need to acquire a deeper understanding of its role in visitors' lives. The IMA surveyed more than 1,000 people in the Indianapolis region to understand the situations that led them to seek out leisure activities.[6] Through the process of multivariate analysis, a research methodology that can uncover patterns and relationships between several variables simultaneously, researchers narrowed the hundreds of motivations down to eight core "jobs" that various leisure activities could be "hired" to do (using the vernacular of JTBD), as shown in Figure 5.1. As defined by the IMA's research study, these eight jobs of leisure activities are:[7]

1. **Outdoor Escape:** Connect with the outdoors, find a change of scenery, and move your body while relaxing your mind in a slow-paced natural environment.
2. **Purposeful Play:** Be playful while expanding one's mind. Do something that everyone can agree upon—allowing everyone to have fun, create fond memories, and make an impression.
3. **Pure Fun:** Indulge yourself and others with the lighter side of life; provoke laughter and fun without having to think too deeply.
4. **Mental Reboot:** Renew yourself and nurture the spirit by seeking individual time in a slow-paced environment to think and reflect, often involving outdoor activity.

5. **Purposeful Pause:** Seek tranquility where it's possible to get away from it all; relax and unwind by immersing in a passion, observing beauty, and appreciating culture and the arts.
6. **Along for the Ride:** Do something for no good reason other than to be social and feel a sense of belonging, where you can almost picture one person asking "What do you want to do?" and another responding, "I don't know, what do you want to do?"
7. **Social Celebration:** Energize and excite through an adventure that is out of the ordinary and indulgent in a way that inspires and feels young at heart in a fast-paced, social setting—focused on needs and desires, not obligations.
8. **Current and Connected:** Seek intellectual stimulation and personal challenge while staying up to date and learning about a subject to feel mature and wise, connecting with others and meeting new people.

The study found that the IMA was serving its current base of visitors and members very well in fulfilling the job of Purposeful Pause. However, the demand for Purposeful Pause activities was only 10 percent of all leisure activities within a given year. In contrast, the job of Purposeful Play and Social Celebration represented 14 and 16 percent of leisure time, respectively. The findings of the IMA's research mirror insights from industry-wide studies: audiences are resistant to the idea of a "museum," but they seek opportunities for "experiences." Newfields director and CEO, Dr. Charles L. Venable, notes that potential museum audiences "go to sports, to restaurants, outdoor hiking, state

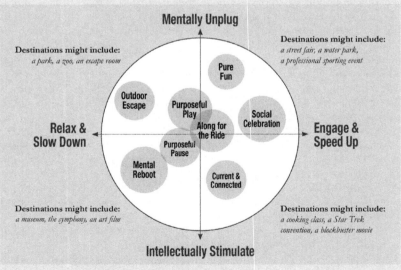

Figure 5.1.   The 8 Jobs of Leisure
Courtesy of Newfields/Halverson Group.

parks. They go to theater. They go to First Friday."[8] Armed with this information, the IMA developed a plan to reach new audiences and capture more of the leisure market.

The first step in the IMA's growth strategy was to protect and nurture its base of current visitors and members by expanding programming to satisfy more opportunities in the job of Purposeful Pause. Next, the IMA turned its attention to engaging new audiences through the creation of a mini-golf course designed by local artists to accomplish the job of Purposeful Play. Lastly, special seasonal events were created to fulfill the jobs of Social Celebration and Pure Fun.

The culmination of the IMA's future-focused initiative was its rebirth as Newfields—a Place for Nature and the Arts. Venable described the museum's vision in this way, "We're looking at how to get people here who want large social gatherings—people interested in 'purposeful play.' That's going to require us to continue to push the envelope. We want to be going in that same direction while still doing enough of the traditional material so core audiences still feel it's the IMA they always loved." To date, Newfields has not experimented with its membership model. The museum offers a traditional membership model with six categories of membership featuring a package of transactional benefits, including:[9]

- Free general admission to the IMA Galleries, The Gardens, and The Virginia B. Fairbanks Park: 100 acres (free to the public and open daily dawn to dusk)
- Member prices on all Newfields programs
- Exclusive members-only viewing times for special exhibitions
- Early registration for programs (some of which fill up fast), like Summer Nights.
- 10% discount at the Museum & Garden Shop and The Café
- Free subscriptions to Newfields magazine and member e-newsletter

With a renewed sense of purpose and an expanded view of how to deliver on its mission, Newfields is gaining momentum. The museum exceeded admission and revenue goals, with Spring 2017 attendance increasing 72 percent over the prior year. Of which, 38 percent of visitors represented what Newfields refers to as "the moveable middle," a large segment of the population identified as potential visitors (Figure 5.2).[10]

Moreover, the museum found that it had successfully increased attendance among younger audiences (54 percent of visitors were between the ages of 18 and 44 years old), with the highest concentration (24 percent) being between 25 and 34 years old. Attendance was also more racially and ethnically diverse. Hispanic or Latino attendance increased by 500 percent, African American attendance increased by nearly 200 percent, and Asian attendance increased by 45 percent.

In November 2017, Newfields launched a holiday lights display in its garden called Winterlights, transforming the museum's lowest-attended season

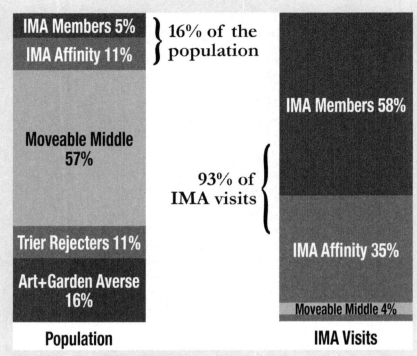

Figure 5.2. The Moveable Middle
Courtesy of Newfields/Halverson Group.

into its highest with nearly 70,000 guests and exceeding revenue projections by 200 percent. The following year in 2018, Winterlights attendance hit nearly 110,000 guests, with 44 percent being guests who had not been to the Newfields campus in at least a year. Membership at the museum has increased by more than 300 percent from about 5,000 when the museum was free to a record high of over 16,500 households in 2019.[11]

With its audience-first approach, Newfields is paving a path for the future of museums. By taking the time to understand the jobs to be done in leisure, Newfields is winning new visitors. As for membership, Venable acknowledges that, as the membership program continues to grow, Newfields will need to turn its attention to defining the purpose, role, and opportunity for membership within its new business model,[12] a conversation that the team at Newfields is looking forward to having.

NOTES

1. Mindy Cultra and Ron Halverson, "How an Art Museum Used the Business Concept of 'Jobs to Be Done' to Segment and Expand Its Audience," *Quirk's*, August

2017, https://www.quirks.com/articles/how-an-art-museum-used-the-business-concept-of-jobs-to-be-done-to-segment-and-expand-its-audience.

2. Charity Counts, "'Newfields' One Year Later: Reflections on Listening to the Community," Association of Midwest Museums, September 3, 2018, https://www.midwestmuseums.org/2018/09/03/newfields/.

3. Ibid.

4. "IMA Strategic Plan, 2015–2025," Indianapolis Museum of Art, updated March 7, 2016, https://discovernewfields.org/application/files/3415/0785/2180/IMA-Strategic-Plan-Board-20May2015.pdf.

5. Domenica Bongiovanni, "Newfields, the New Campus Name for IMA Grounds, Officially Rolls Out," *IndyStar*, October 14, 2017, https://www.indystar.com/story/entertainment/arts/2017/10/15/newfields-new-campus-name-ima-grounds-officially-rolls-out/764476001/.

6. Cultra and Halverson, "How an Art Museum Used the Business Concept of 'Jobs to Be Done' to Segment and Expand Its Audience."

7. Ibid.

8. Lou Harry, "Is IMA Chief Venable Visionary or Misguided?," *Indianapolis Business Journal*, August 31, 2017, https://www.ibj.com/articles/65237-is-ima-chief-venable-visionary-or-misguided.

9. "Join Us," Join, Newfields, accessed September 27, 2019, https://discovernewfields.org/give-and-join/become-member.

10. Charity Counts, "'Newfields' One Year Later: Reflections on Listening to the Community."

11. James Briggs, "Briggs: No, the IMA Is Not Trying to Exclude You," *IndyStar*, October 19, 2017, https://www.indystar.com/story/money/2017/10/19/briggs-no-indianapolis-museum-art-not-trying-exclude-you/779637001/.

12. Andrew Goldstein, "Newfields Director Charles Venable on His Data-Driven (and Maybe Crazy) Quest to Save the Art Museum," *artnet News*, February 12, 2018, https://news.artnet.com/art-world/newfields-director-charles-venable-indianapolis-art-museum-1218602.

Courtesy of Newfields.

MOTIVATIONS OF MUSEUM VISITORS

Most organizations, including museums, suffer from an affliction known as *marketing myopia*, or an overemphasis on selling a product or service rather than focusing on what customers really want or need.[4] Museums spend a significant amount of time and resources enhancing and marketing their products. More often than not, such marketing efforts are based on audience demographics and product features, rather than on the needs of the customer. For example, museums invest heavily in marketing a membership program (a product) that comprises a plethora of prepackaged offerings, programs, events, and discounts (benefits) segmented by type of customer (e.g., individual, families). However, this approach misses a key piece of information: "What is the *job* that our potential member is trying to get done?"

People do not go to a museum just to go to a museum. Calling upon our earlier analogy, that would be like buying a drill solely for the sake of owning a drill. Instead, people are motivated to participate in a cultural activity because it fulfills a specific need—a desire to have fun, to feel less stressed, to experience new things, to learn something, or to spend time with friends or family.[5] Thus, the museum serves as an enabler, helping the visitor accomplish a specific goal—*a job to be done*. This is a crucial distinction that has wide-reaching implications for everything from programming to marketing, membership, and curatorial. As you think about the jobs people are seeking to get done, it is important to remember that all jobs are more than purely functional. Jobs are often rooted in deep, sometimes subconscious, motivations. For example, consumers who "hire" a Prius to do the "job" of transportation may be motivated by the social recognition that stems from their environmentally friendly choice, a behavior known as "conspicuous conservation."[6]

In his ground-breaking book, *Identity and the Museum Visitor Experience*, researcher John Falk introduces a compelling model of museum visitors' identity-related motivations that includes Explorers, Facilitators, Experience Seekers, Professional/Hobbyists, and Rechargers.[7] These five categories of visitors' identity-related motivations represent a clear opportunity of where museums can satisfy consumers' needs and desires. Falk emphasizes that the "identity-related motivations [of visitors] are not qualities of the individual, but temporary roles that visitors enact to fit the specific needs and leisure realities of the moment, including":[8]

- Explorers describe themselves as curious people who enjoy learning and are seeking to expand their intellectual horizons.
- Facilitators are truly altruistic and have a desire to satisfy the needs and desires of someone they care about. For example, Facilitating Parents want their children to get something valuable from the museum visit whereas a Facilitating Socializer believes museums are great places to meet and spend quality time with friends or family.
- Experience Seekers want to "collect" experiences and are looking to check off the must-see destinations and iconic attractions on their bucket list.
- Professional/Hobbyists are motivated by a specific personal or professional interest such as genealogy, photography, education, crafting, model trains, or gardening.
- Rechargers are seeking a tranquil place for reflection and rejuvenation or simply looking to get away from the noise and clutter of the outside world.

Falk makes the case that museums will need to get measurably better at understanding and serving their audiences if they are to remain competitive in the future, asserting that "An enhanced understanding of audience, current and potential, has to be at the heart of any twenty-first century museum's business model."[9] Contextualized by rich personal stories of visitors' experiences and memories, Falk's research illuminates the need for museums to be more responsive to audiences' motivations, as well as the importance of ensuring that marketing reflects how the museum experience can meet visitors' needs. Specifically, Falk admonishes the persistent belief in the museum field that content is what drives a visit, noting that the vast majority of marketing and promotional campaigns are content oriented, often touting what's on display, new exhibitions, featured speakers, and so on. As Falk's research suggests, museum audiences are not principally motivated by content. And other studies have found that museum members are not primarily motivated by the transaction-based benefits of membership, such as retail discounts and free parking.[10]

These findings challenge the long-standing assumption that leading with transactional benefits and content is an effective strategy to promote membership and encourage repeat visitation. Moreover, such studies underscore a pesky problem that is deeply embedded in the typical museum membership model: the practice of benefit stuffing in an attempt to make membership appear like a "good deal" without taking the time to truly understand the deeper motivations behind the decision to join and what job the individual is trying to get done. Consequently, museums find themselves enthusiastically promoting an all-or-nothing package of prescribed "valuable" benefits while remaining entirely unaware of what the customer *actually* values and how that benefit will serve to accomplish a particular job. Such a one-size-fits-none, off-the-shelf membership product is to the detriment of both the customer and the museum's bottom line. Therefore, museums must internalize the concept that it is the *specifics of the job* and its accompanying motivations that matter most. Accordingly, museums need to rethink their offerings, products, and marketing to reflect this new understanding of customer centricity if they are to be successful in attracting and retaining new audiences.

As museum leaders take on the challenge of evolving the concept of membership to reach new audiences, they will inevitably encounter what is known as "The Innovator's Dilemma," a scenario in which an organization must decide to move beyond serving its current customer base to meet the needs of future customers. This is the difficult task of investing today in the ideas and audiences that will sustain museums in the future. As Clayton Christensen warns, "successful companies populated by good managers have a genuinely hard time doing what does not fit their model for how to make money. Because disruptive technologies rarely make sense during the years when investing in them is most important."[11] Technology notwithstanding, figuring out how to evolve and respond to the needs of tomorrow's audiences while acknowledging that membership as it exists today is a vital revenue engine of the museum's current business model places museum leaders at the center of a tricky crossroads. This is no easy path to navigate, but we must take our first steps now in evolving or risk falling victim to our own success.

MAKING THE FUTURE

What do a Winnebago, a team of social workers, and Stanford University have in common? They were all instrumental in improving the well-being of people with developmental disabilities in the San Francisco Bay Area. The story begins in 2014 when students from Stanford's d.school met with a team of social workers from the Golden Gate Regional Center (GGRC) to conduct an experiment—could a multipurpose facility on wheels in the form of a Winnebago decrease the turnaround time for processing disability needs assessments, improve collaboration among departments, ease the frustration and stress felt by families, and help disabled family members receive services sooner?[12] The answer was a resounding yes. With such positive results, you may be surprised to learn that the Winnebago concept was ultimately not implemented by GGRC. But that is beside the point. The goal of the experiment was to push the team outside of its comfort zone to view the organization's processes from a very different perspective—through the eyes of the families it serves. In the end, the experiment encouraged GGRC to rethink what was possible and spurred numerous innovative ideas that are continuing to improve lives.

As we begin to imagine what the museum membership program of the future might look like, it may feel overwhelming. Fortunately, we all have the power to influence what the future looks like. Or, as futurist Jane McGonigal likes to say, we have the potential to "make the future" by asking ourselves "What are the levers that you can push on . . . and move [the industry] purposefully in the direction that you want?"[13] Designing the membership program of tomorrow requires viewing our offering through an entirely new lens—one that prioritizes the viewpoint of the individual and reflects a deeper appreciation of personal needs.

One of the ways museum leaders can begin to envision a more compelling future for membership is to focus special attention on detecting the *signals* of change. You can think of these signals as glimpsing into a crystal ball. They are tangible ideas that you can see, touch, and interact with, yet they feel unusual and enigmatic. Signals are often subtle changes in our environment that provide a clue as to how the future might be different. So what are the signals that may hint at a new and different future for museums and the field of membership? Here are several examples of signals worth exploring in the museum field:

- Rapid adoption of crowdfunding platforms such as GoFundMe and Kickstarter
- Competency-based degrees as an alternative to traditional credit-based degree programs
- Personalized subscription services such as Stitch Fix, Blue Apron, and Ipsy
- The retrofitting and remaking of vacant shopping malls into micro-apartments, college campuses, libraries, community centers, event venues, and amusement parks
- Community tables at restaurants
- ClassPass
- Shared mobility like bikes and dock-less electric scooters
- The growing popularity of virtual assistants and chatbots
- Comprehensive vehicle subscription plans such as Care by Volvo and Mercedes-Benz Collection
- Escape rooms
- Live streaming concerts shown in movie theaters
- The rise of transformative travel and "travel mentors"
- "Digital Detox" retreats

These examples of signals merely scratch the surface of the possibilities for envisioning a membership program of the future. What possible futures do you see in your crystal ball?

SPARK: LOOKING FOR SIGNALS

I'd like to invite you to take a moment to jot down a few signals that you believe may point to a new or unexpected future for museums and membership. Can you imagine an experiment that would build on one or more of these signals?

THE UPSIDE OF EXPERIMENTATION

In February 2014, employees of the London Underground public rapid transit system went on strike, causing a partial shutdown of the network for 48 hours with no services on the Bakerloo, Circle, or Waterloo and City lines.[14] In the chaos of the shutdown, commuters were forced to find new routes to get to work. As it turns out, the particular circumstances of the strike provided an ideal opportunity for researchers at Oxford and Cambridge universities to study the effects of what's known as "forced experimentation," or the requirement to make a change due to unexpected circumstances. After analyzing 20 days of anonymized data from tube travelers, researchers were able to see how the shutdown affected individual behaviors. Remarkably, the study found that, during the strike, one in 20 commuters discovered a more efficient route to work that they then continued using even after the disruption had ended.[15] That is, the commuters who were forced to experiment found an upside to the strike: a better way to get to work.

Experimentation is a new business reality not only for for-profit companies but for nonprofits alike. As audience interests and behaviors continue to evolve, museums will need to fundamentally change their approach to audience engagement to remain relevant. The Wallace Foundation has found that, once an organization has invested time in understanding audience wants and needs, it is important to provide multiple ways for new audiences to participate.[16] One surefire way museums can boost participation among new audiences is to stay open in the evenings.[17]

Through experimentation, museums can tap into what award-winning *New York Times* reporter Charles Duhigg describes as creating a *craving*. A craving is developed through the formation of a habit by way of a simple neurological loop consisting of three parts: a cue, a routine, and a reward.[18] A cue can be anything that initiates the habit loop. For example, the time of day, location, emotional state, and preceding events are often common cues that begin the habit loop. Whatever the cue, this is the trigger for the brain to seek out the next step in the habit loop—the routine. Many times, a routine can be less than ideal, such as turning on the TV, reaching for an unhealthy snack, or scrolling mindlessly through Facebook. For museum goers, a routine might be free time on the weekend, popping into the museum to or from work, or seeking out beauty. The reward is the final part of the habit loop, and it is incredibly powerful because the reward is what satisfies the craving. A reward for people visiting a museum might be the pleasure of spending time with family, the relaxation of strolling the galleries after work, or the sense of peacefulness that comes from gazing at a beautiful painting.

BRIGHT SPOT: FINDING NEW
MEMBERS AT THE EXPLORATORIUM

The Exploratorium, a science center in San Francisco, California, opened up for visitors every Thursday from 6:00 p.m. to 10:00 p.m. and did something quite unique—unlike many museums that offer after-hours events, the Exploratorium took this idea a step further and created a stand-alone membership program around its adults-only nighttime events. Called *After Dark* membership, the concept was the brainchild of Membership Manager Sarah Owens, whose aim was to leverage the evening events to bring a younger and more diverse audience into the museum's membership program.

This need to reach new audiences arose after the museum's grand opening at its new location in 2013. As most museums that experience a grand opening of some type can attest, the Exploratorium saw a huge spike in its membership numbers, growing to nearly 24,000 households by 2014. However, over the next couple of years and as excitement surrounding the new building waned, the Exploratorium's membership totals declined precipitously, dropping to under 15,000 member households in 2016 before climbing back up and leveling off at around 16,000 households in 2018 by way of a membership-focused marketing campaign consisting of direct mail, email, and social media in concert with a larger citywide $1.3 million exhibition marketing campaign (Figure 5.3).

Figure 5.3.   Exploratorium Membership Totals 2014–2018
Courtesy of the Exploratorium.

Recognizing the immediate need to revive membership revenue, Owens was confronted with the uneasy reality of forced experimentation. She needed to come up with an idea to bring in new members that could be implemented quickly without the need for large-scale modifications to the existing membership program. This led Owens to partner with her colleagues in the Museum's education department to design a unique membership product that complemented the Museum's existing membership program. When the Exploratorium launched its new *After Dark* membership, the Museum simultaneously renamed its existing membership program *Daytime*, creating a clear distinction between the two programs. Unlike the standard membership model offered at most museums, the Exploratorium's unique approach allows for the same individual to become a member of one or both programs, thereby offering flexibility to the consumer and the opportunity to cross-sell for the Museum.

Promoted through a robust advertising campaign, Exploratorium *After Dark* members are invited to "join a like-minded community of the engaged, inquisitive, and adventurous . . . [with] unforgettable experiences designed to inspire, delight, and challenge you." Advertising, on-site promotions, and membership materials employed a distinct and memorable creative style with an alluring headline proclaiming "Members See More After Dark" (Figure 5.4). With the ambitious goal of driving repeat attendance and revenue, becoming the market leader of cultural evening experiences for adults, and building the pipeline for future philanthropic support, the Exploratorium's *After Dark* membership offers mission-aligned programs wrapped in music, play, and entertainment.

When designing the *After Dark* membership program, Owens was thoughtful about ensuring that the benefits appealed to younger and nontraditional audiences. The *After Dark* membership touts "endless evenings" with unlimited admission to 50-plus *After Dark* events and free access to *Friday Nights* during

Figure 5.4.   After Dark On-Site Promotion and Membership Card
Courtesy of the Exploratorium.

the summer season, along with VIP treatment, including special members-only bar access and the occasional members-only lounge where *After Dark* members can "find a chill oasis . . . [and] drop in all night long to relax, enjoy free cocktails and beer, and experiment with lasers and phosphorescent paint." For its annual signature event, *Science of Cocktails*, the Exploratorium offers *After Dark* members a discount on tickets. Activities include recipes from local mixologists, cocktail-related science demos, and the chance to "sip and shop" (browsing the Exploratorium's gift shop for fun cocktail-and-science themed items, such as barware, cocktail recipe books, and chemistry kits, all while sipping on a free libation). *After Dark* members are now invited alongside *Daytime* members to all membership parties, including the Exploratorium's annual holiday and summer members-only parties.

After Dark has helped the Exploratorium reach an emerging adult audience by communicating that the science center is not just a place for kids. And because *After Dark* events are an immersive, participatory experience, members have the opportunity to express their identities through their experiences, escape the day to day, and connect socially. This strategy aligns seamlessly with several of Falk's visitors' identity-related motivations, particularly addressing the needs of Explorers, Facilitators, and Experience Seekers by providing an opportunity for discovery, socializing, and #instagramable experiences.

Further, the Exploratorium has created a habit out of its new programming. For example, the cue for *After Dark* attendees might be a text from a friend, the end of the workday, or even a casual glance at a calendar. Whatever the cue, this is the trigger for the brain to seek out the next step in the habit loop— the routine. In the case of *After Dark* members, what otherwise would be an uneventful Thursday night now has an established consistent routine that includes going to the Exploratorium. The final aspect of reward for attending an *After Dark* event at the Exploratorium might be the thrill of learning something new, the emotional boost of spending time with friends, or the relaxation that comes from imbibing a craft cocktail after a long day at the office.

By creating a go-to routine on Thursday nights that delivers a unique reward to the individual, the Exploratorium has been able to shake people out of the familiar and create a new habit among its *After Dark* members. The strategy is paying off, attracting interest and repeat attendance from nontraditional members by offering a perfect pairing of fun and educational experiences hosted after hours. By 2019, the Exploratorium acquired 1,853 *After Dark* members (comprising 636 individual and 1,217 dual memberships), representing approximately 11 percent of the museum's general membership program.

While some might dismiss the addition of these new members as a minimal increase, the result is nothing to scoff at. The *After Dark* membership has not only demonstrated an opportunity to engage a more diverse and younger audience, but early revenue figures indicate that the Exploratorium is on track to recover from recent program deficits. With a clever call to action to "Commit to curiosity and join today," the Exploratorium has taken a big step in the right direction to finding new audiences.

Courtesy of the Exploratorium.

TOMORROW'S SUCCESS STORIES

The increasing costs of doing business, trends in declining participation, and morphing consumer expectations have presented museum leaders with a rare opportunity: the circumstance of forced experimentation and the call to think differently about tomorrow. What will the audiences of tomorrow want? How will museums adapt to meet their needs? Where will museums find the next generation of supporters?

While there is no shortage of ideas when it comes to reversing the trends in attendance and membership, there is little time to waste in finding a viable way forward. Museums must first identify the right target audiences and remove the barriers that are hindering participation.[19] This effort requires prioritizing and investing in research. Such research should include an array of traditional methodologies in the form of exit surveys, member surveys, and focus groups, as well as broader market research, to better understand the needs and perceptions of prospective audiences. However, the standard approach to obtaining insights will not be enough to unearth the possibilities that will shape the future of membership. As we will see in chapter 9, traditional research techniques are inherently flawed and not well suited to generating the kinds of ideas that will propel museums into the future. To be sure, the only way to avoid the trap of an internally focused institutional lens is to deeply understand the needs of tomorrow's audiences.

Museums are at a critical juncture. Many have been relying on the assumption that what works today will continue to work tomorrow. However, the quick fixes that museums have leaned on in the past to generate results will not deliver a long-term solution to what truly ails our organizations. Museum leaders must look beyond near-term tactics such as direct mail campaigns to boost membership numbers and flash sales to fend off unexpected dips in membership revenue. By understanding *why* audiences think and behave the way they do, museums can develop new products that will get the job done. Today's museums are perfectly positioned to find the upside of forced experimentation and begin to make the future.

NOTES

1. Clayton Christensen, "The 'Jobs to Be Done' Theory of Innovation," *Harvard Business Review*, December 8, 2016, https://hbr.org/ideacast/2016/12/the-jobs-to-be -done-theory-of-innovation.

2. Amy Gallo, "A Refresher on Marketing Myopia," *Harvard Business Review*, August 22, 2016, https://hbr.org/2016/08/a-refresher-on-marketing-myopia.

3. Clayton M. Christensen, Scott Cook, and Taddy Hall, "What Customers Want from Your Products," Working Knowledge, Harvard Business School, January 16, 2016, https://hbswk.hbs.edu/item/what-customers-want-from-your-products.

4. Amy Gallo, "A Refresher on Marketing Myopia," *Harvard Business Review*, August 22, 2016, https://hbr.org/2016/08/a-refresher-on-marketing-myopia.

5. LaPlaca Cohen, *Culture Track '17* (New York, NY, 2017), 11, https://culture track.com/wp-content/uploads/2017/02/CT2017-Top-Line-Report.pdf.

6. Rodrigo Flores-Gutiérrez, "The Prestige of Buying Green: The Prius Case," *Yale Environment Review*, August 3, 2015, https://environment-review.yale.edu/prestige-buying-green-prius-case-0.

7. John H. Falk, *Identity and the Museum Visitor Experience* (New York: Routledge, 2016), 64.

8. Ibid., 190–206.

9. Ibid., 21.

10. Colleen Dilenschneider, "Why Effective Membership Programs Are More Important than Ever Before (DATA)," *Know Your Own Bone*, January 2, 2019, https://www.colleendilen.com/2019/01/02/effective-membership-programs-important-ever-data/.

11. Clayton M. Christensen, *The Innovator's Dilemma: The Revolutionary Book That Will Change the Way You Do Business* (New York, NY: HarperCollins Publishers, 2011), 261.

12. Robert I. Sutton and David Hoyt, "Better Service, Faster: A Design Thinking Case Study," *Harvard Business Review*, January 6, 2016, https://hbr.org/2016/01/better-service-faster-a-design-thinking-case-study.

13. Steven Johnson, *The Future of Predicting the Future 4*, "American Innovations," Wondery, August 23, 2018, podcast, https://podtail.com/en/podcast/american-innovations/the-future-of-predicting-the-future-4.

14. Vanessa Houlder, "Tube Strike an Economic Boost, Universities' Study Finds," *Financial Times*, September 13, 2015, https://www.ft.com/content/327c9528-58a9-11e5-9846-de406ccb37f2.

15. Shaun Larcom, Ferdinand Rauch, and Tim Willems, "The Benefits of Forced Experimentation: Striking Evidence from the London Underground Network," University of Oxford, Department of Economics Discussion Paper Series, ISSN 1471-0498 Number 755 (September 2015): 27.

16. Bob Harlow, "The Road to Results: Effective Practices for Building Arts Audiences," The Wallace Foundation, 2014, 49, www.wallacefoundation.org/knowledge-center/pages/the-road-to-results-effective-practices-for-building-arts-audiences.aspx.

17. Janan Ganesh, "The Best Way to Get People to Go to Museums? Open Them at Night," *Financial Times*, November 23, 2018, https://www.ft.com/content/6a5ab94a-ee4a-11e8-89c8-d36339d835c0?fbclid=IwAR3H4B7xF3XceOvHrC4SPXZdi2rV9r wuNJaBw92rz6RXn2XG2jqZTwSqZkE.

18. Charles Duhigg, *The Power of Habit* (New York: Random House, 2012), 49.

19. Harlow, "The Road to Results: Effective Practices for Building Arts Audiences."

Chapter Six

Everything Matters

Before reading further, take a look at the menu in Figure 6.1. What is the first thing you notice?

Besides the sensation of feeling hungrier than you were before scanning the menu, did you notice anything that stood out? How about the filets mignons featured in the upper right-hand corner of the menu? Did your eye instinctively land on the savory fig and prosciutto flatbread? Did you happen to glance at the selections on the wine list and take note of the most expensive bottle?

What you may not realize is that there are many deliberate strategies at play on any given restaurant menu. First, because diners spend less than two minutes scanning a menu, it needs to communicate a lot of information in a short amount of time.[1] Areas of the menu with the greatest eye traffic are where the most profitable items are featured. For example, on a two-column menu, it just so happens that the eye naturally gravitates to the upper right-hand corner. On the menu, the steak selections with the highest profit margin are highlighted in the upper right-hand section. Second, just as newspapers use bold graphical treatments or "callouts" to highlight quotes, statistics, or other key information from a story, the savory fig and prosciutto flatbread is framed in a box that draws attention to this item as a standout in the appetizer section. Third, there is a psychological ploy hidden within the wine list. Although the wine list includes a 2016 Nickel & Nickel Cabernet, Napa Valley for $200, the restaurant does not expect to sell many (if any) bottles of this particular wine. Rather, its inclusion on the menu serves a specific purpose—it provides a reference point against which all other wine prices on the list can be evaluated. When the very expensive $200 bottle of Nickel & Nickel is added to the list of options, the $97 bottle of 2014 Mi Sueno, El Llano, Napa

Main Courses

Appetizers

SAVORY FIG & PROSCIUTTO FLATBREAD
Port Fig Jam, Goat Cheese, Arugula 16

EAST COAST OYSTERS
Cocktail Sauce, Apple Mignonette | Market Price

TUNA TARTARE
Avocado, Cucumber, Ponzu, Wonton Chips 18

WAGYU CARPACCIO
Arugula, Vinaigrette, Shaved Parmesan 23

LUMP CRAB CAKES
Citrus Vinaigrette, Pickled Onion Slaw 21

Salads

STEAKHOUSE WEDGE
Blue Cheese, Bacon, Tomato,
Blue Cheese Dressing 12

TOMATO & MOZZARELLA
Burrata, Preserved Lemon,
Basil Oil, Balsamic Glaze 14

MIXED FIELD GREENS
Cucumber, Watermelon Radish,
Vinaigrette 10

Desserts

CREME BRULEE
Vanilla Bean, Seasonal Fruit 10

KEY LIME PIE
Strawberry Balsamic Reduction, Candied Lime 10

SIGNATURE COCONUT CREAM PIE
Whipped Cream, Toasted Coconut, Caramel 10

Steaks & Chops

Brushed w/ Butter,
Seasoned w/ Salt & Pepper,
Served w/ Saucière of Our
Steak Sauce On Request

FILETS MIGNONS
10 oz. 46

Bone-In 16 oz. 68

Chef's Wagyu Cut | 4 oz. Market Price/oz.

RIBEYES
16 oz. 46

Dry-Aged Cowboy 22 oz. | Bone-In 62

Dry-Aged Tomahawk 32 oz. 108

STRIPS
New York 14 oz. 47

Dry-Aged Kansas City 18 oz. | Bone-In 58

Dry-Aged Porterhouse 36 oz. | Served Carved 90

CHOPS
Berkshire Pork Porterhouse 20 oz
Hand Selected and Carved Tableside,
This Prime Chop Is Cured, Roasted,
Slow-Smoked and Caramelized

Served With Homemade Applesauce 42

Wines

2016 Charles Krug Cabernet, Napa Valley 68

2014 Mi Sueno, El Llano, Napa Valley 97

2014 Inglenook Cabernet, Napa Valley 112

2015 Groth Cabernet, Napa Valley 160

2016 Nickel & Nickel Cabernet, Napa Valley 200

Figure 6.1.   Example of a Menu

Valley seems much more reasonable. As celebrated behavioral economist, Dan Ariely jokes, "Restaurants also know that many of us are cheap—but we don't want to *seem* cheap, which means that almost no one orders the cheapest wine on the menu. The wine of choice for cheapskates is the second-cheapest wine on the list."[2] Finally, you may have found your mouth watering as you read the deliciously detailed descriptions of the dishes. Researchers have found that using descriptive menu labels such as "a succulent Italian seafood filet" or "homestyle chicken parmesan" boosted sales by 27 percent, increased intention to come back to the restaurant in the future, and improved overall satisfaction of the dining experience.[3]

Menus are just one example of how design, pricing, and language can influence decisions. Many of the strategies employed by restaurants and other industries for effective marketing are based on insights from a range of behavioral and social science disciplines, including economics, psychology, sociology, demography, and cognitive science. When it comes to better marketing and more insightful strategy development in membership, museums can learn a lot from behavioral and social science. In a museum setting, it's easy to forget (and, at times, actively dismiss) that our visitors, members, and donors are, in fact, humans. We are motivated by incentives, disproportionately pained by loss, blinded by bias, and plagued by too much choice.

This chapter explores several key theories from the fields of behavioral and social sciences that can assist museums in leveraging the power of design to help audiences make better decisions about how they choose to support the mission through joining, giving, and participating.

NUDGES AND SHOVES

You are probably familiar with the general job description of an architect as someone who determines the aesthetic, functional, economical, and social aspects of a building's design. Most often, when we think of architecture, we tend to think of the visual and functional aspects of the building—the shape of the doorways, the structural embellishments, the roofing material, and so on. However, architecture takes into consideration not only how the building looks but how it will be used, including how the design fits into the broader ecosystem of its city and how it will support goals such as socializing, collaboration, and creativity. If you ask an architect "What is the most important decision when designing a building?," he or she will likely tell you "Every decision." This is because every detail of a physical structure can have an impact on the well-being and productivity of the people who live, work, and play inside the building.

There's an illustrative story about the importance of design that involves the late Steve Jobs and his ideas for a new office building for the film studio Pixar. Jobs pored over every detail of the design believing that the building had the power to affect collaboration among colleagues. With a goal of engineering serendipitous interactions, Jobs envisioned a single pair of "über-bathrooms" located in the center of the building that would increase the chances of impromptu conversation throughout the day. However, Jobs quickly abandoned his restroom centerpiece concept after a group of pregnant women protested, calling attention to how such a design would require them to take long walks to get to the bathroom, frequently.[4] Design, it turns out, can make things much easier or much harder.

In marketing and membership, just as in architecture, every element is important. There is no such thing as *neutral* design—not in a brochure, not in an ad, not on the website, not in the signage that adorns the entrance. Perhaps the most empowering (and paralyzing) aspect of learning that there is no such thing as neutral design is the realization that *everything* has the potential to influence decisions, for better or worse. From the wording and placement of a call to action button on a website to the order of options presented on the sign that hangs above the admission desk—design, whether intentional or not, influences the choices we make.

To fully appreciate the power of design, you first need to understand the concept of a "nudge." A nudge is "any aspect of the choice architecture that alters people's behavior in a predictable way without forbidding any options or significantly changing their economic incentives."[5] The term *choice architecture* is used to describe every opportunity or touchpoint that has the potential to influence the decision-making process. Thus, a choice architect is someone who has "the responsibility for organizing the context in which people make decisions."[6] If you are responsible for any aspect of the marketing or membership strategy at your institution, *you* are a choice architect!

Choice architects can use nudges to help people make better decisions. Importantly, nudges are not decisions that are mandated or forced upon audiences. Rather, a nudge constitutes an intentional intervention that helps to move an individual in a particular direction. A nudge can take many forms, such as specific words or phrases, defaults and options, and what information is presented first as well as the frequency, context, and type of touchpoints employed by an organization. For an overview of various types of nudges, visit membershipinnovation.com.

Choice architects have the power to influence decision-making through design. This is not a responsibility to be taken lightly. Everything—imagery, pricing, category names, messaging, incentives, and more—can either help or hurt your membership program. Choice architects must consider the big picture, the end game, the why behind every decision. From relatively simple decisions, such as the call to action on the website or what image to use in an online ad, to complex and thorny decisions, such as pricing and the mix of benefits offered at various levels.

THE ENDOWMENT EFFECT

There is a fun holiday tradition called the white elephant gift exchange. While there are many variations of the game, the basic concept is the same: The game begins with each player bringing an unlabeled, wrapped gift. Players then draw a number to determine in what order they will choose a gift to open. Once a gift is selected, the player opens the gift and shows it to the other players. The next player in line may then choose to either select from the remaining unopened gifts or steal another player's gift. If you've ever played this game and had your gift stolen, you may have experienced that the feeling is quite disappointing. Why is this?

Science tells us that we tend to overvalue things we already own. It is a bias known as the "endowment effect," and it has a pronounced influence on our feelings about the things we own regardless of how it is that we came to be "owners." The endowment effect shows up when we purchase a product or service; are given something for free, such as a coffee mug or a free trial; or we win something, such as a drawing for a prize or the chance to go behind the scenes.

This overvaluation of owned things results in some pretty peculiar behavior. Numerous experiments have shown that people act irrationally when it comes to selling or trading items they own. In one experiment, researchers gave coffee mugs to every other student in a class to create a real-world marketplace for buying and selling coffee mugs. The results of the study showed that students who owned the mugs (the sellers) were reluctant to sell them, whereas students who did not own a mug (the buyers) were far less interested in buying one. Interestingly, buyers were willing to pay only about half of the price that sellers demanded for their treasured coffee mug.[7]

The endowment effect is so strong that it can even be triggered by exposure to the mere suggestion of ownership. Savvy retailers know that you are likely to experience the endowment effect simply by holding an object in your hands. By picking up that iPhone on display in the Apple store, you are more likely to buy it. The endowment effect can also be experienced virtually. Researchers have found that websites that use haptic imagery or devices with a touch interface, such as a tablet or an iPad, produce the same effect of perceived ownership as physical touch.[8] Surprisingly, simply *imagining* owning something can induce the endowment effect.[9]

The endowment effect is linked to a core tenet of behavioral economics: loss aversion, or the principle that losses are twice as painful as gains. The prospect of loss triggers strong, unpleasant emotions of fear, regret, and disappointment. Even when making a change is in our own best interest, the fear of loss is a powerful counterweight that makes it difficult to take risks. Believe it or not, the magnitude of the risk is irrelevant when it comes to avoiding losses. Any type of loss feels much worse than any type of gain feels good. That is, *getting* something is not the same as *losing* something.

The concept of loss aversion has a significant implication on how museums present information about membership. Consider the following common marketing messages found on nearly every museum website:

- "Join today and receive . . ."
- "As a member you get . . ."
- "Membership is a great value because . . ."
- "Become a member and see it first . . ."

Each message above is "framed" in terms of a gain. In psychology, framing is the way in which problems or options are stated. Information that is positively framed is encoded by the brain as a gain, whereas information presented as a negative is encoded as a loss. Membership is most often framed as a gain: "Become a member and get all these great benefits." Further, membership benefits are frequently described in terms of an equivalent monetary value to be gained, such as "At the $180 membership level, your benefits are valued at more than $275!" Sounds like a great deal, right? Yet the pain of losing $180 to buy a membership will be felt more acutely than the pleasure of gaining the additional value of the benefits.

It may be tempting to simply flip the messaging from a positive frame to a negative frame, such as "Don't miss your chance . . . join today!" However, this approach may be misguided. While the perception of scarcity does heighten the risk of loss—FOMO (fear of missing out), it turns out, is a real thing—reliance on scarcity to sell memberships is a short-term strategy. Audiences will soon catch on to such a tactic and begin to ignore these artificial cries of urgency. Moreover, this type of strategy exploits a limited-time engagement opportunity at the expense of a more meaningful message. Members who joined solely "not to miss out" will be more difficult to keep engaged after the initial reason for joining has passed.

A quirk of loss aversion involves the concept of certainty, or a sure thing. When choosing among various alternatives, people will select a guaranteed positive outcome whenever possible. This is true even when the choice is between a small, certain reward versus the chance of receiving a larger but uncertain reward. Think about how membership is framed at your institution. How would a person who has never been a member interpret the trade-off of joining today in exchange for an unknown experience tomorrow? Recall that there is substantial risk involved in giving up a sum of money (a loss) to buy an uncertain outcome. This idea becomes even more important when thinking about how to engage new audiences who may be entirely unfamiliar with what a museum has to offer. Yet many organizations invest significant resources, both time and financial, aggressively promoting membership to audiences who have never stepped foot inside the museum.

One way to overcome the risk of loss while bestowing ownership at the same time is to offer a free trial. Free trials help to assuage the fear of the unknown by allowing the customers to try before they buy. Because an upfront cost is not required for a free trial, there is no loss experienced at the time of sign-up. Further, the endowment effect is likely to be activated upon owning the membership—even if only temporarily.

Importantly, a free trial is different than a free membership model in which there is no defined end date for the membership. In a free trial model, as the trial period nears its end, audiences will more acutely feel the pain of losing their benefits and thus will be more likely to take action to maintain their membership status (i.e., convert to a paid member). Audiences win because they have an opportunity to experience all that membership has to offer without taking on any risk. The museum wins by introducing new audiences to all that the museum has to offer while creating a sense of ownership from the very beginning. With so many science-backed reasons to offer a free trial membership, why are there so few examples of museums that have adopted this model?

SPARK: CREATING A FREE MEMBERSHIP TRIAL

Using a free trial to introduce new audiences to membership requires a thoughtful strategy to convert free members to paid members. The following steps will guide you through the process of developing a free membership trial that aligns with your museum's goals, infrastructure, and resources.

1. **Evaluate systems infrastructure.** Systems such as email platform, ticketing software, and database(s) must be evaluated for feasibility to support a free trial membership.

2. **Determine what benefits or levels to include.** In most cases, a full-feature version of the membership is preferred so the trial accurately reflects the holistic experience of being a member. However, it is also possible to craft a trial strategy that offers a limited number of benefits to encourage conversion to a full membership.

3. **Set a duration for the trial.** The duration of the trial period must be long enough to allow trial members to experience the benefits of membership but not too long that the incentive to convert to a paid membership is lost. The vast majority of free trials are between 30 and 90 days; however, shorter trial periods have the potential to convert high-propensity trial members more quickly. An extended trial period can encourage procrastination and increase the risk that trial members will choose not to take advantage of membership benefits, ultimately resulting in a much lower conversion rate.

   Additionally, an incentive can be used to entice customers to end their trial early, thereby speeding up conversion cycles. Alternatively, you may consider offering trial members an opportunity to extend their trial period to deepen their experience as a member or to allow customers more time to try out their benefits if they haven't had a chance to use them yet.

4. **Determine what information to collect at the time of sign-up.**

   a. **Credit card.** Some free trials require a credit card at the time of trial initiation. This can be beneficial if, after the trial period, the member will automatically be billed for a paid membership. However, requiring credit card details upon sign-up suppresses sign-up rates. Additionally, data suggest that the end-to-end conversion rate (the percentage of active customers 90 days after transitioning from a free trial to paid customer) doubles if credit card information is not required up front. If you decide to collect credit card information at the time of sign-up, ensure all systems are compliant for securing cardholder data.

   b. **Profile details.** In general, the less information that is required at the time of sign-up, the better. At a minimum, an email address should be required to initiate the free trial. Name, mailing address, and phone number are also reasonable details to require for sign-up. A progressive data capture strategy can be put in place to collect more detailed information about customers over time.

5. **Establish cancellation procedures and communicate regularly.** The cancellation process should be transparent and easy. Open and frequent communication is key to ensuring customers feel the trial is fair and that they won't be tricked into paying for something they don't want. Further, the only way to earn new members is to ensure that they see and experience the value of a membership during the trial period. Reminders about trial expiration and how to cancel will help to encourage customers to use their trial membership.

6. **Create a marketing plan to launch the trial membership.** A trial membership will be successful in attracting new audiences only if it has a well-planned promotional strategy and adequate investment behind it.
7. **Develop a welcome email series.** When a customer signs up for a trial membership, a welcome email should be sent automatically with an overview of how to get the most out of the trial. The welcome email should be personalized and come from an email address that the customer can reply to should they have a question or want to share feedback. Be sure to include contact information for the membership manager, who will be able to assist them with their trial membership.
8. **Design additional touchpoints and track engagement.** Evaluate opportunities to maximize value and establish a connection with new customers. It is critical to focus on building a strong relationship quickly and create touchpoints to nurture trial members during the trial period. Onboarding should include additional outreach and customer service touchpoints to ensure the greatest possible experience for trial members. Measure customer engagement during the trial period to understand visitation patterns and benefits usage.
9. **Develop a post-trial campaign and evaluate performance.** For those customers who choose to cancel or let their trial membership expire, a post-trial survey can provide valuable feedback about the trial and your membership program overall. Additionally, expired trial members can be added to future membership acquisition campaigns as warm leads. Lastly, ensure a thorough evaluation of the trial membership is conducted to understand opportunities for improvement and determine return on investment.

BRIGHT SPOT: EXPERIMENTING WITH A TRIAL MEMBERSHIP AT THE MUSEUM OF FINE ARTS, BOSTON

In 2020, the Museum of Fine Arts, Boston (MFA) celebrates the 150th anniversary of its founding. In recognition of this milestone and with a goal of deepening relationships with new and diverse communities, the MFA has declared a set of priorities aimed at inviting, welcoming, and engaging expanded audiences. Among others, the MFA identified "creative professionals" as a target audience, including artists, designers, architects, musicians and performers; writers, filmmakers, and digital content creators; new product developers; research and development scientists; and advertising and marketing professionals. In alignment with this new vision, the MFA began hosting a series of after-hours parties in 2017, welcoming thousands of guests to its galleries.

Called *MFA Late Nites*, the evening events created an opportunity for the MFA to connect with an expanded audience by creating unexpected experiences in the Museum.

The theme of the first *MFA Late Nites* in October 2017 was Japanese art, designed to introduce the MFA's headline exhibition, "Takashi Murakami: Lineage of Eccentrics." While featuring the work of Takashi Murakami, a contemporary artist who has been compared to Andy Warhol and has collaborated with Pharrell and Kanye West, the exhibition also included items from the Museum's renowned collection of Japanese art. Murakami's irreverent, pop culture–infused art has made him one of the most recognized Japanese artists today. Knowing that the exhibition would attract a new audience to the Museum, the MFA introduced the *XPass*, a six-month trial membership offered during the run of the exhibition (Figure 6.2).

The popularity of the artist and the potential to reach a new audience—younger and nontraditional museum-goers—gave the MFA a unique opportunity to align the concept of the *XPass* with the exhibition. With a clearly defined start and end period, the MFA was thoughtful about how to position and deliver its trial membership. To ensure that the *XPass* would not cannibalize the MFA's existing membership, the trial included a discrete marketing mix, comprising a distinct set of benefits, pricing strategy, promotion, and distribution channel.

Working closely across departments to provide a quality and seamless member experience, the MFA's membership team was strategic about designing the trial membership in a way that would appeal to a new audience. Leveraging the time-bound nature of the *XPass* (October 1, 2017, through April 1, 2018), the MFA took advantage of the opportunity to experiment with many new offerings and approaches. First, the price was intentionally set at an affordable threshold of $40 (or $55 for two) to lower the barrier of participation for younger and nontraditional audiences. Second, the *XPass* aligned with the exhibition run dates and included free tickets to *MFA Late Nites* events, free admission, and an exclusive discount on coveted Murakami merchandise. *XPass* members also were offered the opportunity to preview the exhibition five days before it opened to the general public. The inaugural *MFA Late Nites* event featured a variety of experiential activities, including DJs, a rap slam performance featuring hip-hop artists, Japanese street food, an outdoor beer garden, and, of course, art. Third, promotion was paired with the exhibition marketing strategy, which gave the *XPass* additional visibility. Marketed to a broader audience than its traditional membership program, the MFA leveraged social media and earned media to extend the reach of the campaign. Finally, the *XPass* was designed to leverage a digital membership card using a QR code delivered via email.

Importantly, the *XPass* did not preclude current members from becoming *XPass* members. To the contrary, the strategic design of the *XPass* made it an appealing add-on for current members who were interested in attending the exhibition preview, obtaining free tickets to *MFA Late Nites* events, and

Introducing the XPass

Xperience MFA Membership with an exclusive six-month trial membership, including inside access to curated social events and evening programs.

BUY A SINGLE XPASS

BUY A DUAL XPASS

Xclusives for Takashi Murakami

For just $40 for one person and $55 for two, XPass holders get a taste of MFA Membership from October 1, 2017 through April 1, 2018, timed perfectly with our blockbuster exhibition, "Takashi Murakami: Lineage of Eccentrics." Visit often, as XPass holders receive free Museum admission through April 1! Additional XPass perks include:

- Free admission to the opening party on October 13, a part of the new MFA Late Nites. Be the first to see the exhibition!
- Access to Member Preview, October 15–17, and Member Guest Days, November 9–12
- Snag a 10% discount in the "Takashi Murakami" exhibition shop

For a full list of XPass perks, check out the XPass Frequently Asked Questions.

Xplore More Japanese Culture at the MFA

Can't get enough Japanese art and culture? In addition to our world-renowned Japanese collection, there's more to see and do this season! Don't miss our free tattoo artist demonstration on November 15, or a lecture by famed tattoo artist Chad Koeplinger on November 30. Enjoy the additional XPass perk of member pricing for the lecture!

Figure 6.2.   XPass Trial Membership
Courtesy of the Museum of Fine Arts, Boston.

receiving the special discount at the exhibition museum shop. When the MFA surveyed *XPass* members, the Museum found that 53 percent indicated the primary reason for joining was to gain free admission to the Museum, followed by free *MFA Late Nites* tickets (20 percent of respondents). However, member behavior did not track with this self-reported reasoning. For example, of the 228 tickets sold to *XPass* members, 81 tickets (36 percent) went unused. This was a higher rate of attrition as compared to paid tickets for nonmembers, which was 14 percent. Overall, data showed that, while audiences liked the idea of the merchandise discount, it was not a primary motivator, based on low redemption rates in the Museum shop.

At the close of the six-month trial, 576 individuals had signed up to become *XPass* members. Of this total, 59 percent represented new audiences to the Museum, 16 percent had a prior touch with the MFA either as active general members or ticket buyers, and 7 percent were lapsed general members who rejoined as *XPass* members. The Museum was especially encouraged by the average of 2.3 visits during the exhibition, demonstrating strong interest from *XPass* members given the short duration of the trial membership. During the trial period, the MFA deployed a series of three appeals to *XPass* members to promote general membership, including a 10 percent discount on an annual membership. In the end, 98 trial members upgraded to an annual membership program.

As an experiment, the *XPass* empowered the MFA to become more nimble and forced the Museum to adapt on the fly as unexpected challenges arose. For example, the concept of a digital membership card for the *XPass* was anticipated to be an easier option for the trial, rather than a standard membership card. However, this aspect of the trial ended up being one of the biggest learnings for the MFA. The implementation of the *XPass* digital membership card required customization of technology, tricky integrations, and significant staff resources to deploy and manage. This process of prototyping a digital membership card helped the MFA to realize that the concept as originally envisioned was not a viable full-scale option for the future in its current iteration.

Additionally, the trial membership gave the Museum a chance to experiment with messaging and provided a window into the behaviors and preferences of new audiences. While the *XPass* did not produce immediate return on investment for the MFA, the experiment itself had many positive outcomes. For instance, many of the *XPass* members identified as "creative professionals"—a target audience for the Museum. Moreover, the process of experimentation has enabled the MFA to embrace testing and learning. As Megan Bernard, assistant director of Membership, noted, "We got comfortable with putting something out there that was a little rough around the edges." Perhaps the most valuable aspect of the trial membership was that it led to greater synergy between departments, fostering stronger cross-departmental partnerships and continuing collaboration.

The MFA has found that people tend to think of themselves as members of the Museum, even when this perception does not align with the definition of an "active" or consistent supporter. Recognizing that individuals consider themselves a part of the Museum community in the absence of a financial contribution or transaction-based behavior, such as visiting or joining, has led the MFA to explore the idea of what community means outside of the traditional membership concept. Ultimately, the learnings from the *XPass* have laid the foundation for future experimentation and helped shape new initiatives for engaging with an expanded audience.

Courtesy of the Museum of Fine Arts, Boston.

INFLUENTIAL BY DEFAULT

One way to overcome the challenge of inertia, or the tendency we all have to go along with the status quo, is to intentionally create a path of least resistance. A default is a way to create this path, as it eliminates the need for a consumer to make a decision. To truly be considered a default, no additional action must be required on the part of the individual. For example, as shown in Figure 6.3, Design A displays the traditional method for marketing membership, in which the individual is prompted to opt in to join, whereas Design B utilizes a default for joining, requiring the individual to explicitly opt out if he or she does not wish to become a member.

One of the best examples of the power of the default is the advent of automatic enrollment in defined contribution plans to increase participation and retirement savings rates. Prior to 2006, employees were required to explicitly opt in to be enrolled in defined contribution plans, such as 401(k) programs at their company. However, that all changed when the US House of Repre-

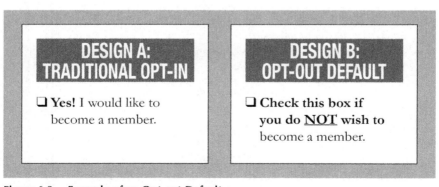

Figure 6.3. Example of an Opt-out Default

sentatives passed landmark legislation to encourage more employers to adopt automatic enrollment. The Pension Protection Act of 2006 established safe-harbor protections for employers who automatically enroll employees in certain retirement savings plans at specified contribution rates.[10] With automatic enrollment as the default, employees must now take steps to opt out should they choose not to participate. A seemingly small change, data on the impact of automatic enrollment suggest that the practice has nearly doubled participation rates among workers from 47 percent to 93 percent.[11] Thus, an opt-out default can be implemented as a nudge to encourage greater participation.

Interestingly, researchers have found that disclosure of the use of a default did not change the decisions of participants.[12] However, disclosure did affect attitudes. Participants who were told about the intent behind the default up front perceived its use to be more ethical. That is, transparency may improve customer loyalty without making the default any less effective.

SPARK: MEMBERSHIP AS THE DEFAULT

In museums, the default way of participating is some form of admission, be it paid or free. That is, when a visitor arrives on-site, the assumed starting point is to obtain a ticket for admittance into the museum (or, in the case of free admission, a ticket may not be required for entry). Membership is an *optional* way to participate. Upon arrival, a visitor may choose between buying a daily admission ticket or purchasing a membership, but membership is not presumed to be the preferred way to participate. Instead, membership is presented as an "upgrade" option.

Use the following questions to explore what making membership the default might look like at your museum.

1. Why would we want to make membership the default at our museum?
2. What level of membership would work best as a default?
3. Do we need to consider creating a new level of membership that could serve as a default for visiting?
4. How would our admissions desk and entry process need to evolve to support a default membership model?
5. What would need to change to communicate that membership is the default to all visitors (e.g., signage, website, brochures, etc.)?
6. How would making membership the default change the way we talk about visiting, joining, and giving?
7. What's at risk by making membership the default?

THE PARADOX OF CHOICE

When it comes to choices, are more options better? It seems like a logical and straightforward concept: the more access people have to a variety of options (e.g., flavors of ice cream, brands of athleticwear, or health insurance plans), the better off they will be because each person can select the option that best meets his or her needs. That is, more choice equals happier customers. The problem is, more choice *isn't* always a good thing. In fact, there are circumstances in which increasing the number of options actually makes people less satisfied and, in some cases, reduces the likelihood that a person will make any selection at all.

Known as "the paradox of choice," too many options can create a paralyzing effect in which the person feels overwhelmed and confused by the number of choices available, resulting in a reluctance to make a decision. In one study, researchers set up two distinct tables with jams for sale. The first table displayed a variety of six flavors, the second, twenty-four. While the second, larger display attracted much more browsing and interest, the table with the smaller array led to ten times more sales.[13] In another unintended experiment, an office supplies company reduced the total number of products in its catalog to save on printing and postage costs. Unexpectedly, the company found that sales increased in nearly every category where the number of choices had been reduced.[14]

Every decision that we make takes attention and energy—it's called "cognitive load." Much like a computer, human cognitive processing is limited by the capacity of our working memory which constrains the amount of information we can process at any given time.[15] Cognitive load theory describes how people filter, process, store, and retrieve information to facilitate decision-making. When our mental resources are depleted by complexity, tedious tasks, stress, or too much unnecessary information, decision-making is negatively affected. Too many options can overwhelm, leading to choice overload and decision fatigue.

Think about how visiting, joining, and giving are communicated at your institution. If your museum is like most, upon entering the museum itself or accessing its website, visitors are bombarded with admission options, prices, and competing messages. At best, the visitor will try to absorb as much information as possible within a few minutes and stumble through making a choice that is "good enough."[16] At worst, the organization will lose a critical opportunity for an intentional intervention. By simplifying choice attributes and the number of available options, as well as how and when information is presented, choice overload can be diminished, and both the visitor and the museum will benefit.[17]

Finally, there is an ongoing debate about what constitutes the ideal number of options. Certainly, fewer options help to ease cognitive load, resulting in better decision-making. However, researchers also have found that *increasing* the number of options can help people make better choices. Research suggests that this is likely due to the fact that more options allow an individual to make a more sensible choice that is ultimately easier to justify. The study authors note that "This unanticipated benefit of assortment can potentially be used to improve consumer welfare—but with caution. Giving consumers more options should increase their reliance on justifications for choice, however, this will only improve their welfare in cases in which those reasons point them to better options."[18] Of course, because each organization and situation is unique, it is incumbent upon museums to experiment with and evaluate how the number, order, and description of options presented either help or harm decision-making. Ultimately, choice architects must ensure information is presented in the right way and at the right time to help guide visitors and users toward the best option for their needs.

SPARK: CHOICE ARCHITECTURE AUDIT

While it is challenging to be an objective observer of our own environments, it is important for museum professionals to step back and look at their marketing, experience, and membership programs through the eyes of their audiences. A choice architecture audit can help museums take off their blinders and notice the influences shaping audience decisions that may or may not be intentional. To conduct a choice architecture audit, select an audience touchpoint, such as your museum's website, brochure, email campaign, or admissions desk, and consider the following questions to identify opportunities for interventions:

1. What is the very first thing you see?
2. Why do you think this was the first thing that caught your attention?
3. What is the first decision someone would need to make to move forward from this point in any direction?
4. What words and phrases are used to describe various options?
5. In what order are the list of options presented?
6. What is the default for participating?
7. What images (if any) accompany the message?
8. What decision or step preceded arriving at this point?
9. What does the visitor or user need to do to make a choice?
10. How much information is presented at one time?
11. Is there anything confusing, difficult to read, or inaccessible that could create friction to being able to make a good decision?
12. What other environmental factors are present that might distract or confuse a visitor or user?

13. Are there opportunities to limit the number of available options to reduce the visitor's/user's cognitive load?
14. How long would it take for someone to understand the full range of options available and the benefits or risks associated with each?
15. Can you think of a quick, low-cost intervention that would help guide a visitor or user toward making a better decision?

THE DECOY EFFECT

Decision-making is dependent on many factors, including the context and alternatives presented. The "decoy effect" occurs when consumers change their preference between two options when a third option (the decoy) that is *asymmetrically dominated* is introduced to the choice set. The term asymmetric domination refers to the strategic positioning of the decoy that makes one of the other options appear more attractive in terms of perceived value.

The decoy is often an irrelevant alternative that is not intended to be a desirable option. Rather, the decoy is included within the choice set to create contrast between the original options and nudge the consumer toward the upper end of the choice set (Figure 6.4). Since 1982, the decoy effect has been observed across a wide range of fields, including consumer products, political campaigns, job hiring, and public health. The decoy effect has even been shown to increase donations in crowdfunding campaigns.[19]

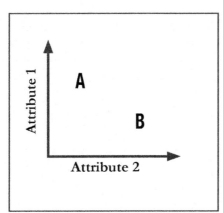
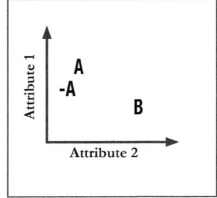

Figure 6.4. The Decoy Effect

SPARK: CREATING A DECOY

In museums, choice architects have an opportunity to intentionally design the choice set to differentiate among options and to nudge visitors and users toward an optimal choice. Take a few minutes to brainstorm how a decoy might be developed to make a particular alternative look more appealing. Refer to Figure 6.4 as a guide, and plot two existing membership categories along an axis with the y-axis representing the attribute of "benefits" and the x-axis representing the attribute of "price," where option A is desirable because of its high value of benefits and option B is desirable because of its low price. Consider how a decoy (option −A) could be introduced to provide contrast between the original two options within the choice set. *Hint: To leverage the decoy effect, do not include more than three alternatives within a single choice set.*

INFLUENCING CHOICES

In the early twentieth century, psychologist Kurt Lewin developed the theory that behavior is driven by two types of external forces, driving forces and restraining forces.[20] Driving forces are those that encourage or drive action, whereas restraining forces are those that inhibit or restrain action (Table 6.1). As Nobel Prize laureate Daniel Kahneman wisely observed, "instead of asking, 'How can I get him or her to do it?' it starts with a question of, 'Why isn't she doing it already?' Very different question."[21]

In museums, the most used marketing strategies are those that focus on driving forces—the membership acquisition campaign that uses a promotional discount to spur interest in joining (e.g., How can I get her to join? Offer a discount!). It is far less common to see a museum working to address

Table 6.1. Driving vs Restraining Forces

Driving forces	Restraining forces
Advertising	Lack of money
Discounts	Lack of time
Events	Lack of transportation
Free admission	Not for someone like me
Free parking	No one to go with
Free tote bag	Uncertain about the experience

restraining forces, such as lack of time, perceptions of belonging, lack of transportation, or uncertainty about the experience. These are the barriers to participation that are slowly atrophying cultural institutions. Addressing the restraining forces that are keeping audiences from participating is far more important than investing time and resources into driving forces. However, asking "Why isn't she doing it already?" requires more time and intentional inquiry. Identifying and developing solutions to diminish restraining forces requires systematic evaluation at every step of the customer journey. Choice architects have the power to address restraining forces to make it easier for people to make the right choice.

Think about the most recent decision—large or small—that you made about your membership program or marketing strategy. Did you increase membership prices to "keep up" with the last ticket price increase? Did you offer a discount or free gift to promote membership during the spring acquisition campaign? Did you select the word used as the call to action for joining during the recent website redesign? What about the decisions that were made outside of your department or work group (e.g., a decision about where and how to install signage, to present admission prices before membership at the box office, or to be closed on Mondays)?

If your institution is like most, very little *intentional* design is applied when it comes to membership. This statement is not intended to dismiss the strategic capabilities, good instincts, or thoughtful decisions of museum professionals who are responsible for managing and marketing the membership program. Rather, it is an acknowledgment that the vast majority of museums have inherited membership programs with pricing strategies, benefits structures, and marketing frameworks that were established long ago. Moreover, the pace at which museums operate allows little time for reflection. Although decisions with significant implications are made daily, few organizations take the time to step back and assess the impact of such decisions on the long-term viability of the museum. A nondecision about the choice architecture may be unintentional, but unintentional influence is influence, nonetheless.

Museum audiences are fallible and susceptible to a wide range of biases that affect how they make decisions. People find it difficult to make choices if they have trouble understanding how that decision will translate into an experience. Membership is a big ask when a person does not have a prior experience to serve as a frame of reference for what becoming a member will entail. Worse yet, past experiences as a member of other organizations may creep into the frame of reference for what becoming a member at your institution may involve. As a choice architect, it is incumbent upon you to help translate membership into a choice set and attributes that can easily be understood.

THE ETHICS OF NUDGING

Discussion of nudges and choice architecture necessitates a discussion of ethics. Rightfully, there is concern about whether such techniques are manipulative and may be used to exploit cognitive biases. Critics argue that nudges and choice architecture compromise autonomy and undermine human agency. Additionally, there is risk that nudges may be used for self-serving purposes that benefit the organization and harm the individual. For example, an organization may nudge people to choose its most profitable product solely to benefit from the increased revenue.

These concerns are valid. Yet the reality is that choice architecture is inevitable. If an organization is not involved in intentionally designing the choice architecture for its audiences, then it is leaving the choice architecture to evolve haphazardly on its own. Either way, the choice architecture will still exist. Therefore, museums must be conscientious in designing choice architecture that is ethical. Ethical nudging is *not* manipulation. Behavioral economist, Richard Thaler outlines three principles to guide ethical nudging:[22]

- All nudging should be transparent and never misleading.
- It should be as easy as possible to opt out of the nudge, preferably with as little as one mouse click.
- There should be good reason to believe that the behavior being encouraged will improve the welfare of those being nudged.

As museum leaders begin to embrace their role as choice architects, they will need to give careful consideration to design decisions. By better understanding the motivations and desires of museum audiences, membership and marketing professionals can help people act on their intentions and make better choices. Armed with insights from the behavioral and social sciences, choice architects are positioned to develop intentional interventions that will support the long-term goals of their museums—keeping in mind Thaler's emphatic plea to always "nudge for good."[23]

NOTES

1. Yun Wang, "Designing Restaurant Digital Menus to Enhance User Experience," Graduate Theses and Dissertations, Iowa State University, 2012, https://doi.org/10.31274/etd-180810-2790.

2. Dan Ariely, "Ask Ariely: On the Bordeaux Battlefield, Irrationality Impact, and Ruminating While Running," *The Blog*, Dan Airely, August 16, 2014, http://danariely

.com/2014/08/16/ask-ariely-on-the-bordeaux-battlefield-irrationality-impact-and-ru minating-while-running/.

3. Brian Wansink, James Painter, and Koert van Ittersum, "How Descriptive Menu Labels Influence Attitudes and Repatronage," *Advances in Consumer Research* 29 (2002): 168–172, http://acrwebsite.org/volumes/8588/volumes/v29/NA-29.

4. Tim Harford, *Messy: The Power of Disorder to Transform Our Lives* (New York: Riverhead Books, 2016), 87.

5. Richard H. Thaler and Cass R. Sunstein, *Nudge: Improving Decisions about Health, Wealth, and Happiness* (New York: Penguin Group, 2009), 6.

6. Ibid., 3.

7. Richard H. Thaler, *Misbehaving: The Making of Behavioral Economics* (New York, NY: W.W. Norton & Company, Inc., 2015), 154.

8. Joann Peck, Victor A. Barger, and Andrea Webb, "In search of a Surrogate for Touch: The Effect of Haptic Imagery on Perceived Ownership," *Journal of Consumer Psychology* 24, no. 2 (April 2014): 226–33.

9. Joann Peck, Suzanne B. Shu, and John Deighton, "The Effect of Mere Touch on Perceived Ownership," *Journal of Consumer Research* 36, no. 3 (2009): 434–47, doi:10.1086/598614.

10. 109th Congress 2d Session, H.R. 4, Pension Protection Act of 2006, Washington, DC: GPO, July 28, 2006, accessed September 26, 2019, https://www.govinfo .gov/content/pkg/BILLS-109hr4cph/pdf/BILLS-109hr4cph.pdf.

11. Jeffrey W. Clark and Jean A. Young, "Automatic Enrollment: The Power of the Default," Vanguard Research, February 2018, https://institutional.vanguard.com/ iam/pdf/CIRAE.pdf.

Mary Steffel, Elanor Williams, and Ruth Pogacar, "'Default' Choices Have Big Im12. pact, But How to Make Sure They're Used Ethically?," *The Conversation*, April 3, 2017, https://theconversation.com/default-choices-have-big-impact-but-how-to -make-sure-theyre-used-ethically-65852.

13. Barry Schwartz, *The Paradox of Choice: Why More Is Less* (New York: HarperCollins, 2004), 19–20.

14. Barry Schwartz, "Is the Famous 'Paradox of Choice' a Myth?," *PBS News-Hour*, January 29, 2014, https://www.pbs.org/newshour/economy/is-the-famous -paradox-of-choic.

15. John Sweller, Jeroen J. G. van Merriënboer, and Fred Paas, "Cognitive Architecture and Instructional Design: 20 Years Later," *Educational Psychology Review* 31, no. 2 (June 2019): 261–92, https://doi.org/10.1007/s10648-019-09465-5.

16. In 1956, economist and cognitive psychologist Herbert Simon introduced the term *satisficing*, a portmanteau of satisfy and suffice, to describe how decisions are made when an optimal option cannot be determined.

17. Eric J. Johnson et al., "Beyond Nudges: Tools of a Choice Architecture," *Marketing Letters* 23 (2012): 487–504, doi:10.1007/s11002-012-9186-1.

18. Aner Sela, Jonah A. Berger, and Wendy Liu, "Variety, Vice, and Virtue: How Assortment Size Influences Option Choice," *Journal of Consumer Research* 35, no. 6 (April 2009): 941–51, https://ssrn.com/abstract=1150853.

19. "Matthias Tietz, Alexander Simons, Markus Weinmann, Jan vom Brocke, "The Decoy Effect in Reward-Based Crowdfunding: Preliminary Results from an Online Experiment," *37th International Conference on Information Systems* (December 2016), https://www.researchgate.net/publication/308611392_The_Decoy_Effect_in_Reward-Based_Crowdfunding_Preliminary_Results_from_an_Online_Experiment.

20. Kurt Lewin," Business and Management, British Library, accessed September 26, 2019, https://www.bl.uk/people/kurt-lewin.

21. Stephen J. Dubner, *How to Launch a Behavior-Change Revolution*, "Freakonomics Radio," produced by Greg Rosalsky (Ep. 306), October 25, 2017, http://freakonomics.com/podcast/launch-behavior-change-revolution/.

22. Richard H. Thaler, "The Power of Nudges, for Good and Bad," *New York Times*, October 31, 2015, https://www.nytimes.com/2015/11/01/upshot/the-power-of-nudges-for-good-and-bad.html.

23. Evan Nesterak, "Nudge Turns 10: A Q&A with Richard Thaler," *Behavioral Scientist*, September 25, 2018, https://behavioralscientist.org/nudge-turns-10-a-qa-with-richard-thaler/.

Chapter Seven

Members, Motives,
and Mixed Messages

Classical music fans represent about 35 percent of consumers globally. The majority of these classical music fans still use radio and CDs as the primary mediums for listening to classical music.[1] In recent years, streaming services such as Spotify and Pandora have boosted the accessibility of classical music, helping to create a new generation of fans. Yet, for the most passionate of classical music fans, dubbed classical aficionados representing just 4 percent of the market, mainstream music platforms leave much to be desired.[2] This is because, unlike popular music that can be easily sorted by song title, album, and artist, a single classical composition may have hundreds of nearly identical versions based on a multitude of factors, such as composer, conductor, orchestra, and recording. Moreover, classical song titles are often very long and can include additional composition features, such as the movement number and tempo. This multitude of variables can make searching for a specific version of a classical song on a mainstream music platform an exercise in futility. Seeing an opportunity to better serve classical aficionados, a German-based start-up has developed a new streaming music service called IDAGIO to fill this gap in the marketplace.

IDAGIO caters to a sophisticated consumer, offering a robust catalog of classical music for users whose discerning ears can distinguish adagio from andante. The platform offers more than 1.2 million recordings from 2,500 orchestras, 6,500 conductors, and 60,000 solo artists.[3] However, its extensive selection of music is not the most important feature of the platform. Recognizing that its users would be interested in not just listening to a wide range of classical music but also being able to listen to a specific version of a composition, IDAGIO created the ability for users to search by criteria such as ensemble, conductor, soloist, instrument, date of performance, period, and so on. The platform even enables searching by "works," allowing users to listen to every version of a composition, such as Aaron Copland's *Appalachian Spring*, filtered by popularity, release date, or performer. It is this nuanced search functionality that sets IDAGIO apart from other streaming music services. With this seemingly small tweak to the traditional streaming music service, IDAGIO has been able to address the unmet needs of a unique niche of music lovers. *Bravo!*

ONE MEMBERSHIP, TWO VERY DIFFERENT CUSTOMERS

The origin story of IDAGIO demonstrates the importance of truly understanding your customers to better tailor products to meet their unique needs. Further, by identifying the key differences between general classical music fans and classical aficionados, IDAGIO has been able to define a differentiating value proposition for its service. Concentrating on this sweet spot has allowed IDAGIO to focus its marketing, product features, and customer experience on an underserved and highly valuable customer—one who will happily pay a $10 monthly subscription fee for its service.

IDAGIO's business model taps into the power of market segmentation (or customer segmentation) by identifying and clustering customers into subgroups based on similar needs, interests, behaviors, and motivations. Segmentation helps an organization see how its products and marketing can be tailored to a distinct and clearly defined audience. There are a number of ways to conduct segmentation, including by geography, demographics, behavior, and psychographics. Each of these segmentation strategies can be layered and combined to develop a profile of customers who look, think, feel, and act in the same way. To be profitable, market segments must be identifiable, substantial, accessible, stable, differentiable, and actionable.[4]

SIX CHARACTERISTICS OF MARKET SEGMENTS

1. **Identifiable**—For market segmentation to be useful, a museum must be able to identify the customers within a particular segment. For example, if an organization is unable to track member visitation, then it will be difficult to create a customer subset around this behavior.
2. **Substantial**—The market segment must be large enough that it makes business sense to invest the resources necessary to develop a unique marketing strategy or product to serve the subgroup of customers.
3. **Accessible**—A museum must be able to reach the market segment. For example, a marketing strategy to reach a market segment defined as

teenagers between the ages of 14 and 18 may include text messaging and Instagram.

4. **Stable**—The market segment must be stable enough to allow time for the museum to develop a product and implement a marketing strategy to reach the customer subset.

5. **Differentiable**—To be effective, the customers included within the market segment must possess the same characteristics that make them uniquely different from other customer segments.

6. **Actionable**—The museum must be able to act on its market segmentation strategy through the development of new products or marketing designed to meet the unique needs of the newly identified segment.

Market segmentation is an essential part of a successful business model. In the museum sector, there may be many customer segments that an organization wishes to serve, such as parents, teachers, gardeners, makers, art lovers, or history buffs. Museums may also segment customers by purchase behavior. For example, many organizations view "members" as a customer segment. However, the practice of segmenting customers by purchase behavior conceals a critical piece of information: members are not homogeneous.

MARKET SEGMENTATION CRITERIA

Geography: Segmentation by geography includes location-based identifiers, such as city, state, zip code, or region. For example, a zoo might offer a community membership to residents who live within a defined radius around the zoo.

Demographics: Museums traditionally have segmented customers based on demographics. What is the age, income, educational background, ethnicity, occupation, and family status of the person? What language(s) do they speak? These are all demographic factors that can be used to segment customers. A membership category that is based on the number of children in the household or a membership level for young professionals are examples of demographic segmentation.

Behavioral: Patterns of behavior, such as previous purchases, visitation frequency and recency, past event attendance, and who they visit with, are data points that can be used to develop a customer segment profile. Behavioral segmentation may also include aspects of preference, occasion, buyer readiness, and user status. For instance, one customer may prefer a boisterous coffeehouse environment, while another seeks a quiet, calm ambience in which to enjoy his or her espresso. Occasion refers to the timing of a decision, such as planning for a family activity or purchasing a birthday gift. Where the customer is in terms of the purchasing process is known as buyer readiness and includes mental states such as awareness, interest, and intent. User status refers to the relationship of the individual to the organization, such as a first-time visitor, current member, donor, or defector.

Psychographics: Motivations, values, beliefs, lifestyle, perceptions, social identity, and attitudes are aspects of psychographic segmentation. Psychographics is one of the most important components of a market segmentation strategy because it reveals the fundamental distinctions about why customers behave the way they do.

As the studies presented in this chapter demonstrate, members can have very different motivations, values, and needs. Importantly, research shows that members fall into two distinct categories:

1. Transactional, or value-based, members who are motivated by the "value" that membership offers—free admission, free parking, free member events, the free tote bag, member discounts, and so on. These members are unlikely to think of their membership as a donation and make decisions based on a cost-benefit analysis.
2. Philanthropic, or mission-based, members who are motivated by a sense of belonging and commitment to the cause. Mission-based members are more likely to renew, join at higher levels, and get more value from their membership.[5] These members likely have higher intrinsic motivations and, therefore, are at greater risk for conflict between philanthropic motives and market incentives.

The existence of this two-headed membership monster reveals an opportunity to develop a market segmentation strategy. Museums have been challenged in the past to build offerings tailored to niche audiences due to limited resources, imperfect research methods, and inadequate customer data; however, the future of membership will be built on a strategy that leverages robust market segmentation. Without such a strategy, museums not only are missing out on revenue, but they also are doing a disservice to stakeholders by not fully meeting their needs. Inaction may result in audiences finding other leisure activities and organizations that are a better fit.

The absence of market segmentation in museum membership is a cardinal sin of marketing. As museums seek to engage new audiences and deepen relationships with current stakeholders, they must adopt a more proactive approach to meeting member needs. The path forward will not be easy. Developing a market segmentation strategy requires that museums begin the hard work of listening, understanding, and developing new products. Just as IDAGIO rose to meet the needs of classical aficionados, museums must rise to the challenge of becoming truly customer centric.

Today, museums market to and serve members as if they all share the same motivations, values, and needs. While the tiering of categories to include higher levels of membership seeks to address these differences, this is not a holistic segmentation strategy. Rather, the use of membership tiers is a passive approach that attempts to facilitate self-selection among audiences who have differing motivations, values, and needs. We are social, vibrant, complex beings—it's time that our approach to membership and marketing reflects this truth.

SPARK: FINDING A NEW MARKET SEGMENT TO SERVE

No single approach to market segmentation is best. Market segmentation may include a combination of analyzing existing data, primary research, and secondary research. The following provides an example of how a museum may approach a market segmentation analysis.

Step 1: Establish an objective. What is the goal of conducting a market segmentation analysis? Does the organization have the ability and commitment to serve a new market segment? How will you prioritize potential customer segments?

Step 2: Gather available data, draw out possible segmentation variables, and establish a hypothesis. For example, a museum may be able to uncover hidden, unmet needs by analyzing how users navigate or search for content on the institution's website. Behavioral data may also be available based on visitation patterns, membership lifecycle, and benefits usage. Email campaign analytics may provide information about differing interests among current subscribers. A zip code analysis can reveal patterns in visitors, members, and website or mobile users. Institutional databases may provide the ability to cluster customers with similar needs, buying patterns, or other relevant characteristics. Understanding where gaps in data exist and capturing any meaningful insights from available data sets will help guide further customer discovery.

Step 3: Identify customer segments. Research design, data collection, analysis, and validation are all necessary to finding a new market segment. Customer segments must be identifiable (sharing similar characteristics, needs, and behaviors), substantial (large enough to grow and the ability to generate revenue), accessible (able to be reached via marketing), stable (can be marketed to over a long period of time), differentiable (divergent from other potential customer segments), and actionable (the museum can feasibly serve the segment).

Step 4: Cluster and rank potential customer segments. Based on the stated objective, rank the potential customer segments on the dimensions of revenue, accessibility, and priority. This step will help answer questions such as What is the market size and potential of each segment? Which segments offer the highest revenue and profit potential? Do we have existing customers in any of these segments? Which segments have the best potential for opportunity *and* return on investment?

Step 5: Profile customer segments. Conduct research to determine customers' unmet needs and motivations. This step may include focus groups, in-depth interviews, surveys, social media listening, customer journey mapping, empathy maps, and ethnographic research.

SMILES AND FROWNS

Which of the following messages do you think will be most effective in encouraging more hotel guests to reuse their towels?

1. HELP SAVE THE ENVIRONMENT. You can show your respect for nature and help save the environment by reusing your towels during your stay.
2. JOIN YOUR FELLOW GUESTS IN HELPING TO SAVE THE ENVIRONMENT. Almost 75 percent of guests who are asked to participate in our new resource savings program do help by using their towels more than once. You can join your fellow guests to help save the environment by reusing your towels during your stay.

You may be surprised to learn that people who were exposed to the second message reused their towels 26 percent more often than those who saw the general environmental protection message.[6] Why? The second message taps into an important hidden motivator we all share: social norms. "Social norms" refer to the perceptions of what is commonly done in a particular situation and what is generally approved or disapproved of within a society. We're social creatures by nature so, when there is a strong sense of social obligation and reciprocation involved in a decision, people are more likely to participate in behaviors that are viewed as prosocial.[7] Calling upon social norms can encourage behavior that benefits the individual and his or her community.

Despite evidence to the contrary, the most common way hotels promote involvement in conservation programs is by focusing on the importance of environmental protection. Yet, by simply tweaking the wording to emphasize social norms, hotels would be able to significantly improve towel reuse rates. The nuance of language matters.

Testing the power of social norms, researchers created a brilliantly simple intervention that used emoticons to encourage energy conservation. In the experiment, a smiley face was placed on a customer's energy bill to indicate that the household's energy usage was less than their neighbors'. If the household were consuming more energy than the neighborhood average, researchers would place a frowny face on their energy bill to indicate the bad behavior.[8] The results were compelling. Households that received a smiley face for below-average energy usage continued to conserve energy, while those households that received a frowny face reduced their energy usage.

There was, however, an unexpected finding in the study: In the control condition of the experiment, households did not receive emoticons on their energy bill. Instead, only information about their own energy usage along with the average neighborhood energy usage was provided. In this group, while households that were consuming more energy than their neighbors reduced their usage, the energy-conservers *increased* their consumption. Researchers attributed this undesirable behavior to the "boomerang effect," in which people adjust their behavior—even good behavior—to be more in line with the norm. Without the smiley face to praise their good prosocial behavior, these energy conservers felt like they were going above and beyond what was expected of them. In response to this new information that highlighted how their behavior compared to their neighbors', the households that were working hard to conserve energy lowered the bar they had set for themselves. So, as behavioral economist Richard Thaler warns, "If you want to nudge people into socially desirable behavior, do not, by any means, let them know that their current actions are better than the social norm."[9]

Social norms can be a potent device in communicating the prosocial behavior of being a member. While inclusion of social norms messaging may seem like an obvious strategy in a nonprofit setting, countless museums miss out on using this influential technique when marketing membership. This is not the time to be humble or ambiguous. Messaging that explicitly draws attention to social norms, such as the popularity of membership, how members are part of a "growing movement" supporting the mission, and the impact of membership, help to convey the type of participation expected from a community.

BRIGHT SPOT: LEVERAGING SOCIAL PROOF
AT THE ARKANSAS ARTS CENTER

The foremost expert on the psychology of persuasion, Robert Cialdini, classi-fied "social proof" as one of six weapons of influence, along with reciprocity, commitment and consistency, authority, liking, and scarcity.[1] Social proof is the tendency we have to view a behavior as more appropriate when we see others doing it. The concept of social proof can influence behavior by signal-ing to others that a particular action or decision is the right thing to do.

To leverage the concept of social proof, the Arkansas Arts Center conduct-ed an experiment in 2014 by placing yard signs in front of members' houses that would conspicuously show their support of the Center. In preparation for the experiment, the Center analyzed its membership database and identi-fied the zip code with the largest concentration of members. Speaking about the goals of the campaign, Spencer Jansen, manager of Member Experience, said "I wanted to give affirmation of belonging to our current members, and I wanted the non-members to want to be a part of the Arkansas Arts Center through membership."

To visually map out the member houses into four quadrants, the Center pur-chased a 34- by 44-inch map of the target zip code with members' addresses highlighted for $11 from the Pulaski County Department of Planning and Development. Next, the Center emailed members asking for permission to post a sign in their yard for one month, emphasizing that the purpose was for members to "show their love" for the Center. Of the 625 members asked, 144 agreed to display signs in their yard.

The campaign was ingenious. As people drove to and from home, they couldn't help but see "I'm a Part. Because Art." signs posted on virtually every street in their neighborhood (Figure 7.1). While the signs were displayed, the Center implemented a direct mail campaign to nonmembers within the target zip code that included a $10 discount on membership.

While the results of the experiment appeared lackluster at first—the overall response rate from the direct mail campaign was just 0.44 percent—the five-year return on investment from the effort has been incredible. Of those who joined during the campaign, several were first-time or recently lapsed mem-bers who have become long-standing supporters of the Center. In one case, a first-time member upgraded his membership the following year and has contributed a total of $515 since 2014. In another case, a first-time member who had never previously taken a class at the Center has renewed every year since the campaign, totaling $270 in membership dues, and regularly enrolls in multiple classes annually, totaling $3,510 in tuition to date. Importantly, the campaign was successful in reactivating numerous long-lapsed mem-bers—some of whom had not been a member for 10 to 20 years. Overall, the campaign generated a total of $3,325 in membership dues and $3,785 in

Figure 7.1. Yard Sign and Letter
Courtesy of the Arkansas Arts Center

revenue for activities such as annual fund gifts, tributes, and tuition, representing a $1.85 return on investment to date.

While the experiment required a significant amount of staff resources and did not initially generate a return on investment, it demonstrated the potential of applying social proof to promote membership. Case in point, Jansen chuckled as he recalled a woman who was visiting a friend in the neighborhood where the signs were displayed and said she wanted one for her yard. "She joined over the phone," he said, "and I drove to the other side of the city and placed a sign in her yard!" Social proof is a powerful weapon of influence indeed.

NOTE

1. Robert B. Cialdini, *Influence: The Psychology of Persuasion* (New York: HarperCollins e-books, 2009), 120, Google Play.

Courtesy of the Arkansas Arts Center.

IDENTITY AND A SENSE OF SELF

As highly social creatures, we belong to many social groups that have their own distinct identities. We define ourselves by our affiliations—our sports teams, our profession, our hobbies, our religion, our neighborhood, our alma mater, our political views, our ethnicity, our nationality. Identity shapes the purchases we make, what we read, how we spend our time, and the causes we support.

The mental image we have of ourselves is called our "self-concept," and social identity is a part of this construct of our sense of self.[10] Social identities can be activated based on the context and circumstance of a given moment. It is our social identity that helps us decide how to act in a way that validates our distinctiveness as a certain type of person. For example, an individual who shops at a natural foods market may have several social identities that influence purchasing decisions, such as being health conscious, eco-friendly, and a good parent.

Research in the field of psychology has established that there are certain *prescriptions* associated with an individual's sense of self that, when followed, affirm one's self-concept.[11] Findings suggest that people will adjust their behavior to more closely reflect these prescriptions when they are reminded of their identity. Further, the use of specific words, messages, or imagery—known as "priming"—can influence behavior without the individual's conscious awareness of the prime. For instance, priming a potential donor for "generosity" increases the likelihood of a donation. In a study conducted by the American Red Cross, researchers found that fundraising appeals that primed an individual's identity as a previous donor generated more donations.[12]

Priming can take many forms, including asking questions that create an association to a desired behavior. For example, when researchers asked passersby if they would participate in a marketing survey without compensation, only 29 percent agreed to participate. However, if the researcher first asked the individual "Do you consider yourself a helpful person?" the rate of participation shot up to 77 percent.[13] Once an individual was primed with the characteristic of being a helpful person, they were more likely to agree to help out with the survey. Thus, priming can influence audiences to behave in ways that are congruent with their aspirational identity.

Because social identities are formed by a collection of behaviors that reinforce an individual's affiliation within a particular group, when consumers have a well-defined social identity with a positive image, they are likely to select products that enhance and signal their affiliation. Consider the social identity evoked by the outdoor brand Patagonia. As a long-standing advocate of natural lands preservation, Patagonia urges its customers to enjoy, respect, and protect nature. The brand emphasizes the kinds of behaviors that reinforce this identity, including sponsoring petitions for public land preservation, encouraging involvement with environmental action groups through its Patagonia Action Works program, promoting reuse and upcycling of clothing, and offering its own line of foods that address environmental issues and support local producers. These identity-aligned activities deepen Patagonia's relationship with its customers and also provide clear direction to its audiences about how to live into their social identity of being a nature lover.

In recent years, membership in social identity–related organizations has been thriving. For example, the American Civil Liberties Union (ACLU) has seen its membership grow from 400,000 to 1.84 million in 2017, with online donations surging from between $3 and $5 million annually to nearly $120 million.[14] Likewise, the Environmental Defense Fund reached a record level of $223 million in revenue in 2018 with a 5 percent growth in membership over the previous year.[15] Overall, giving to environmental and animal organizations is estimated to have increased by 13.5 percent between 2016 and 2018.[16] There are no transactional benefits associated with membership in such organizations. Rather, membership is deeply tied to personal values and social identity.

Importantly, social identities are not just preexisting constructs that can give marketers greater insight into the motivations behind decision-making and behavior. Identity can also be formed. That is, museums have an opportunity to craft a new social identity for audiences to adopt, opening the door for deeper engagement among current audiences and the ability to attract new ones. Moreover, identity can be aspirational, allowing organizations to inspire and direct behaviors that align with a desired set of values just as Patagonia has established identity-related actions associated with its brand. For example, a botanical garden may wish to build a new social identity around being a pollinator activist. This social identity might include supporting behaviors, such as planting regional milkweed to support the Monarch butterfly population, stopping use of pesticides in home gardens, and purchasing ecologically sustainable products. To define this new identity, the garden might create a series of classes about pollination, moderate a social media–driven community for activists, and build a separate membership program that emphasizes the social identity of being a friend of butterflies, naming them the "Pollinator Pals." (That's a freebie!)

The implication of social identity for museums is clear, and marketing must shift toward strategies that activate an individual's social identities within the context of participation. Such a shift will require deeper understanding of museum audiences and their underlying motivations and social identities. Uncovering such motivations and identities requires a different approach to research. Because traditional research methodologies will not be able to reveal when a particular social identity is activated, it will be necessary to observe consumers in real time as they make decisions.

GIFTS AND GLOWS

One of the more fascinating aspects of human psychology involves the entanglement of generosity and incentives. When someone does something kind without the expectation of anything in return, they get what is colloquially described as "the warm fuzzies" caused by the reward centers of the brain lighting up. In fundraising, nonprofit organizations can leverage this warm fuzzy feeling that a donor gets when he or she gives. Known in academic circles as the "warm glow," museums often attempt to tap into this good feeling by piggybacking the idea of philanthropic support onto the membership purchase.[17]

As shown in Figure 7.2, a cursory review of marketing materials promoting museum membership shows the prevalence of this dual messaging strategy. A museum Facebook post touts "Members gain access to benefits such as curator-led tours, exclusive exhibition openings, and special members-only events. Plus, your membership supports the museum's dedication to access and excellence, and it helps ensure a strong future for the institution and those

Figure 7.2.   Examples of Membership Messaging

we serve." Another exclaims "Our memberships pay for themselves in less than two visits. Your support benefits the care of about 1,165 species at the Zoo and the efforts of 50 field conservation projects and 20 research projects annually." A website proclaims "A Zoo membership offers unlimited visits plus benefits all year round while supporting the Zoo's educational programs and conservation efforts." A membership brochure promotes "Unlimited Admission . . . Exclusive Benefits . . . Valuable Discounts . . . Support the National Aquarium." Another describes how "Museum membership supports one of the world's finest museums and gives you many benefits to be enjoyed through the year." This dual messaging strategy is so ingrained in the nonprofit membership world that it is difficult to find an example where membership is promoted without a philanthropic angle.

There are many reasons why museums have adopted this approach. First, membership can be considered a form of philanthropic support because the profit produced from the membership program is allocated to further the organization's mission. As the levels of membership increase, the gap between the value of the benefits received and the cost of the membership also increases, leading to a greater portion of the membership price being considered a donation. Indeed, the industry standard is to include a tier of "donor members" who *give* at higher amounts than lower-level members. Second, the use of such philanthropic terminology is intended to create a sense of belonging and foster future support from members. Third, the warm glow associated with supporting the mission makes members feel really good about their decision to join. By becoming a member, members feel like they are giving in support of a cause they care about.

But there is a challenge that arises when a philanthropic message is paired with a consumer-driven decision (i.e., evaluation of the transactional benefits of membership)—a blurring of the line between altruism and a purchase transaction that creates an entanglement in the mind of the consumer. This entanglement can be problematic because it can crowd out a member's altruistic motivations for joining. Here's how it happens: Museums promote membership by highlighting the market incentives associated with joining—these are the extrinsic rewards that come with being a member, such as a coffee mug, scooter rental, or member magazine, as well as the intangible benefits of membership, such as free admission, free parking, and member events. By touting these types of perks in exchange for financial support, the exchange becomes a quid pro quo scenario. It is this exchange of benefits for membership dues that can crowd out the intrinsic motivation of a member. In other words, when a philanthropically oriented member receives benefits, the transactional benefits can overwhelm the member's good intentions, causing him or her to think only in terms of cost-benefit.[18]

At this point, you may be thinking "Wait a second; isn't that exactly what membership is? A cost-benefit equation?" Therein lies the rub.[19] Museums like to describe membership as a philanthropic "gift," based on the gap between the market value of the benefits and the cost of the membership, which is considered a charitable donation to the organization. However, membership is explicitly designed to offer conditional incentives in exchange for a contribution. It is this emphasis on the transactional benefits of membership—particularly at higher membership levels—that is likely to shift a potential member's mindset. That is, intrinsic motives of giving will give way to a more calculative mindset, resulting in less philanthropically oriented decision-making. In a nonprofit setting where members are highly intrinsically motivated to give, incentives can be counterproductive. Thus, by giving philanthropic members benefits, the museum risks convoluting altruistic motives and crowding out the warm glow. Fundamentally, museums are robbing these philanthropically motivated members of the good feeling that comes from the act of giving.

███

BRIGHT SPOT: FLEX TICKETS AT THE DENVER MUSEUM OF NATURE & SCIENCE

In 2011, the Denver Museum of Nature & Science began pioneering work to collaborate with communities to understand the ways in which its community connects with nature and science, including learning what is important to them in leisure-time activities and what they hope to see in future Museum experiences. From this research, numerous insights about how the community wants to connect with nature and science were identified, and a vision for *Community Themes and Values* was created. One of the themes that caught the attention of the membership team was that people want to "create their own" experiences—to be able to decide how to engage with the Museum and to have the freedom to define their own experience in a way that is relevant and meaningful to them.

This finding was an aha moment as the Museum realized that its most generous members—those giving annually $300 or more through the Giving Club membership—were being prescribed a package of benefits. For example, members received a set number of tickets for general admission, IMAX, Planetarium, and traveling exhibitions—regardless of whether they had any interest in these experiences. Thus, members were not able to customize their experience based on their interests.

In 2016, the Museum began a planning process to increase prices for both general admission tickets and membership. As part of this process, the membership team performed a market scan, reviewed benchmarking reports, and considered key learnings from staff and member surveys. Importantly, member surveys highlighted that Giving Club members had different motivations for joining and desired a different set of benefits than transactional members. Giving Club members indicated that the primary reason for joining was to support the Museum's mission and the scientific research, whereas free admission was the primary driver for members in the General Membership program. Further, Giving Club members indicated that the most important benefit (other than free admission) was free tickets. While an argument could have been made at that time that the prescribed set of benefit tickets was adequately meeting the needs of Giving Club members, the membership team believed there was an opportunity to be more customer centric.

Armed with data, the membership team made a recommendation to increase the price of the base level of the Giving Club (Curator) to $500, a 66 percent increase. To justify such a significant price increase, the membership team decided to explore the possibility of empowering members to "create their own experience." With this goal in mind, the Museum introduced "Flex Tickets," which can be used for *any* lecture, traveling exhibition, IMAX, Planetarium, or other program priced at $15 or less. *Flex* means the ticket can be used at any time for any experience. No reservations are required—even for ticketed venues, such as IMAX. In fact, the member is guaranteed entry even if the experience is sold out.

The Museum promotes its new Flex Tickets as a way for Giving Club members to curate their own experience (Figure 7.3). For instance, members might use all of their Flex Tickets for a single one-time experience, such as at the Museum's VR Arcade, or they might use their Flex Tickets for a mix of

Dear Giving Club Member,

Spring is in full swing at the Museum! With all sorts of exciting offerings right now, I wanted to answer some Frequently Asked Questions about Flex Tickets.

Flex Tickets may be used to attend any surcharged exhibition, as well as any show or program that costs $15 or less. No advance reservations are needed, and your Flex Ticket will get you in even if the program is "sold out."

This means that you can use your Flex Tickets for:

- *Dead Sea Scrolls* (admission to the exhibition is currently offered between 10 a.m. to 3:40 p.m.)
- Science Lounge and After Hours* lectures
- IMAX and Planetarium shows
- Family programs*
- And more!

Figure 7.3. Frequently Asked Questions About Flex Tickets
Courtesy of the Denver Museum of Nature & Science.

evening lectures and IMAX films. Whatever members are most interested in, they can use their Flex Tickets to get them in. An additional feature of Flex Tickets is that they can be given away, allowing members to share their love of the Museum with others.

While approximately 10 percent of Giving Club households were lost due to the price increase, revenue in the program increased by more than $150,000 overall in the first year. Since the inception of Flex Tickets in September 2017, Giving Club member retention has decreased by 5 percent compared to the prior year, and upgrades into the Giving Club have increased by 20 percent compared to the prior year. Flex Ticket redemption stands at 10 percent on average, and tickets are primarily used for traveling exhibitions and IMAX films. However, redemption of Flex Tickets is also occurring at unexpected venues and experiences, including lectures and the VR Arcade, indicating that members are now creating their own experience based on the introduction of this new benefit. With time, the membership team hopes to encourage members to experiment with designing their own experience by exploring even more of what the Museum has to offer.

A leader in the sector, the Denver Museum of Nature & Science is constantly evaluating its membership offering to ensure that its programs remain an important part of its members' lives. The Museum's belief in taking measured risks by testing new ideas has led to numerous initiatives that have helped deliver on its mission to ignite a passion for nature and science in everyone. It is this innovative mindset that has allowed the Museum to introduce Giving Club members to a more personalized experience. Members are loving their new benefit. Just ask the happy members who used all of their Flex Tickets so early in their membership year that they asked if they could purchase more.

Courtesy of the Denver Museum of Nature & Science.

Another counterintuitive challenge is that members—even transactional members—believe they are financially supporting the mission by purchasing a membership. Why? Because museums intentionally (and frequently) thank members for their financial support of the mission, when, in fact, revenue from membership alone is not enough to sustain an organization's operations. Moreover, it is rare for transactional members to provide additional donations above and beyond their membership dues likely because they have been taught (mistakenly) to think of their membership purchase as a proxy for a philanthropic gift. The result is that the museum inadvertently thwarts its ability to cultivate new donors because members feel like they're already doing their part.

Transactional members are first and foremost consumers. They may feel good about supporting a cause they care about; however, transactional members are quick to dismiss this sensibility come renewal time if they do not believe that they "got their money's worth." Kent Dove, formerly a top development officer at Indiana University, shared some prudent advice in *The Chronicle of Philanthropy* regarding the challenge of transactional members who wrongly believe their membership fee is a gift, recommending that organizations "let members know that getting a membership is not the same thing as making a donation."[20] Museums would be wise to do more to help transactional members understand that there is an important distinction between joining and giving.

THE ONE-FOR-ONE MODEL

A rising trend in cause marketing is the advent of the one-for-one business model, made popular by brands such as TOMS, Bombas, and Warby Parker, which overtly pairs a charitable donation with a for-profit product purchase. Although the one-for-one business model is relatively new, there has been an immense appetite for such products, resulting in the sale of billions of dollars' worth of shoes, eyeglasses, coffee, health bars, socks, backpacks, watches, and soccer balls. The goal of such cause-marketing business models is to turn a profit while helping communities in need. The buy-to-give construct of one-for-one companies leverages several consumer behavior concepts, including conscious consumerism and conspicuous giving. In particular, the purchase of charity-aligned products offers consumers the opportunity to align their purchase with a social identity and exhibit their prosocial behavior by signaling to others that they are doing good.[21]

Compare how museum membership is marketed today with TOMS shoes, a one-for-one company (Figure 7.4). While the difference between the two marketing approaches is extremely subtle, there is an important distinction. Museum membership is frequently marketed as a mash-up of a vague philanthropic message layered with a consumer-driven value proposition. For example, membership marketing often includes messaging such as "Join today to take advantage of exciting membership benefits. Plus, your support will help bring groundbreaking exhibitions and programs to diverse audiences for years to come" and "In addition to all the great benefits above, your membership contribution supports the museum's mission to . . ." In contrast, TOMS shoes are clearly marketed as an identity-driven purchase.

Moreover, because research shows that a significant portion of visitors and members are *unaware* that museums are nonprofits, they may not equate purchasing a membership with making a donation at all. Instead, it is likely that many members think of their membership more in terms of a buy-to-give concept, similar to a for-profit social good product like TOMS. This presents

I VOTE
I GIVE BLOOD
I

FOR EVERY PAIR PURCHASED,
TOMS GIVES A PAIR OF SHOES
TO A CHILD IN NEED.
ONE FOR ONE. www.TOMSshoes.com

Figure 7.4.   TOMS Advertising

an interesting opportunity for museums: If members already think of their membership as a "do good by buying" type of product, then it may be possible to shift the marketing message to explicitly promote membership as a buy-to-give concept, thereby allowing the museum to create a stronger distinction between giving and joining. Further, membership marketing has the potential to activate an individual's social identity if it is positioned with the right message. Additionally, reframing membership as a one-for-one could create an opportunity for museums to educate visitors about the cause behind the mission and offer members the chance to pay it forward by "giving" the museum experience to an individual or family in need.

Cause-marketing companies have begun giving consumers more options for how their charitable donation is directed. For example, TOMS customers can now choose from one of five causes to support.[22] This strategy further strengthens the identity bond between customers with its brand by allowing customers to exercise control over how their donation is applied. Moreover, by providing customers with a path to become affiliated with a specific cause, TOMS is leveraging the strong emotional connection that comes from being part of an affinity group.

Despite decades-old research into member retention that links participation in special interest groups to higher renewal rates, museums have not fully integrated this concept into their membership business model.[23] Of those museums that do offer special interest groups, such programs are often promoted as an add-on to the traditional membership program, rather than as a distinct membership product in and of itself. For example, Women and the Kemper is a special interest group of the Mildred Lane Kemper Art Museum that is offered for an additional annual fee with a current membership to the museum.[24] As museums begin to explore a more tailored approach to membership, special interest groups can be a great place to start.

WHY DO MEMBERS JOIN?

If you have sensed that members join for very different reasons at your own institution, your gut is right. Museum leaders have long surmised that members have varied motivations for joining, and the data are starting to confirm this intuition. However, while there is a substantial body of literature exploring the motivations of *donors*, research into museum *members* is fragmented and sparse. Thankfully, new studies are under way that will begin to shed light on the distinctions between the motives and behaviors of members related to philanthropy, membership, and consumerism. Such research will help to answer questions like Why is it that some audiences choose to join, while others abstain? What are the barriers to joining? And what does it truly mean to be a member?

Notably, research to date has found that museum members initially join for pragmatic and economic reasons, specifically, for the tangible benefits of membership, such as free admission and early and expedited access to programs and events, as well as other members-only perks. Further, members tend to renew their membership only if these tangible benefits continue to be delivered *and* if the members' "emotional and psychological needs are fulfilled" through various aspects of the experience, including "attachment to a particular venue, its ambience and facilities; status attached to belonging to a prestigious organization; social interaction and friendship; a wish to attain and develop . . . knowledge and awareness; need for activity, for attainment and educational development; and economic benefits such as free admission."[25]

In a study of museum members in the UK, two of the most-cited reasons for joining were personal interest and free admission, and, not surprisingly, members tend to value the benefits that they use the most.[26] These results suggest that members view their membership more as a transaction—money in exchange for benefits—rather than as a charitable donation. However, in this same study, financial support was also listed as a primary reason for joining, and a third of respondents expressed a willingness to give beyond their membership fee.[27] Other studies find the strange phenomenon of members who join (and renew) but never take advantage of their benefits.[28] What is the explanation for this odd behavior? It is very likely that these members view their membership fee as a proxy for a donation. These findings indicate that we are witnessing an active process of a member-driven market segmentation occurring within membership—museums should be paying attention and begin taking steps to capitalize on this opportunity.

The studies highlighted in this chapter make it clear that museum members lack homogeneity and exhibit a wide range of motivations. Members may be driven by altruistic, egoistic, or hedonic motives, such as philanthropy and preservation (altruistic); social recognition, children's benefits, and tangible benefits (egoistic); and a love of art or the experience of connecting with nature (hedonic).[29] As one might suspect, the higher the membership level, the greater the altruistic motive. However, higher levels of membership are also used to signal status and prestige. Members who join at higher levels demonstrate higher scores for social recognition motives. For example, when the names of members are publicly displayed, contributions tend to meet the minimum amount required to qualify within a particular category.[30] And, as expected, members who join at lower-priced levels tend to be motivated more by transactional benefits. Thus, there are a number of intrinsic and extrinsic factors that affect how an individual decides to support an organization. Moreover, members' motivations and behaviors may change over time. Therefore, museums must be diligent in listening, understanding, and responding to audiences' diverse needs throughout their various stages of involvement with the organization.

LOYALTY AND MEMBER INVOLVEMENT

Customer loyalty impacts every metric that matters. In membership, loyalty is often confused with member retention, yet loyalty and membership tenure are not the same thing. While it is easy to equate a membership renewal to a relationship with the museum, length of membership itself is not a predictor of member commitment. This reality upends a strong belief in the museum sector that longevity of membership status alone correlates with a deeper relationship to the organization.[31] That said, there is research to suggest that members who identify with an organization tend to feel more involved, attend more frequently, and have a higher likelihood of renewing their membership.

So, while not all long-term members feel a sense of connection to their museum, there is a subset of members who identify deeply with the organization and feel a strong sense of belonging through their membership. To ensure they are focused on building relationships with those members who are truly committed to the organization, museums will need to get better at distinguishing between those members who are long serving but apathetic and those who are loyal and impassioned.

As museums work to build stronger and more meaningful relationships with members, they must develop capabilities in the areas of four core drivers of loyalty, including identity, satisfaction, trust, and commitment.

- **Identity.** A critical aspect of loyalty, research finds that strengthening the identification bond can lead to improved member retention.[32] Focusing on identity is an imperative for museums operating in an increasingly competitive and resource-limited environment. Moreover, customer retention has been proven to reduce marketing costs, increase revenue through upgrading and cross-selling, improve customer satisfaction, and increase word-of-mouth referrals.
- **Satisfaction.** Studies on satisfaction in the nonprofit sector to date have focused primarily on donors, rather than members. Such research has identified a positive correlation between satisfaction and loyalty among donors. For instance, donors who indicated that they were "very satisfied" with the quality of service were found to be twice as likely to give a subsequent gift.[33] Moreover, satisfaction is positively linked to future intentions and behavior, including increased giving.[34] One of philanthropy's premier scholars, Adrian Sargeant, notes that "a 10 percent improvement in [donor] attrition can yield up to a 200 percent increase in projected value, as with lower attrition significantly more donors upgrade their giving, give in multiple ways, recommend others, and, ultimately, perhaps, pledge a planned gift to the organization."[35] Further, only 22 percent of donors stop giving due to a change in financial circumstance.[36] Thus, there are more reasons than money that cause the majority of donors to stop giving. Along with these compelling facts comes an opportunity for museums to better measure loyalty and invest in improving member satisfaction in a meaningful way.
- **Trust.** As a core driver of loyalty and giving behavior, trust is essential for building long-term, successful relationships with members. Trust is

established when organizations demonstrate good judgment, competence, a set of core principles, and high-quality service.[37] Museums can build trust when they proactively create opportunities for open dialogue, listen to audiences, and take action to respond to feedback.

- **Commitment.** In contrast to satisfaction, which is a measure of past experiences, commitment comprises two dimensions: emotional attachment based on an individual's personal identification with the organization (affective commitment) and the perceived economic and psychological benefits of being in a relationship with the organization (continuance commitment).[38]

Whereas satisfaction is a primary driver of future intentions among more transactional members, studies show that trust and commitment are critical factors in the future intentions of "high relational customers," or consistent members.[39] Therefore, museums seeking to improve relationships with high relational members must focus on marketing strategies and experiences that prioritize building trust and commitment.

Finally, research into museum members has identified six characteristics that provide important distinctions among member involvement as signified by their motivations, values, and needs, including (1) centrality and pleasure; (2) desire to learn; (3) escapism: spirituality and creativity; (4) sense of belonging and prestige; (5) physical; and (6) drivers of involvement.[40]

SIX CHARACTERISTICS OF MEMBER INVOLVEMENT

1. **Centrality and Pleasure**—members who enjoy visiting and feel that the museum is an integral part of their life. Importantly, the museum itself is not necessarily a primary feature of the decision to join. Rather, membership to the museum facilitates the freedom and flexibility to experience art in their lives.
2. **Desire to Learn**—members who are curious and looking for experiences that are enlightening, encouraging them to learn new things and see the world in a new way. Those who have a desire to learn view their membership as a facilitator to unlocking greater understanding of art.
3. **Escapism: Spirituality and Creativity**—members who seek to escape from their personal or work lives. Membership enables access to a sanctuary, a place to relax, to fulfill creative or spiritual needs.
4. **Sense of Belonging and Prestige**—members seeking connection, acceptance, and relationship with others, including with the museum. There is a sense of belonging as being part of a community and, also, that the muse-

um belongs to them. Members who feel a sense of belonging may have a strong desire to be part of a cultured and prestigious club. Membership provides feelings of honor, pride, and satisfaction.

5. **Physical**—members who value the multifaceted physical spaces that a museum provides. Membership facilitates an immersive experience, a "third space" comprising a range of diverse sensory and visual environments.

6. **Drivers of Involvement**—the exhibitions, lectures, cafes, shops, digital content, and communications all serve as a reminder and connection to the museum, and membership is viewed as a "good value" for the money. In this way, membership itself is a driver of involvement, encouraging participation and more frequent visitation. For members who aspire to become more involved, membership makes it easier to participate and reduces the perceived risk associated with visiting on a pay-per-visit basis. Thus, membership is a means to an end.

These characteristics shed light on additional reasons why members join and what they gain from their membership. Further, the core drivers of loyalty underscore that renewal rate is not the only metric museums should be paying attention to. Ultimately, it is member loyalty that matters. Museums would benefit greatly from capitalizing on these findings in their marketing and new product development efforts.

WHY MEMBERSHIP?

Membership is an important part of the museum business model. Depending on the museum, membership may represent 3 to 20 percent or more of earned revenue. Members have a much higher lifetime customer value, approximately four-and-half times greater lifetime value than the average visitor ($726.83 in member revenue compared to $160.20 for the average visitor over a 10-year period).[41] Nevertheless, membership is an expensive undertaking for a museum. Generally speaking, it takes one dollar for every two dollars raised to run an effective membership program. Significant resources must be invested in customer service, programming, acquisition, retention, and upgrade strategies to maintain a traditional membership program. While members are worth more to an organization than a general-admission visitor, a traditional membership program has higher costs associated with customer acquisition, retention, program management, and member servicing.

These realities can make museum membership a double-edged sword. And, because museums may have competing goals for membership, the purpose of

membership must be clearly stated to ensure alignment. For example, an organization that wishes to increase involvement from nontraditional audiences
will likely not be able to also have a compatible objective of increasing revenue—at least, not at the outset. Likewise, if a membership program is nothing
more than a glorified parking pass, then museum leaders must understand that
this type of membership will naturally attract transactional members who are
not joining with the same intent as a philanthropically oriented member. Each
museum leader will need to define the purpose of membership for his or her
own institution and ensure that the marketing strategy, pricing strategy, and
product portfolio align with this objective.

Consider, for example, a concept that has long been vilified by our industry—the season pass. A season pass that includes nothing more than free
admission would be an attractive option to those transactional members who
join for purely economic reasons, offering flexibility and a lower cost per
visit. A season pass could also lower the cost of servicing such transactional
members, allowing museums to focus more time and attention toward cultivating more valuable mission-based members. And a season pass could
generate participation from new audiences who otherwise would not join
due to the significant investment and unknown value of a traditional membership program. Of course, the financial implications of introducing such a
product into the membership mix would need to be evaluated, as the majority
of transactional members would likely select this option over a more robust
(and expensive) membership category. However, as part of a comprehensive
membership strategy, a museum could leverage a season pass to address a
specific market segment that, at present, is not being served.

The key takeaway is that museums must get better at understanding and
responding to customer needs. We are only just beginning to understand the
motives that drive the decision to join, renew, donate, and become more involved. As some scholars have astutely observed, "museum membership is
complex and multi-dimensional and not entirely economic-based."[42] Therefore, deciphering the motivations, values, and needs that underpin the decisions of museum audiences is of paramount importance. Luckily, as museum
leaders look ahead, there is ample room for growth in membership if they are
willing to test their assumptions.

It's clear that the traditional membership model is an amalgamation that
attempts to serve the needs of multiple market segments. Therefore, as
museums evolve to meet the needs of tomorrow's audiences, so too must
the field of membership. Today, membership represents a single arrow in
the museum's quiver. However, through new product development and an
intentional market segmentation strategy, museums have the opportunity
to create many new arrows, each with its own unique shape, that can be
utilized to target new audiences.

NOTES

1. Mark Mulligan, Keith Jopling, and Zach Fuller, "The Classical Music Market," MIDiA Research, May 2019, 7, https://www.midiaresearch.com/app/up loads/2019/06/MIDiA-Research-IDAGIO-Classical-Music-Market_June19.pdf.

2. Ibid., 23.

3. Benedikt Kammel, "This Berlin Startup Is Spotify for Classical Music Buffs," *Bloomberg Businessweek*, May 19, 2019, https://www.bloomberg.com/news/ar ticles/2019-05-20/berlin-startup-idagio-is-spotify-for-classical-music-buffs.

4. Gretchen Gavett, "What You Need to Know about Segmentation," *Harvard Business Review*, July 9, 2014, https://hbr.org/2014/07/what-you-need-to-know -about-segmentation.

5. Colleen Dilenschneider, "Mission Motivated vs. Transaction Motivated Members: What Your Cultural Organization Needs to Know (DATA)," *Know Your Own Bone*, July 6, 2016, https://www.colleendilen.com/2016/07/06/mission-motivated-vs -transaction-motivated-members-what-your-cultural-organization-needs-to-know-data/.

6. Noah J. Goldstein, Robert B. Cialdini, and Vladas Griskevicius, "A Room with a Viewpoint: Using Social Norms to Motivate Environmental Conservation in Hotels," *Journal of Consumer Research* 35, no. 3 (2008): 472–82.

7. Brent Simpson and Robb Willer, "Beyond Altruism: Sociological Foundations of Cooperation and Prosocial Behavior," *Annual Review of Sociology* 41 (August 2015): 43–63, https://doi.org/10.1146/annurev-soc-073014-112242.

8. P. Wesley Schultz, Jessica M. Nolan, Robert B. Cialdini, Noah J. Goldstein, and Vladas Griskevicius, "The Constructive, Destructive, and Reconstructive Power of Social Norms," *Psychological Science* 18, no. 5 (2007): 429–34.

9. Richard H. Thaler and Cass R. Sunstein, *Nudge: Improving Decisions about Health, Wealth, and Happiness* (New York: Penguin Group, 2009), 69.

10. Americus Reed, "Social Identity as a Useful Perspective for Self-Concept–Based Consumer Research," *Psychology & Marketing* 19, no. 3 (February 28, 2002): 235–66, https://doi.org/10.1002/mar.10011.

11. George A. Akerlof and Rachel E. Kranton, "Economics and Identity," *The Quarterly Journal of Economics* 115, no. 3 (August 2000): 715–53, https://doi .org/10.1162/003355300554881.

12. Judd B. Kessler and Katherine L. Milkman, "Identity in Charitable Giving," *Management Science* 64, no. 2 (2018): 845–59, https://doi.org/10.1287/mnsc .2016.2582.

13. Dan Schawbel, "Robert Cialdini: How to Master the Art of 'Pre-Suasion,'" *Forbes*, September 6, 2016, https://www.forbes.com/sites/danschawbel/2016/09/06/ robert-cialdini-how-to-master-the-art-of-pre-suasion/#346218cf7445.

14. Joel Lovell, "Can the A.C.L.U. Become the N.R.A. for the Left?," *New York Times*, July 2, 2018, https://www.nytimes.com/2018/07/02/magazine/inside-the -aclus-war-on-trump.html?smtyp=cur&smid=tw-nytimes.

15. "Our Finances," Financial Information, Environmental Defense Fund, accessed September 27, 2019, https://www.edf.org/finances.

16. Giving USA: The Annual Report on Philanthropy for the Year 2018 (2019). Chicago: Giving USA Foundation.

17. Economist James Andreoni introduced the theory of "impure altruism" to address the extra utility donors receive (i.e., the warm glow) from the act of donating.

18. Matthew Chao, "Demotivating Incentives and Motivation Crowding Out in Charitable Giving," *PNAS* 114, no. 28 (July 11, 2017): 7301–306, www.pnas.org/cgi/doi/10.1073/pnas.1616921114.

19. The expression "therein lies the rub" is a misquotation from Shakespeare's Hamlet, "To die, to sleep—to sleep, perchance to dream—ay, there's the rub, for in this sleep of death what dreams may come." The term *rub* originated from a game called bowls or lawn bowls, a game once played in ancient Egypt and still played today, in which players attempt to get their bowls (or balls) as close as possible to a small white ball called the "jack." A rub is an imperfection in the surface of the green that prevents a bowl from rolling smoothly toward its target. Thus, a rub is an obstacle on the course.

20. Holly Hall, "Ask an Expert: Turning a Nonprofit's Members into Generous Donors," *The Chronicle of Philanthropy*, November 9, 2012, https://www.philanthropy.com/article/Ask-an-Expert-Turning-a/226667.

21. Amihai Glazer and Kai A. Konrad, "A Signaling Explanation for Charity," *The American Economic Review* 86, no. 4 (September 1996): 1019–28, https://www.jstor.org/stable/2118317.

22. Cynthia Robinson, "Toms Lets Customers Choose Which Causes Their Shoes Support," PSFK, May 10, 2019, https://www.psfk.com/2019/05/toms-customers-choose-nonprofit-support.html.

23. C. B. Bhattacharya, "When Customers Are Members: Customer Retention in Paid Membership Contexts," *Journal of the Academy of Marketing Science* 26, no. 1 (January 1998): 31–44, https://doi.org/10.1177/0092070398261004.

24. "Women and the Kemper Is a Special Interest Group Open to All Museum Members," Women and the Kemper, Kemper Art Museum, https://www.kemperartmuseum.wustl.edu/WAK.

25. Daragh O'Reilly, Ruth Rentschler, and Theresa A. Kirchner, *The Routledge Companion to Arts Marketing* (New York: Routledge, 2013), 235.

26. Audhesh K. Paswan and Lisa C. Troy, "Non-Profit Organization and Membership Motivation: An Exploration in the Museum Industry," *Journal of Marketing Theory and Practice* 12, no. 2 (2004): 1–15, https://doi.org/10.1080/10696679.2004.11658515.

27. Ibid.

28. Mary Ann Glynn, C. B. Bhattacharya, and Hayagreeva Rao, "Art Museum Membership and Cultural Distinction: Relating Members' Perceptions of Prestige to Benefit Usage," *Poetics* 24, no. 2-4 (November 1996): 259–74, https://doi.org/10.1016/0304-422X(95)00011-8.

29. Paswan and Troy, "Non-Profit Organization and Membership Motivation: An Exploration in the Museum Industry."

30. William T. Harbaugh, "What Do Donations Buy? A Model of Philanthropy Based on Prestige and Warm Glow," *Journal of Public Economics* 67 (1998): 269–84.

31. Paswan and Troy, "Non-Profit Organization and Membership Motivation: An Exploration in the Museum Industry."

32. C. B. Bhattacharya, Hayagreeva Rao, and Mary Ann Glynn, "Understanding the Bond of Identification: An Investigation of Its Correlates among Art Museum Members," *Journal of Marketing* 59, no. 4 (1995): 46–57, doi:10.2307/1252327.

33. Adrian Sargeant and Elaine Jay, *Building Donor Loyalty: The Fundraiser's Guide to Increasing Lifetime Value* (San Francisco, CA: Jossey-Bass, 2004), 24.

34. Roger Bennett and Anna Barkensjo, "Causes and Consequences of Donor Perceptions of the Quality of the Relationship Marketing Activities of Charitable Organisations," *Journal of Targeting, Measurement and Analysis for Marketing* 13, no. 2 (January 2005): 122–39.

35. Adrian Sargeant, "Donor Retention: What Do We Know and What Can We Do about It?," *Nonprofit Quarterly*, August 15, 2013, https://nonprofitquarterly.org/donor-retention-nonprofit-donors/.

36. Adrian Sargeant, "Relationship Fundraising: How to Keep Donors Loyal," *Nonprofit Management & Leadership* 12, no. 2 (2001): 177–92.

37. Sargeant, "Donor Retention: What Do We Know and What Can We Do about It?"

38. Heiner Evanschitzky, Gopalkrishnan R. Iyer, Hilke Plassmann, Joerg Niessing, and Heribert Meffert, "The Relative Strength of Affective Commitment in Securing Loyalty in Service Relationships," *Journal of Business Research* 59, no. 12 (November 2006): 1207–13, https://doi.org/10.1016/j.jbusres.2006.08.005.

39. Ellen Garbarino and Mark S. Johnson, "The Different Roles of Satisfaction, Trust, and Commitment in Customer Relationships," *Journal of Marketing* 63, no. 2 (1999): 70–87, doi:10.2307/1251946.

40. Alix Slater and Kate Armstrong, "Involvement, Tate, and Me," *Journal of Marketing Management* 26, no. 7 (2010): 727–48.

41. Colleen Dilenschneider, "Crunching the Numbers—Just How Valuable Are Your Members? (DATA)," *Know Your Own Bone*, April 9, 2019, https://www.colleendilen.com/2019/04/09/crunching-the-numbers-just-how-valuable-are-your-members-data/.

42. Glynn, Bhattacharya, and Rao, "Art Museum Membership and Cultural Distinction: Relating Members' Perceptions of Prestige to Benefit Usage."

Chapter Eight

The Perfect Mix

In August 2016, Chase introduced the Sapphire Reserve credit card, offering an unprecedented 100,000 points for new card members.[1] Ostensibly a mundane commodity, the credit card gained a cult following among millennials who took to social media, uploading videos of themselves unboxing their Sapphire Reserve cards on YouTube, and posting on Twitter with the hashtag #SapphireReserve.[2] Within two weeks, the card had exceeded its 12-month sales target.[3] In the frenzy, Chase actually ran out of the special metal alloy used to make the card itself.[4]

With more than half of its new customers under 35 years old, the Sapphire Reserve reflected what young consumers wanted—flexibility, VIP access, and rewards.[5] Pam Codispoti, president of Chase Branded Cards, described the points structure in this way, "For millennials, 'travel' might mean a once in a lifetime trip around the world or it could mean taking a Lyft to a hole-in-the-wall restaurant in Chinatown and then riding the subway to karaoke, and then catching a taxi home. So, we decided to give customers accelerated rewards on all those purchases . . . the emphasis is on what you can do, rather than what you can buy."[6]

There are parallels between the financial services and museum sectors. Much like the museum market, the financial services market is highly competitive, and there's little differentiation among providers in the mind of the consumer. This makes acquiring new customers difficult. Just as museums struggle to reach new audiences, financial services firms have had a similar challenge in attaining top-of-mind awareness, not to mention overcoming the inertia of switching credit cards.

Chase wanted to attract the next generation of customers, but millennials are not using credit in the same way as previous generations. Growing up in the shadow of the Great Recession, millennials are particularly credit leery.

They carry on average two fewer credit cards than Gen Xers (at the same respective ages) and tend to maintain lower balances on those cards.[7] Chase realized that to break through and become the credit card of choice for this younger audience, they would have to find a way to force consideration (with an eye-popping incentive that would be irresistible) and induce repeat behavior (by ensuring the Sapphire Reserve would become the top-of-wallet choice for daily spending).

Following the success of the Sapphire Reserve, Chase has now turned its attention to retention. In exchange for the benefits card members receive, there is a substantial $450 annual fee. From the beginning, the company acknowledged that it would not immediately make money on new card members. Instead, it knew that the payoff would come over time as card members became long-term customers.

Like any business, younger consumers represent substantial growth for the financial services sector over the course of their lifetime. For Chase, understanding the needs and motivations of the next generation of consumers is critical to building deep, long-lasting relationships. In the future, as these new customers seek a broader range of financial services, such as mortgages, banking, and investing, Chase plans to be their bank of choice.

THE PERFECT MIX

In the field of marketing, there is a fundamental concept known as the "marketing mix," which represents the set of components necessary to build a successful business model. Comprising the "4 Ps,"—product, place, promotion, and price—the marketing mix includes the essential ingredients needed to create a viable marketing strategy (Figure 8.1).[8] While technology, marketing channels, and access to vast amounts of data have all increased exponentially in recent years, the 4 Ps remain an immutable aspect of marketing strategy.[9]

In designing the new Sapphire Reserve, Chase invested considerable time and resources to blend together the perfect marketing mix.

- **Product.** The Sapphire Reserve credit card consists of a set of research-driven, customer-centric benefits paired with a heavy metal alloy card and premium packaging. As Sean McQuay, credit card expert at the personal finance website NerdWallet, notes, "Chase has basically realized that the weight [of the card] raises customers' dopamine levels."[10] The product also includes all of the aspects of servicing card members, including a focus on concierge-style member services, access to a robust rewards program and website, a mobile app, and regular communications with card members.
- **Place.** Because it is a credit card, the Sapphire Reserve requires new customers to apply for and be approved to obtain the product. Consumers can

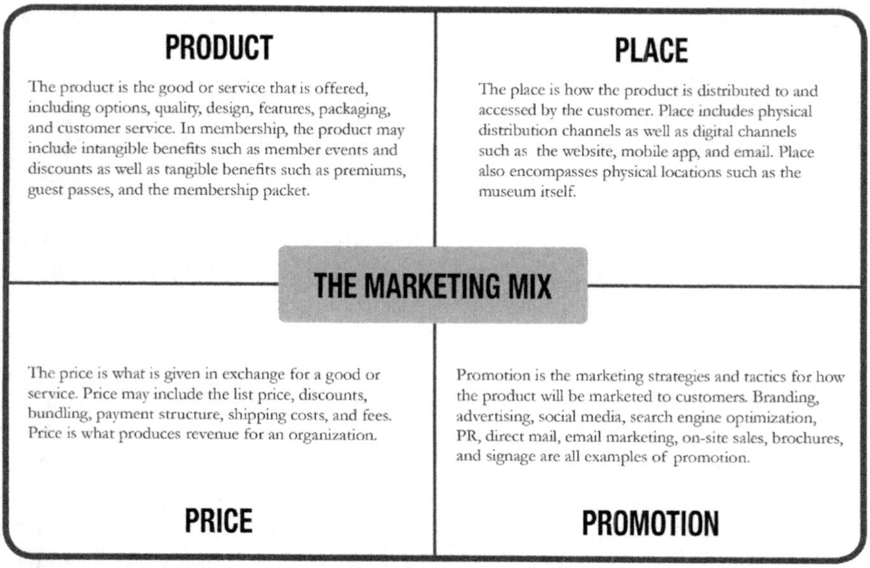

PRODUCT

The product is the good or service that is offered, including options, quality, design, features, packaging, and customer service. In membership, the product may include intangible benefits such as member events and discounts as well as tangible benefits such as premiums, guest passes, and the membership packet.

PLACE

The place is how the product is distributed to and accessed by the customer. Place includes physical distribution channels as well as digital channels such as the website, mobile app, and email. Place also encompasses physical locations such as the museum itself.

THE MARKETING MIX

The price is what is given in exchange for a good or service. Price may include the list price, discounts, bundling, payment structure, shipping costs, and fees. Price is what produces revenue for an organization.

Promotion is the marketing strategies and tactics for how the product will be marketed to customers. Branding, advertising, social media, search engine optimization, PR, direct mail, email marketing, on-site sales, brochures, and signage are all examples of promotion.

PRICE

PROMOTION

Figure 8.1.   The 4 Ps

access the application process through the Chase website, via a direct mail solicitation, or in person at a bank branch.
- **Price.** The Sapphire Reserve comes with an annual price tag of $450 and double-digit APR.
- **Promotion.** When Chase launched the Sapphire Reserve, the company decided not to use traditional advertising or public relations for promotion. Instead, Chase invested its marketing budget in building relationships with social media influencers and bloggers to spread word-of-mouth referrals.

The Sapphire Reserve card demonstrates the need for organizations to innovate and invest in developing the marketing mix. Peter Drucker, the father of modern business management, emphasized that "Because its purpose is to create a customer, the business enterprise has two—and only these two—basic functions: marketing and innovation."[11] While marketing is often equated with *advertising*, its role within an effective organization encompasses a much broader purpose. As defined by the American Marketing Association, marketing is "the activity, set of institutions, and processes for creating, communicating, delivering, and exchanging offerings that have value for customers, clients, partners, and society at large."[12] The Chartered Institute of Marketing (CIM) offers the following definition for marketing: "The management process responsible for identifying, anticipating and satisfying customer requirements profitably."[13] Unpacking these two definitions reveals the true role of marketing as a driver of business model innovation. And, because marketing and membership share responsibility for anticipating customer needs; creating value; and managing the systems, relationships, and processes necessary to ensuring an effective membership program, the membership department also needs to be involved in driving innovation.

Explicit within each definition of marketing is the need for identifying, satisfying, and anticipating customer needs—areas in which both marketing *and* membership should be involved. Each definition speaks to the importance of marketing as a multifaceted business discipline with a focus on management of the full life cycle of a customer. As the member life cycle is directly managed by the membership department in partnership with the marketing department, both teams assume the role of product managers in a museum setting. The term *set of institutions* implies that there are systems, processes, internal and external audiences, and societal aspects that are central to the success of a business model, including technology, vendors, and funders, as well as influences, such as social norms and institutional priorities, that affect both marketing and membership. Lastly, each definition emphasizes an exchange process in which value is created and transferred between stakeholders. This exchange includes value creation for the organization, its internal and external customers, its partners, and the broader community—value that is inherent in a membership program.

In many organizations, the roles of marketing and membership have been relegated to the narrow functions of customer acquisition and retention, involved in little more than the downstream tactics of advertising, communications, renewal processing, and database management. However, the key to developing a successful business model is ensuring that audiences are offered the right product, at the right price, in the right way. To do this, the roles of marketing and membership must be elevated to be drivers of innovation, including responsibility for uncovering unmet customer needs; understanding customer perceptions, motivations, and behaviors; managing the customer experience ecosystem; and developing the full range of the marketing mix.

AN ESSENTIAL INGREDIENT

As an essential ingredient of the marketing mix, new product development is integral to maintaining a successful business model. Product development in museum membership can be conducted within any of the following six categories:[14]

1. **New-to-the-world products** are revolutionary goods or services never seen before that lead to the creation of entirely new markets, such as the microwave or personal computer.

2. **New product lines** represent new products that an organization has not offered before that allow access to an existing market. For example, Gatorade gained entry into the sports nutrition market with its introduction of an array of products formulated to help athletes enhance performance before, during, and after training, including energy chews, carbohydrate drinks, protein shakes, vegetable-based nitrate boosts, and smart chip–enabled refillable water bottles that track fluid intake, sodium, and electrolyte levels in real time.

3. **Product line extensions** supplement an existing product line with new features, flavors, or formats, such as Starbucks' introduction of its Pumpkin Spice Latte in the fall of 2003.

4. **Improvements or revisions of existing products** are modifications that improve performance or add functionality, such as Colgate 2-in-1—a toothpaste plus mouthwash.

5. **Repositioned products** are existing products targeted at new markets, such as aspirin being repositioned as heart attack prevention, or how Pedialyte, originally developed as an electrolyte replenishment drink for sick kids, is now being marketed to dehydrated adults as a cure for everything from dry airplane air to hangovers.

6. **Lower-priced products** involves modifying existing products in order to cut costs and offer them at a lower price to customers, such as a generic brand or a self-service gas station.

Most often, museums focus their time and resources on #4—improving or revising existing products. For example, a museum might tweak its membership program benefits by adding an event or a tote bag, or it may adjust the categories of its membership program by adding or removing a level. However, to evolve and extend the reach of their missions, museums must make investments in the other five product development categories as well.

■

SPARK: NEW PRODUCT DEVELOPMENT EXPLORATION

Product development is both an art and a science. While new products should not be developed in a vacuum without proper market research and customer input, the following exercise is a valuable first step to stretch your imagination by exploring a few ideas for new membership products. Using the matrix in Table 8.1, practice thinking about new products for each of the four categories listed. *Hint: Beginning with the job to be done will help fuel your brainstorming and generate ideas to address an unmet need.*

Table 8.1. New Product Development Exploration

	New Product Line	Product Line Extension	Repositioned Product	Lower-Priced Product
Your Organization **Existing Market** (Choose an existing market to target)	Example: Botanic garden Example: A local farmer's market			
Customer Segment (What audience do you want to reach within the chosen market?)	Example: Health-conscious, budget-strapped millennials who shop at the local farmer's market			
Job to Be Done (What is the job they are trying to accomplish?)	Example: To feed their family with food they feel good about	Example: To be a part of their community by supporting local business	Example: To nourish their body with nutrient-rich food	Example: To buy fresh produce in small amounts to save money and limit waste
New Membership Product Idea (Brainstorm ideas to get the job done)	Example: A new community supported agriculture (CSA) program that allows members to pick up their locally sourced, fresh vegetables on a weekly basis at the garden	Example: Introduction of an add-on option to any membership level that offers monthly events hosted at the garden featuring guest speakers from the community and catering by local businesses	Example: Membership is repositioned as a self-care ritual touting "Indulge at the garden and find your moment of bliss." Members have access to a complimentary fruit-infused hydration bar and designated "quiet spaces" for reflection.	Example: A new $5 monthly membership level that provides real-time gardening, eco-friendly living, and money-saving cooking tips from garden staff via mobile text messaging

Every product has a life cycle that follows a bell-shaped curve, from introduction and growth to maturity and, eventually, decline. Signals from across the museum industry strongly indicate that the traditional membership model is entering the stage of decline. In response to this reality, museums have tried to rejuvenate their membership programs by layering new benefits on top of the old. However, this approach is often unsuccessful, as the process of continuous enhancement dilutes the value proposition of the original product over time. More is not always better. As senior associate dean for strategy and innovation at Harvard Business School, Youngme Moon, observes, organizations can successfully restart their business model by "shedding product attributes the rest of the industry considers sacred" to reposition the product for growth.[15] "Reverse positioning" is a bold strategy that can allow a museum to expand further into existing markets and prepare to enter new ones (Figure 8.2).

When Chase took on the challenge of designing the Sapphire Reserve card, the company made a decision early on to "make perfect the enemy of good." Smartly, the company built on the assets of its core business model to create a new product that disrupted the premium card category. Keenly focused on growth, Chase took the time to listen to potential customers to truly understand their needs and motivations. By doing so, Chase was able to uncover the key drivers that would make a difference for young consumers when considering applying for a credit card.

Importantly, the company did not make assumptions about what this new audience would and would not place value on. The insights gleaned from

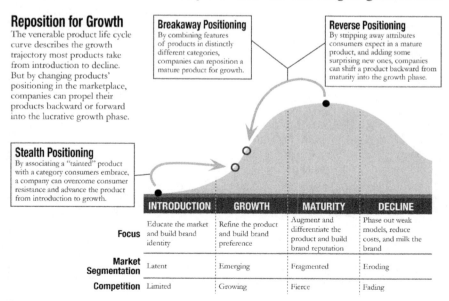

Figure 8.2. Reposition For Growth

Reprinted with permission from "Break Free from the Product Life Cycle" by Youngme Moon. Harvard Business Review, May 2005. Copyright 2005 by Harvard Business Publishing; all rights reserved.

research led to a new definition of dining and travel that included services millennials already used frequently, such as Uber and Grubhub. Chase also identified the opportunity to pair rewards with perks that made cardholders feel like VIPs, such as skipping security lines, relaxing in swanky airport lounges, and accessing exclusive experiences at music festivals and concerts.

The Sapphire Reserve card shines a light on the importance of reinventing to stay relevant. The company could have just continued marketing its existing products to millennials, hoping that one day they would "age into" using the services it offers. Instead, Chase took a proactive approach and made the prescient decision to invest in creating a new product specifically designed to meet its customers' needs.

The success story of the Sapphire Reserve card provides an important lesson for museums: attracting new audiences *must* include the development of new products. Without such an investment, marketing dollars will be wasted, falling on the deaf ears of an audience who is unable to see how your museum and its membership offering fit into their lives.

TEXTBOX 8.2

BRIGHT SPOT: COLUMBUS MUSEUM OF ART GETS *LOUD & PROUD* WITH A NEW MEMBERSHIP PROGRAM

Ask Gabriel Mastin, leadership giving officer with the Columbus Museum of Art (CMA), about the Museum's *Loud & Proud* membership program, and he will tell you, "Doing something important is hard work. It involves countless hours, taking big risks, overcoming fears, and above all, authenticity." The concept for CMA's *Loud & Proud* membership began in 2016 when Mastin organized an informal guided tour of the Museum's Picasso exhibition led by chief curator, David Stark, with a small group of LGBTQ+ community members. Dubbed the "Big Gay Tour," the event was well received and led to a more formal program being developed in 2017 called *Mysteries of the Museum*, which featured a tour of artworks in the Museum's permanent collection to highlight LGBTQ+ artists and their stories. Led by CMA's executive director, Nannette Maciejunes, the tour was emotionally moving, connecting participants to the joys and struggles of the artists.

Recognizing an opportunity to develop a deeper and more meaningful relationship with members of the LGBTQ+ community, the Museum hosted a series of meetings to solicit input from stakeholders with the goal of understanding the unique needs and perspectives of the community. Through this qualitative research, CMA learned firsthand about the devastating HIV/AIDS epidemic of the 1980s and how this crisis impacted the LGBTQ+ community. Moreover, the Museum came to understand the significance of the equal rights movement and the need for a safe space where the LGBTQ+ and Allied community could come together in solidarity.

Armed with insights from its outreach efforts, CMA saw an opportunity for the Museum to play an important role in meeting the needs of the LGBTQ+ community. As CMA's collection encompasses artists from diverse backgrounds, the Museum decided to leverage this to share inclusive stories about the human experience and connect art with subject matter relevant to the LGBTQ+ community. Propelled by the enthusiasm and dedication of its team, CMA took on the challenge of developing an entirely new membership program, specifically tailored to the LGBTQ+ community. Complete with its own discrete marketing mix, the Museum's *Loud & Proud* membership launched with fanfare in September 2018, welcoming more than 800 attendees at its inaugural party, exceeding expectations by 167 percent.

CMA's *Loud & Proud* membership program offers seven categories ranging from $250 for an individual to $10,000 for its Royalty level, described as perfect for "a King, Queen, or anything In Between." The *Loud & Proud* membership features an abundance of audience-focused benefits, such as invitations to two annual cocktail parties, champagne at member openings, and evening tours led by local drag personalities, docents, and leaders in the community. Sponsored by Equitas Health, *Prizm Magazine*, and many others, the *Loud & Proud* membership program is promoted with a clever and playful tone that resonates with audiences. For example, the Celebrity level of membership offers a "Private Museum tour for you and 6 of your favorite people given by a docent in sparkling attire. (Hopefully sequins, depends on the day). Sparkle not guaranteed," and "You are fancy. And, we like you."

Awareness and participation in CMA's new membership program is growing. *Loud & Proud* has been successful in creating a safe space where members can come together to celebrate LGBTQ+ artists, learn about LGBTQ+ history, hear untold stories of LGBTQ+ artists, and feel empowered to be themselves. By designing a new offering with intentionality to meet the needs of the LGBTQ+ community and their allies, CMA is engaging new audiences, generating support for its mission, and facilitating a sense of belonging among its members.

Courtesy of the Columbus Museum of Art.

RIGHT PLACE, RIGHT TIME, RIGHT MESSAGE

The places where a product is marketed, sold, delivered, and consumed are all critical aspects of a marketing strategy. These channels may be physical or digital. In the marketing mix, place encompasses the ideas of awareness and access, and it involves decisions about how and when the product will be offered to the customer. In a museum setting, the place where membership is sold may include the website, the admissions desk, direct mail solicitation, or even the phone. It may also be sold via a partner organization, such as a school, or made available for sale via a third-party platform, such as Groupon.

A museum membership may be delivered via a direct mail packet that includes the membership card. When members visit the museum and use their membership card to gain access to the exhibition, they are consuming the product on-site. Whereas a membership that provides the member with exclusive access to online content, the place of delivery and consumption may be the museum's website or mobile app. In the marketing mix, it's important to note that there are a variety of places that may have a role in other aspects of the membership product, such as email communications or a member newsletter.

When we think of marketing, the aspects related to promotion are usually what come to mind. Promotion includes all of the tools available to the museum to market its membership program, such as brochures, direct mail, social media, earned media, email marketing campaigns, and pay-per-click advertising. The brand strategy, messaging, creativity, and tactics to raise awareness, generate interest, create desire, and motivate action are all part of promotion. In the marketing mix, promotion also includes the utilization of research, data, software, and technology necessary to reach audiences with the right marketing message at the right time.

In addition, promotion encompasses a wide range of systems and mediums to reach a target market. For instance, marketing automation makes it possible to trigger marketing messages based on behavior, and dynamic content allows for landing pages to be tailored to a specific user. Cross-device tracking, pixels, and big data allow marketers to reach a user across multiple devices, apps, and platforms, as well as the ability to target advertising to look-alike audiences based on shared online behavior. Search engine optimization, voice search, personal assistants, semantic intent, and machine learning are all technologies that will affect how museums reach audiences in the future.

Promotion is a vital aspect of the marketing mix. Consider how Chase launched the Sapphire Reserve card without any traditional advertising or public relations. In fact, the company spent zero dollars on traditional advertising (yes, you read that right—zero). Instead, Chase took advantage of the power of Instagram influencer marketing, partnering with celebrities, such as photographer Alice Gao, model Chrissy Teigan, and food and travel creator No Leftovers. The campaign leveraged the hashtag #SapphireOnLocation to showcase exciting dining and travel experiences that could be earned while using the card. The marketing strategy was about more than just a credit card. The messaging emphasized how the Sapphire Reserve card could open doors to a lifestyle—full of glamour, adventure, and Instagram-worthy memory making.

PRICING PSYCHOLOGY

Disclaimer: The following includes an overview of several price-related theories, as well as studies from across a wide variety of industries and fields. At times, these findings may seem contradictory, incomplete, and confounding—they are. More research is needed in the museum sector overall and within the field of membership specifically to develop a holistic understanding of how price influences audience participation, membership uptake, customer satisfaction, and long-term involvement. In many cases, an argument can be made to employ one strategy or another depending on the particular goals of an institution.

The Power of Price

An often overlooked and undervalued revenue lever in the marketing mix is price. Pricing can convey many things to audiences, such as quality, prestige, institutional priorities, and relevance. Understanding how pricing fits into a membership and marketing strategy is essential to the financial health of an organization. In membership, there are three well-established pricing approaches:[16]

- **Market Value Method** sets the price of membership based on the fair market value of benefits.
- **Actual Cost Method**, also known as "cost plus pricing," uses the actual out-of-pocket cost of membership benefits and adds on a markup to attain a desired profit margin.
- **Program Cost Method**, the simplest pricing strategy, is calculated by dividing the entire membership program budget by the number of member households in an effort to price membership high enough to cover the total cost of attracting, servicing, and retaining members.

While these approaches are valuable for budgeting and forecasting purposes, none are an ideal way to arrive at an effective pricing strategy. Because all three approaches begin with an existing product (the membership program) and its associated costs, each is inherently inward facing. Even a market value method for pricing can be ineffective if appropriate research is not done to understand consumers' perceptions and willingness to pay. For example, while an IMAX movie ticket or canvas tote bag may have an established market value, without testing and data, assumptions are being made about a customer's perceived value of such benefits. Thus, museums that employ such insular and assumptive membership pricing strategies risk, at best, leaving money on the table and, at worst, pricing membership in a way that presumes value where there is none.

Museums would benefit greatly from a more strategic method of price optimization. Today, the vast majority of museums arrive at a membership price by benchmarking against similar organizations within their market or balancing the value proposition of membership with the cost of admission (e.g., membership pays for itself in just two visits). These approaches to pricing are predicated on established market prices for what membership is "expected" to cost. Thus, it is difficult for a museum to price its membership program higher than what membership costs at similar organizations within its market. Pricing membership based on comparator benchmarks can result in a race to the bottom, where museums are competing solely on price.

BRIGHT SPOT: REVAMPING A MEMBERSHIP PROGRAM AT LONGWOOD GARDENS

Spanning 1,000 idyllic acres in Chester County, Pennsylvania, Longwood Gardens welcomes more than 1.5 million guests a year. In 2007, Longwood transitioned 16,000 households from a frequent visitor pass to a more robust membership model. After expanding benefit offerings and focusing on the customer experience, membership reached approximately 65,000 households in 2016. While growth in the membership program was extraordinary, Longwood began questioning whether its membership program could support additional growth while continuing to deliver an exceptional customer experience. In addition, membership pricing had not kept pace with increases in admission prices, resulting in a high number of transactional members joining for value, rather than a desire to support the organization's mission.

To develop a road map for the future, Longwood embarked on a multiyear project to evaluate and reimagine its membership program with the goals of simplicity, flexibility, loyalty, and profitability. The first step in the process, a data mining study to understand current member behavior and visitation patterns, uncovered a negative trend related to first-time members. Data showed that, while overall member households were increasing, the number and percentage of first-time members was declining. And a series of focus groups and surveys confirmed that access to the Gardens was the primary driver for joining. To understand willingness to pay, interest in new membership levels, and which benefits were most important, three membership models were tested with a sample of more than 4,000 current and lapsed members.

Armed with findings from the comprehensive research study and modeling, Longwood launched its new membership program in August 2016. Implementation consisted of a complete refresh of the program, including updated branding, restructured levels and benefits, and increased pricing. Active members were transitioned to new levels, and key performance indicators were developed for the new program. Longwood also enacted an internal and external communications plan, including staff training, welcome packets with new membership cards, and a messaging platform highlighting the increased flexibility of the new program.

Longwood planned for a decrease in the total number of member households after the new program was introduced. A low of 58,000 households occurred eight months after the program launch. This shrinking member base, however, was short lived, and membership now stands at 69,000. Importantly, while the new membership program pricing reflected approximately a 40 percent increase, testing showed that there was not a high degree of price sensitivity and Longwood felt strongly that the price increase was necessary for delivering an exceptional customer experience and ensuring the financial viability of the program. Moreover, by restricting some benefits to higher levels, the new structure encouraged members to move up the membership ladder. This increased revenue from members joining at higher levels, coupled with the new pricing strategy, has resulted in members supporting a larger percentage of operating expenses, with revenue goals being exceeded each year since the program launch.

Longwood found that understanding member needs and behavior was key to determining how best to design its new membership program. Importantly, the process allowed Longwood to understand which aspects of its offering were under- or overvalued in order to discontinue those benefits that did not enhance the member experience or proved to be too costly. While the idea of the membership restructure seemed a daunting task, Longwood has found that the initiative was a much-needed journey for both the organization and its members. Through the development of a new membership model, Longwood has been able to increase revenue, better serve its members, and ultimately improve member loyalty.

Courtesy of Longwood Gardens.

The Rise of New Admissions Models

The pricing strategy a museum applies to membership requires a deep understanding of its product(s) and market(s) as well as the psychology of price. Historically, museums have priced membership with the goal of accomplishing three primary objectives: encouraging repeat visitation, generating earned revenue, and building a pipeline for future donors. This means that membership is most often priced relative to ticket prices to make membership look like "a good deal." However, the introduction of new revenue and admissions models is challenging the traditional value proposition of membership.

In the right circumstances and with the right strategy, free or discounted admission has the potential to spur new donors in support of the mission. However, museums must be cognizant of how new admissions strategies will impact other revenue streams, including membership. In a free admissions model, for example, the greatest benefit of membership and its biggest selling feature—free admission—is eliminated. Further, data indicate that free or discounted admission leads not only to lower satisfaction rates but also can increase the time before a return visit.[17]

Similarly, dynamic pricing for admission—a variable, algorithm-driven ticket-pricing strategy, such as those employed by airlines and hotels—directly undercuts the traditional value proposition of membership on days when admission prices fall below static membership prices. And while membership managers everywhere dread the notion of dynamic pricing, like it or not, the practice is quickly being adopted within the museum sector.

The news is not all bad. Dynamic pricing shows many areas of promise for museums. For instance, dynamic pricing for admissions can offer opportunities for smoothing out visitation peaks by encouraging advance purchasing of tickets online, as well as improved accessibility for visitors looking for low-cost times to visit. Moreover, the introduction of dynamic pricing has a surprise benefit—it forces an organization to look holistically at its product portfolio, pricing strategies, and marketing strategy, especially with respect to its membership program. As museums seek to become all at once more profitable *and* more accessible, experimentation with new revenue models and admissions strategies will continue to emerge.

BRIGHT SPOT: INTRODUCING DYNAMIC PRICING AT THE CHILDREN'S MUSEUM OF INDIANAPOLIS

Over the past several years, the Children's Museum of Indianapolis has seen a significant decline in paid attendance, which correlated with increasing ticket prices each year. In 2016, the price for an adult ticket had reached $23.50. Price-sensitive audiences with household income between $30,000 and $65,000 were especially affected by the ticket price increases. In an effort to win back this demographic and improve community accessibility, the Museum introduced a dynamic pricing ticketing model in 2017.

The introduction of dynamic pricing allowed the Museum to encourage audiences to "buy ahead and save" by selecting a date to visit in advance to "lock in" their ticket price. By purchasing in advance on the website, visitors are able to enjoy savings of up to 25 percent off the day-of box office prices for general admission tickets. Further, to better serve lower-income families, the Museum established a minimum number of days in which the daily ticket price would not rise above $12. Based on demand, historic visitation patterns, weather, and a number of other factors, ticket prices on any given day could range from $12 to $36 for an adult admission. Thus, the Museum has been able to simultaneously prioritize access while maximizing revenue. And the Museum is seeing success in winning back the price-sensitive audience with visitation from this segment increasing by at least 25 percent.

The introduction of dynamic pricing also has impacted membership. In the past, the Museum leveraged a traditional value proposition to sell memberships, namely, that membership is a great deal. Prior to dynamic pricing, this messaging approach was prominently featured in marketing messaging and was employed to upsell membership at the box office. However, with the dynamic pricing model, ticket prices varied from day to day, making the traditional value proposition of membership more complex. On some days, ticket prices were so low that the Museum could no longer claim that membership "pays for itself in two visits or less!" Conversely, on higher demand days, when the ticket prices were higher, the value proposition was much stronger.

With the adoption of dynamic pricing, the Museum had to rethink its entire marketing strategy for selling membership. In particular, the membership team needed to counteract the effect of more visitors buying admission tickets in advance. Because this shift in behavior allowed visitors to bypass the box office by purchasing tickets online, dynamic pricing put the membership department's most crucial conversion point—the box office—at risk. Historically, on-site conversion accounted for 60 percent or more of membership sales.

Additionally, as dynamic pricing has driven more consumers online, the museum needed to strategically increase the visibility of membership throughout the website. To do so, the Museum reframed the value proposition of membership from saving money to emphasizing the convenience and flexibility that membership offers. Now, the Museum's "Plan Ahead Pricing" messaging highlights the ability to visit anytime by reminding visitors that membership offers "one year of unlimited indoor/outdoor fun!" (Figure 8.3).

Figure 8.3. New Membership Marketing
Courtesy of the Children's Museum of Indianapolis.

To reinforce the message of convenience and flexibility, the Museum incorporated a dynamic cart pop-up that mimics the box office experience online by displaying exactly how much more it would cost (or, in some cases, how much visitors would save) to get unlimited visits for a year by becoming a member. This strategy has shown the biggest impact, with a 30 percent increase in online membership revenue in 2018. Moreover, the Museum plans to continue building on its new membership messaging platform by promoting the value of membership as an opportunity to visit anytime without having to plan ahead, as well as building upon a new audience built through more online data collection by utilizing highly targeted marketing efforts, including SMS and dynamic email content to engage with more diverse audiences who have different buying behaviors and motivations.

Courtesy of the Children's Museum of Indianapolis.

Anchors Aweigh!

In behavioral economics, the term *anchor* is used to describe a reference point from which we make adjustments when evaluating the price of goods or services. When we are exposed to a price by way of a price tag or an ad and purchase (or merely contemplate purchasing) the product at that specific price, an anchor is imprinted in our mind. From that point forward, the anchor shapes not only what we are willing to pay for that particular product but also how much we are willing to pay for other goods and services.

Beyond ads and price tags, expectations of price are influenced by many things, including previous purchases and the cost of other products and services within the same or a similar category. For example, the price of a zoo membership creates an anchor for membership to a history museum within the same market. That is, visitors will judge the price of membership at the history museum relative to the cost of membership at the zoo. Similarly, the cost of admission creates an anchor because visitors will use the ticket price as a reference point when evaluating the cost of becoming a member.

The effects of anchoring are why new product development is vital. By redefining the product category, museums have an opportunity to introduce a new type of membership that is disassociated from preexisting anchors. Creation of a new product changes the game by removing any previous reference points, allowing for a more strategic pricing strategy to be implemented. When Chase introduced the Sapphire Reserve card, consumers believed that the card was not only different but better so that its hefty $450 annual fee was not a barrier to signing up—even for the cash-strapped, debt-laden millennial. As Eileen Serra, senior advisor and former CEO of Chase Card Services for

JPMorgan Chase, explained, "One thing we learned is that you sometimes have to challenge conventional wisdom. Everyone said that millennials won't pay a high fee for anything. And then, you realize well, that's not actually true. They'll pay for value."[18]

When it comes to anchors, the manufacturer's suggested retail price (MSRP) is a good example. While savvy consumers realize that an auto dealership's advertised MSRP is a fabricated value, this arbitrary number still influences the price range potential buyers are willing to pay for a car. The MSRP serves as an anchor that benefits the seller, prompting the buyer to negotiate *down* from the MSRP, as opposed to forcing the dealer to negotiate up from a lower price offered by the buyer.

In the nonprofit sector, studies have found a similar strategy at play when large suggested donations are used to encourage donors to give more (Figure 8.4).[19] Even when donors do not match their donation to the highest suggested amount, their gifts are higher than they would be without the anchor. It would seem that the prediction of the anecdote "the more you ask for, the more you get" holds true. Yet, while it may be tempting to include an extremely large suggested donation with the hope of raking in ever higher gifts, larger suggested donations can discourage first-time donors to give. So, while a larger suggested donation can boost average gift amounts, a smaller suggested donation can engage a broader base of donors. Thus, an organization must consider its goals and be intentional about which strategy to employ.

The Pain of Paying

For those who aspire to visit more often and stay connected to the museum, membership offers a tantalizing proposition: an opportunity to buy today in order to visit for "free" tomorrow. Similar to products such as Amazon Prime

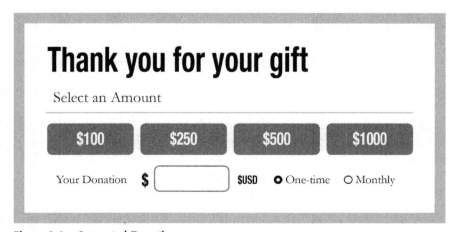

Figure 8.4. Suggested Donation

and timeshares, museum members are likely justifying the up-front cost of a membership as an "investment" that grants free enjoyment of benefits, rather than as an out-of-pocket cost in the moment. Tricking ourselves into thinking of something as an investment that will pay off in the future helps to offset a psychological phenomenon called "the pain of paying." As it turns out, paying for things up front helps to avoid the agony of spending money on something by decoupling the consumption (i.e., usage) of a product from the pain of the initial purchase. Interestingly, the form of payment used to buy can also affect the pain of paying. For example, using a credit card helps to disassociate the purchase from consumption by deferring payment until a later date.

While paying for things up front mitigates the pain of paying, doing so also can have a significant impact on how members use their benefits. Museums often charge the full price of membership up front to take advantage of the immediate cash flow from sales and to streamline management of benefits usage. Yet research shows that this type of pricing strategy is likely to *discourage* consumption, diminishing the likelihood that members will make use of their benefits.[20] In turn, the less members use their benefits, the less likely they are to renew their membership. That is, while charging for the full cost of membership up front reduces the pain of paying, thereby generating an increase in immediate sales, this approach can result in a devaluation of benefits, leading to lower engagement among members.

Perhaps counterintuitively, when consumers are made acutely aware of the cost—when the pain of paying is accentuated—they are *more* likely to consume the product. To avoid feeling like they've wasted money, people will do whatever is necessary to "get their money's worth."[21] Think back to the last time you ate the entire dessert even though you were already full or sat through a terrible movie because you had already paid for the ticket. "Masking" the true price of a product *reduces* the pain of paying, making the importance of consumption less urgent. In the museum space, a traditional membership program is an example of a pricing strategy that masks the true price of the product. How? By bundling numerous benefits together and not explicitly listing the associated price of each item included within the package, the consumer is shielded from the pain of paying. Thus, the typical approach to membership pricing likely reduces the pain of paying, thereby *decreasing* engagement among members.

To illustrate how the pain of paying affects participation, consider the findings from a health club study that found consumption tracked directly with payments. As Figure 8.5 shows, usage was highest in the months immediately following payment and declined steadily until the next payment stimulated activity. So, for those organizations seeking to encourage repeat

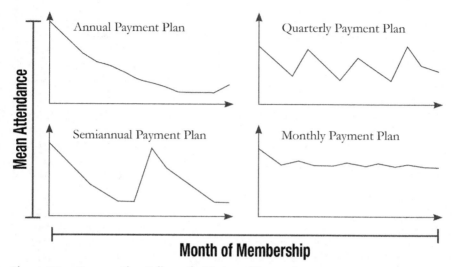

Figure 8.5. Consumption Follows the Timing of Payments

visitation and increase member engagement, amplifying the pain of paying can really, *ahem*, pay off.

All of this is to say that museum leaders need to be thoughtful about how membership is priced and paid for. If an institution seeks to deepen engagement among members, museum leaders need to be aware of how an ill-fitting pricing strategy can stifle participation. Likewise, if the goal is to drive sales and encourage an "investment" mindset, then bundling membership benefits and charging the full price of membership up front could help to offset the pain of paying.

You Really Do Get What You Pay For

Price is powerful. The price of a product conveys a substantial amount of information and can serve as a signal of quality—the higher the price, the higher the perceived quality. People expect higher-priced wines to taste better than less expensive wines, so it may not come as a surprise that participants in a study who tasted wines labeled by only price consistently rated a $90 wine higher than a $10 wine.[22] However, unknown to the participants, those two wines were identical. But there is more to the story; this taste test was conducted while the participants' brains were being scanned using functional magnetic resonance imaging, or fMRI. The scans showed increased activity in the medial orbitofrontal cortex, a region of the brain associated with pleasure. Exposure to the $90 price tag lit up the pleasure center in their brains, so the participants experienced greater enjoyment while drinking the higher-priced wine.[23] Not only did the participants subjectively think the more expensive wine tasted better, it actually *did* taste better.

Museum leaders often fear that charging for admission will result in fewer people visiting and lower overall visitor satisfaction. However, data suggest the exact opposite is true. Not only is cost not a primary barrier for visitation; visitor satisfaction is actually *higher* when visitors pay for admission.[24] As famed economist Milton Friedman wisely observed, "people value what they pay for and will pay for what they value."[25]

In addition to signaling quality, price can also influence decision-making and intent to purchase. For instance, when a purchase decision is driven by feelings such as spending time with family, prices ending in round numbers (e.g., $200) have been found to encourage consumers to rely more on emotion for decision-making.[26] Moreover, rounded prices have been shown to increase intent to buy.[27] Unfortunately, round numbers tend to make price increases difficult to conceal. Because many museums must increase membership prices to keep up with increasing operational costs, nonrounded numbers can help to make price increases less noticeable over time. Further, and in disagreement of the round number findings, a nonrounded price ending (e.g., $212) may lead consumers to conclude that such an unconventional price is the result of a very precise price-setting process, such that they are more likely to believe the cost accurately reflects the value.[28] Further confusing the issue are prices ending in uneven numbers, which can produce contradictory inferences about a product's quality. For example, prices ending in 9 or 99 may connote low quality and "tackiness" or high value (i.e., a bargain).[29]

The practice of discounting is another aspect of pricing strategy that reveals a dichotomy of findings. Studies suggest that discounts may drive demand by serving as a quality signal by announcing the "regular" higher price and creating the perception of savings. In one experiment, researchers tested the following three pricing treatments for a nonprofit membership campaign:

- Control: "Become an [organization] member with a gift of $35 or more."
- Treatment 1: "Become an [organization] member with a gift of $25 or more."
- Treatment 2: "Become an [organization] member with a gift of $25 or more—that's a $10 discount off our normal membership."

The results of the study found that Treatment 2, which framed the membership price of $25 as a special discount, prompted a larger number of people to join (an 18 percent increase).[30] Further, whereas Treatment 2 did not negatively impact the total dollars raised, reducing the price to a minimum $25 donation without applying the frame of a special discount led to fewer donors and a lower average gift amount. In this experiment, the use of a discount to promote $10 savings on a "regularly priced" membership increased the overall size of the nonprofit's donor base without sacrificing profitability.

This type of discounting is prevalent in museum membership marketing. However, data indicate that discounting is not a sustainable strategy. Discounting has been shown to erode price integrity, decrease customer satisfaction, and contribute to an overall lower perception of quality.[31] Discounts tend to attract the wrong kinds of customers, leading to higher attrition rates and more expensive acquisition costs.[32] Moreover, this type of pricing strategy can create an environment of "discount waiting," whereby customers will postpone making a purchase until the next discount arrives.[33] So, while museums may be able to increase short-term sales by discounting the price of membership, the impact of such a pricing strategy has a detrimental effect on long-term profitability.

Although studies into the psychology of pricing have identified many important findings, there is still much investigation to be done to understand the implications associated with the pain of paying, perceptions of quality, and discounting. To date, studies into the effects of various pricing strategies at museums, particularly in the field of membership, are limited. As a result, many museums employ new pricing strategies based on intuition or market benchmarks, neither of which is an objective, data-informed approach. As museums take on the challenge of developing effective pricing strategies, investment in research and ongoing evaluation must be a part of the process— for their own benefit and for the broader benefit of the industry as a whole.

The Irresistible Allure of Free

While price is deeply tied to perceptions of quality, there is another price point that creates an inescapable pull—zero. Numerous studies have revealed that people find the allure of zero nearly impossible to resist. Getting something for free is so tantalizing that people often ignore the associated opportunity costs. In one experiment, participants were offered a choice between a $20 Amazon gift card for the cost of $7 or a $10 Amazon gift card for free. Even though the value of the discounted $20 gift card was $13 ($20 − $7 = $13), all 65 participants chose the $10 free card.[34] It's hard to say no to free.

The concept of free is deeply embedded within the traditional membership model. Free is the primary message that museums use to communicate the value of membership—free admission, free parking, free events, free exhibition tickets, free scooters. Membership marketing frequently touts free swag, such as tote bags, baseball caps, and T-shirts, to entice new members

128   *Chapter Eight*

to join. While the concept of free can certainly be used as a device to boost membership sales, data suggest that there are inherent risks associated with such a model. Freebies, whether tangible or intangible, encourage members to consider their relationship with the organization as a consumer-driven purchase transaction—as money in exchange for benefits. And, because of this exchange, they are less likely to view their membership fee as a donation. Such a model can attract transactional members who are more fickle, cost more to retain, and generally have lower lifetime customer value scores. Thus, basing a membership program on value-driven messaging and freebies can be an untenable scenario.

There is still much to question, test, and learn about whether the concept of free is an ideal strategy for membership in the museum industry. There is no denying that the concept of free works—at least in the short term and for certain audiences. However, if an institution's goals are to cultivate philanthropically minded members, emphasizing the freebies of membership can be counterproductive. Further, museums have an opportunity to build a membership product that is more responsive and tailored to the unique needs of the individual. In doing so, the concept of membership can be redefined as something more than merely a mechanism that dispenses freebies.

Making Membership Easy to Say Yes To

How museums price membership and structure payments can have significant implications not only for revenue but also for participation. Making museums more accessible and encouraging involvement from a broader audience could be as simple as offering a monthly subscription model for membership. The trend in monthly giving shows the immense opportunity that such a subscription-type program could offer for museum membership. In 2018, one-time gifts decreased by 2 percent while monthly giving revenue increased by 17 percent.[35] While offering a monthly membership would seem like a straightforward pricing strategy in today's subscription-focused economy, the museum sector has lagged behind other industries in implementing such programs. Museum leaders who argue against a monthly membership program typically articulate two main challenges: benefits usage control and payment processing capabilities, neither of which is insurmountable nor a valid reason to dismiss a growth-oriented opportunity.

Organizations such as the World Wildlife Fund and National Public Radio have been highly successful in acquiring new members through monthly membership programs. The Human Rights Campaign (HRC) has steadily grown its monthly supporter base to 83,000, representing more than $1.1 million in revenue per month.[36] In the UK, museums have benefited greatly from monthly membership payments via the ease and high adoption rates of direct debit. Data for nonprofit monthly giving show that retention rates for monthly donors are between 62 and 94 percent with a donor life span of five to seven years.[37] Monthly donors give 42 percent more annually than those who give one-time gifts.[38] Further, monthly giving can attract a younger audience.[39]

Developing a monthly membership program will require a shift in mindset, technology, marketing mix, and institutional protocols. However, the promise of monthly membership as one of the quickest and surest revenue levers for museums is too important for inaction. As museums seek to attract new audiences, membership must be affordable and easy to say yes to.

BRIGHT SPOT: THE MUSEUM OF CONTEMPORARY ART DENVER REACHES NEW AUDIENCES WITH ITS BROKE HEART CLUB

Paving a new path for a twenty-first century museum that is "both/and," the Museum of Contemporary Art Denver (MCA Denver) is advancing the field of contemporary art and providing a platform for creative expression, in the broadest sense of the term. Presenting both world-class exhibitions and quirky events, serious lectures and epic parties, MCA Denver is unapologetically *both* sophisticated *and* unpretentious.

MCA Denver has expressed a goal to become part of the hearts and minds of Denverites, driven by the belief that everyone should have access to the Museum's offerings, including exhibitions and programs. For example, MCA Denver offers an art-sharing program called the *Octopus Initiative*, which allows Denver-area residents the opportunity to enter a lottery for the chance to receive an artwork by a local artist and keep it in their home over a 10-month period. In addition to its nearly 100 adult-focused programs offered annually, the Museum is cultivating the next generation of museumgoers through a wide range of teen programs, including free admission, designed to create a home away from home for many of the city's high school students.

In 2017, MCA Denver began exploring the possibility of adding a new membership level that would prioritize accessibility and affordability. Based on the interest demonstrated by hundreds of visitors attending the Museum's monthly "Penny Admission Saturdays," MCA Denver decided to add a new membership level that would offer full access to the Museum for less than $2 a month. With a radical approach to pricing and a desire to capture the distinct voice of the Museum, MCA Denver christened its new membership program the *Broke Heart Club*, a quirky play on the Museum's highest membership level, the *Heart Club*.

Intended for audiences who love the Museum but do not have the disposable income to enroll in MCA Denver's $45 annual individual membership, the *Broke Heart Club* is an impossible-to-say-no-to offer. *Broke Heart Club* members receive all of the same benefits as the Museum's individual members, with the exception of bringing a guest for free. Members choose from two payment options: (1) an annual payment of $23.40 or (2) a $1.95 per month subscription plan. For those who select the monthly subscription plan, members can cancel any time after the initial six-month period has passed.

MCA Denver's *Broke Heart Club* quickly saw strong interest from new members, particularly among the Museum's primary audience of adults between the ages of 18 and 35 years old. During its first month, the Museum saw enrollment of 113 members, with 126.5 percent growth in the following month, bringing the total count to 256 members. By the end of 2018, the *Broke Heart Club* had grown to 656 members, surpassing the program's initial projections. As of August 2019, MCA Denver has enrolled 1,000 *Broke Heart Club* members, resulting in $25,000 in revenue since the program's launch.

Directly tied to its vision to provide "art for all," MCA Denver intends to continue evolving and growing its *Broke Heart Club*. With its pricing strategy of incredibly small monthly payments, the *Broke Heart Club* is allowing the Museum to reach a wider audience by meeting people where they are financially. As the Museum considers future efforts to improve accessibility and member satisfaction, one thing is certain: MCA Denver is getting lots of love from new audiences through its new membership program.

Courtesy of the Museum of Contemporary Art Denver.

MIXING IT UP

The marketing mix for membership is ripe for reinvention. The traditional membership model is falling short of meeting the needs of different audiences. New product development, intentional pricing strategies, and innovative marketing approaches are needed to help museums attract new and more diverse audiences. As museums look to remove the barriers for participation, reimagining membership is a logical and opportune place to start.

The success of the Sapphire Reserve credit card demonstrates that the seemingly elusive millennial consumer can, in fact, be wooed given the right product and marketing strategy. And as Marianne Lake, chief financial officer at Chase, explains, "These are the customers that everybody wants to acquire. . . . We now have them, and we intend to deepen relationships with them."[40] To that end, in 2018 Chase launched a new service called Sapphire Banking, an extension of its popular credit card, with the goal of capturing more of its newly acquired customers' financial business. Jenn Piepszak, CEO of Chase Card Services noted, "We're serving our customers and taking the view of the customer—not the view of the product. . . . These products require a lot of attention, focus, and strategy in their own right, but we have to be able to put ourselves in the mind of the customer."[41]

Museums need to become more customer centric, viewing their offerings through the lens of the job to be done. Developing new products that address customers' unmet needs is how museums will be able to thrive in the rapidly changing landscape of the twenty-first century. Situated at the intersection of audience engagement, philanthropy, technology, and marketing—membership is uniquely positioned to lead the way forward.

NOTES

1. Ben Steverman, "Cult of Chase Sapphire: Credit-Card Churners Have a New Love," *Bloomberg*, September 2, 2016, https://www.bloomberg.com/news/articles/2016-09-02/chase-sapphire-reserve-deal-seeking-obsessives-have-a-new-favorite-credit-card.

2. Jeffry Pilcher, "Millennials Go Bananas for Super Cool, Very Pricey Metal Credit Card," *The Financial Brand*, October 17, 2016, https://thefinancialbrand.com/61696/chase-sapphire-reserve-millennial-travel-rewards-credit-card/.

3. Emily Glazer, "Sapphire Reserve Cards Aren't Very Rewarding for J.P. Morgan," *Wall Street Journal*, July 28, 2017, https://www.wsj.com/articles/sapphire-reserve-cards-arent-very-rewarding-for-j-p-morgan-1501239601.

4. Steverman, "Cult of Chase Sapphire: Credit-Card Churners Have a New Love."

5. Shelle Santana, Jill Avery, and Christine Snively, "Chase Sapphire: Creating a Millennial Cult Brand," Harvard Business School, 9-518-024, November 15, 2017, 1.

6. Ibid., 8.

7. TransUnion, "Decoding Millennial Financial Health: Generation Revealed," August 30, 2017, https://solutions.transunion.com/millennials/resources/files/TransUnion-Millennial-Study-Campaign-Report.pdf.

8. William Perreault, Jr., Joseph Cannon, and E. Jerome McCarthy, *Basic Marketing: A Marketing Strategy Planning Approach*, 19th ed. (New York: McGraw-Hill/Irwin, 2014), 35.

9. Over the years, some have tried to add additional Ps to the marketing mix, such as people, processes, and physical evidence, among others. However, the 4 Ps model has stood the test of time because its construct is flexible enough to accommodate changes in technology, the marketing landscape, and the customer experience.

10. Sam Grobart, "How Chase Made the Perfect High for Credit Card Junkies," *Bloomberg*, September 22, 2016, https://www.bloomberg.com/news/features/2016-09-22/how-chase-made-the-perfect-high-for-credit-card-junkies.

11. Peter F. Drucker, *People and Performance: The Best of Peter Drucker* (New York: Routledge, 2011), 90.

12. "Definitions of Marketing," American Marketing Association, accessed September 28, 2019, https://www.ama.org/the-definition-of-marketing/.

13. The Chartered Institute of Marketing, "Marketing and the 7Ps: A Brief Summary of Marketing and How It Works," 2015, https://www.cim.co.uk/media/4772/7ps.pdf.

14. O. C. Ferrell and Michael D. Hartline, *Marketing Strategy: Text and Cases*, 6th ed. (Mason, OH: South-Western Cengage Learning, 2011), 156.

15. Youngme Moon, "Break Free from the Product Life Cycle," *Harvard Business Review*, May 2005, https://hbr.org/2005/05/break-free-from-the-product-life-cycle.

16. Patricia Rich, Dana S. Hines, and Rosie Siemer, *Membership Marketing in the Digital Age: A Handbook for Museums and Libraries* (Lanham, MD: Rowman & Littlefield, 2016), 362–63.

17. Colleen Dilenschneider, "Why Offering Discounts through Social Media Is Bad Business for Nonprofit Organizations," *Know Your Own Bone*, May 21, 2012, https://www.colleendilen.com/2012/05/21/why-offering-discounts-through-social-media-is-bad-business-for-nonprofit-organizations/.

18. Shelle Santana, Jill Avery, and Christine Snively, "Chase Sapphire: Creating a Millennial Cult Brand," Harvard Business School, 9-518-024, November 15, 2017, 9.

19. Lisa Ward, "The Art of Suggested Donation Amounts," *Wall Street Journal*, updated December 11, 2016, https://www.wsj.com/articles/the-art-of-suggested-donation-amounts-1481511960.

20. John T. Gourville and Dilip Soman, "Pricing and the Psychology of Consumption," *Harvard Business Review*, September 2002, https://hbr.org/2002/09/pricing-and-the-psychology-of-consumption.

21. This phenomenon is known as the sunk-cost effect.

22. Leonard Mlodinow, *Subliminal: How Your Unconscious Mind Rules Your Behavior* (New York: Vintage Books, 2013), 24.

23. In a follow-up experiment, conducted by researchers at the California Institute of Technology and Stanford University, participants tasted wines without any price labels—when the prices were later disclosed, the study results revealed that everyone liked the cheapest wine the best.

24. Colleen Dilenschneider, "Distraction: Blaming Admission Cost for Lack of Cultural Center Attendance (DATA)," *Know Your Own Bone*, January 11, 2017, https://www.colleendilen.com/2017/01/11/distraction-blaming-admission-cost-for-cultural-center-attendance-data/.

25. Milton Friedman, "'Free' Education," in *Milton Friedman on Freedom: Selections from the Collected Works of Milton Friedman*, ed. Robert Leeson and Charles G. Palm (Stanford, CA: Hoover Institution Press Publication, 2017), 192.

26. Monica Wadhwa and Kuangjie Zhang, "This Number Just Feels Right: The Impact of Roundedness of Price Numbers on Product Evaluations," *Journal of Consumer Research* 41 (February 2015): 1172–85, doi:10.1086/678484.

27. Ibid.

28. Ji Youn Jeong and John L. Crompton, "The Use of Odd-Ending Numbers in the Pricing of Five Tourism Services in Three Different Cultures," *Tourism Management* 62 (2017): 135–46, http://dx.doi.org/10.1016/j.tourman.2017.04.002.

29. Robert M. Schindler, "Symbolic Meanings of a Price Ending," *Advances in Consumer Research* 18 (1991): 794–801.

30. Andreas Lange and Andrew Stocking, "Charitable Memberships, Volunteering, and Discounts: Evidence from a Large-Scale Online Field Experiment," Working Paper 14941, *National Bureau of Economic Research* (May 2009), doi:10.3386/w14941.

31. Colleen Dilenschneider, "Do Discounts Attract New Visitors to Cultural Organizations? (DATA)," *Know Your Own Bone*, May 30, 2018, https://www.colleendilen.com/2018/05/30/discounts-attract-new-visitors-cultural-organizations-data/.

32. Amy Gallo, "The Value of Keeping the Right Customers," *Harvard Business Review*, October 29, 2014, https://hbr.org/2014/10/the-value-of-keeping-the-right-customers.

33. Colleen Dilenschneider, "Why Discounting Hurts Your Cultural Organization and What to Do Instead (DATA)," *Know Your Own Bone*, October 14, 2015, http://www.colleendilen.com/2015/10/14/why-discounting-hurts-your-cultural-organization-and-what-to-do-instead-fast-fact-video/.

34. Kristina Shampanier, Nina Mazar, and Dan Ariely, "Zero as a Special Price: The True Value of Free Products," *Marketing Science* 26, no. 6 (November–December 2007): 742–57.

35. Will Valverde et al., "2019 M+R Benchmarks Study," accessed September 28, 2019, https://mrbenchmarks.com/numbers/fundraising.

36. "Best Sustainer Retention Rates Are Online," *The Nonprofit Times*, May 14, 2019, https://www.thenonprofittimes.com/donors/best-sustainer-retention-rates-are-online/.

37. Erica Waasdorp, "Erica Waasdorp: Monthly Giving Is Buzzing: The First Three Stages in a Monthly Donor's Life," Association of Fundraising Professionals, June 20, 2019, https://afpglobal.org/news/erica-waasdorp-monthly-giving-buzzing-first-three-stages-monthly-donors-life.

38. "Why Recurring Giving Matters," The Ultimate Recurring Giving Course, Network for Good, accessed September 28, 2019, https://www.networkforgood.com/lesson/why-recurring-giving-matters/.

39. The Case Foundation, "2013 Millennial Impact Report: Connect, Involve, Give," 6, https://casefoundation.org/wp-content/uploads/2014/11/MillennialImpactReport-2013.pdf.

40. Emily Glazer, "Sapphire Reserve Cards Aren't Very Rewarding for J.P. Morgan," *Wall Street Journal*, July 28, 2017, https://www.wsj.com/articles/sapphire-reserve-cards-arent-very-rewarding-for-j-p-morgan-1501239601.

41. Tanaya Macheel, "Chase Wants to Be the 'Amazon Prime of Financial Services,'" *Cheddar*, August 24, 2018, https://cheddar.com/media/chase-wants-to-be-amazon-prime-of-financial-services.

PART THREE

Chapter Nine

Asking the Right Questions

In the early afternoon of December 5, 1945, a squadron of five TBM Avenger torpedo bombers took off from the Naval Air Station in Ft. Lauderdale, Florida, to perform a routine training flight. Known as Flight 19, the planes were scheduled to fly east from the coast, conduct a series of bombing exercises at a designated point, turn north for the second leg of the flight plan, and then change course and head southwest to return to the base.[1] Led by Lieutenant Charles C. Taylor, an experienced pilot and veteran of several combat missions in World War II, the first part of the training flight ran smoothly as planned. However, shortly after successfully completing the practice bomb drop, Lieutenant Taylor became convinced that his compass was malfunctioning and the planes were flying in the wrong direction. Disoriented, he directed the pilots northeast, taking the squadron farther out to sea. Sadly, this decision sealed the fate of Flight 19, and all 14 airmen were lost that day.[2]

NEVER LET THE FACTS GET IN THE WAY OF A GOOD THEORY

The tragic story of Flight 19 demonstrates a powerful cognitive bias known as "confirmation bias." Despite evidence to the contrary, Lieutenant Taylor *believed* that his flight had gone off course, which led him to a flawed conclusion about the squadron's location. This tendency to search for and interpret information that confirms our expectations is a well-documented danger in aviation.[3] While confirmation bias by pilots and other professionals, such as doctors and engineers, can have life-threatening consequences, we are all susceptible to such biases, which can affect how we make decisions in our everyday lives.

Confirmation bias not only affects how information is gathered but also limits our capacity for objective analysis, influencing how we interpret and recall information. This can result in serious errors in judgment and flawed decision-making. The tendency to seek out and emphasize data that support our hypothesis and dismiss evidence to the contrary often leads to the cherry-picking of information that corroborates our preconceived assumptions. In his seminal book on decision-making, *Thinking Fast and Slow*, behavioral psychologist Daniel Kahneman explains how people tend to jump to conclusions on the basis of limited information. Kahneman describes this phenomenon as "what you see is all there is" or WYSIATI, for short. This focus on *perceived* evidence results in a tendency to ignore "absent" evidence and allows our brains to quickly shape a coherent and believable story (an explanation for what is happening) based on past associations, memories, assumptions, and patterns. Because of WYSIATI, the human brain "automatically and effort-lessly identifies causal connections between events, sometimes even when the connection is spurious." In other words, we are able to convince ourselves that our deep-rooted values and beliefs are based on clear causes and inten-tions, even when there is no evidence to support these connections.

In membership, confirmation bias comes into play when managers have established views about how marketing dollars should and should not be spent, why people join, and what role membership should serve within the broader context of audience development and fundraising. Once exposed to an idea that appears to be verified with an anecdote or data point, it remains locked in our brain as an immutable truth, causing museum leaders to rely on past patterns of behavior and long-held beliefs to guide strategy. This is how confirmation bias works. It tricks our brains into thinking that what we know is true and valid, even when it's not. Those winning marketing strategies, best practices in membership management, the right way to design a reply device, the proven tactics that show how incentives and discounts work are all susceptible to confirmation bias. For this reason, confirmation bias inevitably leads to decisions that end up reinforcing the status quo.

The ill effects of confirmation bias are rampant in the fields of marketing, membership, and fundraising. Consider the firmly held belief in museum fundraising that the greater the ratio for a challenge gift, the greater the results for a campaign. That is, a 2:1 match in which every dollar that a donor gives is matched by two dollars "greatly adds to the match's attractiveness."[4] The 2:1 match is often touted as doubling the donor's contribution. Such a pro-motion is akin to the two-for-one deals offered by retailers to increase sales of everything from candy bars to bath soap. The anecdotal evidence of the power of this fundraising tactic is so widespread that many in the field have accepted it as a commandment. So it may come as a surprise to learn that the size of the match really doesn't matter. In fact, a 1:1 challenge appears to be just as effective as a 2:1 or even a 3:1 match.[5]

Another common refrain among museum leaders is that their institution's status as a nonprofit is not only top of mind but of paramount importance for visitors and members. The attitude that audience perceptions are impacted by an organization's nonprofit status permeates websites, membership brochures, email campaigns, and direct mail letter copy. Given the strong adoption of this principle throughout the industry, it may seem a bit absurd to ask the question, "Does being a nonprofit even matter to potential and current cultural audiences?" Yet that is just what the National Awareness, Attitudes, and Usage Study went about asking. The findings are sure to be unnerving: more than half of all potential and current visitors are unaware that nonprofit cultural organizations are nonprofits.[6] Further, audiences are becoming increasingly "sector agnostic," caring less about an organization's tax status and more about its overall social impact. Many for-profit companies, such as Patagonia, TOMS, Disney, and Dove, have capitalized on this concept by creating highly successful "cause-marketing" programs that raise awareness, drive donations, and promote social good. The good news is that consumers are increasingly prioritizing companies that are socially responsible (86 percent), caring (85 percent), advocate for issues (81 percent), protect the environment (79 percent), and give back to important causes (73 percent).[7] The bad news is that, while a majority of consumers prefer to support brands and organizations with a social good impact, most do not distinguish between nonprofit and for-profit status. Museums don't *own* social good. And despite all the urging by museums to get audiences to recognize their nonprofit status, this factor is not a key driver of the decision to support. Museums today are competing for mission mindshare against companies with much deeper pockets for advertising and much higher consumer brand affinity.

To paraphrase an old adage, the museum sector seems to never let the facts get in the way of a good theory. If museum leaders, membership managers, and marketing professionals can fall victim to so many supposed industry certainties, how many decisions have been corrupted by faulty assumptions, false validations, and flawed past behaviors? Too many membership programs and marketing departments rely on hand-me-down formulas and industry best practices that are being artificially propped up by confirmation bias. Do you really know why members join? Are you offering the right kinds of experiences that will entice new audiences to participate? Is membership pricing optimized with the right mix of benefits? Do your supporters consider themselves members, donors, or both? How can you be sure?

THE TROUBLE WITH ASKING QUESTIONS

Traditional methods of market research, such as surveys, interviews, and focus groups, are inherently prone to all sorts of bias. The effects of these biases are far reaching and pervasive in museum research studies. While highly skilled professional researchers can mitigate the effects of these biases, it is impossible to entirely stop them from creeping into research findings. One of the most prevalent risks associated with market research involves the unintentional use of problematic techniques, which can result in inaccurate and misleading data. Five common mistakes that result in flawed research are leading questions, loaded questions, double-barreled questions, absolutes, and sampling bias.

Leading Questions

Leading questions use non-neutral wording that can influence the respondent to answer in a certain way. This type of question suggests the answer the organization is looking for and is used to confirm a particular viewpoint by implying or prompting a specific type of response. For example, a survey may include coercive questions designed to elicit positive feedback, such as "What is your favorite member benefit?" This is a leading question because it assumes that the respondent favors one or more of the available benefits and doesn't allow for an alternative viewpoint. Another example of a leading question is one that informs the respondent as part of the question, such as "Are you aware that members receive exclusive discounts on special exhibitions?" Well, if I were not before, I am now! While this may be a good way to educate audiences about the benefits of membership, it's a very bad way to conduct objective research.

Leading questions can also signal to respondents that they should or shouldn't like something. Consider the following examples:

1. "How likely are you to attend programs in our new state-of-the-art theater?"
2. "Should concerned parents expose young children to the arts to encourage creative thinking?"

In the first example, the description of the theater as "new" and "state-of-the-art" is likely to induce a more positive view of the programs than a question that does not include these adjectives. In the second example, the phrase "concerned parents" suggests how the respondent should answer this question.

Loaded Questions

Loaded questions include emotionally charged words or phrasing that forces the respondent to answer in a way that doesn't accurately reflect the individual's situation or opinion. Often, loaded questions are based on underlying assumptions that make it difficult for respondents to answer objectively. For example, "How much did you enjoy your interaction with the curator at the member reception?" assumes that the member had an opportunity to interact with the curator and it was an enjoyable experience. Another example is a question that includes a false premise, such as "Do you think museums are a good way to relax from a stressful day at work?" In this example, the respondent is required to agree with the assumption that work is stressful to be able to answer.

Double-Barreled Questions

Also known as a "compound question," a double-barreled question forces the respondent to answer two questions at once. For example, "Was the member event held at a convenient time and location? Yes/No." This question includes two distinct topics (time and location) but allows for only one answer. Suppose the respondent found the location to be convenient, but the time was not. Because there are two separate questions embedded within a single question, it may be difficult for the respondent to answer truthfully to either.

Absolutes

Often, questionnaires or interviews may inadvertently include absolutes—using words such as *every*, *always*, *all*, *never*, or *ever*. Absolutes can make respondents feel that their responses need to be black or white. Consider the statement, "I always spend time with family on the weekends: Yes/No." In this example, the inflexibility of the statement forces a response that individuals may not feel accurately represents their situation. Perhaps most weekends are spent with family, but sometimes there are obligations that require the family to be apart. Does watching TV together count as "spending time" with family? Also, how do you define "family"? Suppose a respondent considers a close friend as family—is the organization prepared for an individual to define "family" on their own terms? Or is the organization's use of the term "family" intended to mean "with children"? If the aim of the question is to understand whether children are present in the household on Saturdays, then that is a very different question.

Sampling Bias

A dangerous error in market research is sampling bias, also referred to as sample selection bias, which occurs when a sample—the group of respondents participating in the study—is not randomly selected. That is, certain people are more or less likely to be included in the sample, leading to results that do not accurately reflect the target population. In membership, sampling bias often arises when managers send out a member survey. There may be significant differences between those members who completed the survey and those who did not. Moreover, members will likely differ greatly in many respects from nonmembers and potential visitors. Thus, generalizations about members should not be applied to all visitors or the general public. Additionally, surveys and focus groups tend to attract people who like to participate in surveys and focus groups, leading to a biased sample that excludes a broad swath of nonparticipants.

One famous example of sampling bias occurred during the 1948 United States presidential race. To gauge voter intent, a political telephone survey was conducted nationwide in which Thomas Dewey was predicted to win over Harry S. Truman in a landslide victory. On November 3, 1948, the day after the election, the front page of the *Chicago Daily Tribune* emphatically pronounced, "Dewey Defeats Truman."[8] While the final vote had yet to be tallied at press time, the newspaper's editors felt confident that Dewey was favored to win based on the results of the telephone poll. Yet it was Truman who ultimately defeated Dewey, winning 28 of the 48 states and 303 out of 531 electoral votes. How could the pollsters have gotten it so wrong? In 1948, telephones were a relatively new and expensive technology. Due to the high cost, only a small number of wealthy families had telephones in their homes. The researchers failed to take this into account when they analyzed the results. Today, Truman's unexpected victory is the stuff of legend, and we know that sampling bias was responsible for a very wrong conclusion about who would win the election.

LIES AND THE LIARS THAT TELL THEM

People are liars. They lie about how often they go to the gym. They lie about how much they drink. They lie about what they watch on TV. They lie about how happy they are. They lie about being vegetarians. They lie about how much they give to charity. They lie to their friends and doctors. And they most definitely lie in surveys. Social scientists refer to this tendency by respondents to lie as "social desirability bias." It happens when people answer questions in a way that they think will be viewed more favorably by others.

Social desirability bias can affect many forms of quantitative and qualitative research, including telephone or in-person interviews, focus groups, and on-line surveys—even when the responses are anonymous.

When people are asked about their behaviors, beliefs, or motives, they often feel a need to present themselves in a positive light. Thus, results can see an exaggeration of socially desirable behaviors and attitudes and an understatement of behaviors and attitudes that would be considered less socially acceptable. Importantly, while social desirability bias is usually associated with highly sensitive or embarrassing topics, such as drug use or sexual behavior, people will also adjust their responses about the most trivial of subjects based on what they think the researcher or organization wants to hear. In some cases, respondents are not even aware that they are responding in a biased way, or they may simply be lying to themselves out of guilt or an idealized self-identity.[9]

Acquiescence bias, as the name suggests, is often called the "yes" bias or "yea-saying" because respondents are more likely to agree with statements regardless of the content. This happens for many reasons. First, we take mental shortcuts when answering questions, and answering in the affirmative is simply easier than disagreeing. Second, people are prone to go along with the crowd and are unlikely to challenge others or a moderator in a group setting. Third, respondents often feel that it is impolite to disagree, so they are more likely to acquiesce, even when responses are anonymous. Acquiescence bias is more common in questions that are formatted as yes/no, true/false, or agree/disagree statements. One way to mitigate the effects of acquiescence bias is to use a "forced choice" format in which respondents are asked to choose between two statements, rather than answering based on a binary scale.

Another bias that wreaks havoc in marketing and membership is called hyperbolic discounting, or present bias, and it's the reason for a whole lot of broken New Year's resolutions. Present bias is the idea that people prefer a smaller immediate reward compared to a larger reward later. Research shows that people consistently fail to follow through on the plans they make for themselves, especially if those plans require an up-front cost with benefits that aren't realized until sometime in the future. In other words, given the choice between two rewards, people have a tendency to prefer the reward that arrives sooner. Present bias is why we indulge in ice cream now and plan to eat vegetables later.

Present bias can result in inflated responses when audiences are asked about their intentions to do certain things. This is because humans are naturally aspirational creatures. Tomorrow, we will give more, eat healthier, exercise more, and spend more time with friends and family. Clearly, we are all much better people in the future. These idealistic versions of our future selves can cloud findings related to intentions, including whether a person plans to join, renew, or donate. So the next time you ask people about their intentions, remember that they are unlikely to say that they *intend* to spend money on frivolous things, rather than supporting a cause they care about, or they *plan* to sit on the couch binge watching the latest docuseries instead of going to a museum.

WHEN TO ASK WHY

Why did you decide to become a member? This is such a routine survey question that it hardly feels out of place. Yet asking "Why?" can make people feel blamed or challenged, as if they have to defend their decision. Why questions can also be difficult for respondents to answer because they may not even know why they did or didn't do something. Because decisions are influenced by numerous factors on a subconscious level, people are poor witnesses to their own behavior and motivations. Moreover, market research often takes place in an environment that is far removed from the actual decision-making experience. That is, asking someone why they made a particular decision out of context will not accurately reflect their frame of mind at the time.

In addition to being bad at understanding our own behavior, people are also generally pretty terrible at predicting what they will want in the future. As Henry Ford reportedly once quipped, "If I had asked people what they wanted, they would have said faster horses." It is this same type of innovation challenge that Apple encountered as the company was developing the iconic iPhone, and it is why traditional research often leads organizations astray. While audiences may be responding truthfully about their desires and intentions, their future actions don't always match their responses. And, because it is extremely difficult to articulate what you want before you see it, consumers are not able to honestly answer the questions "What do you want?" and "Why do you want it?"

All of this is not to say that traditional market research, such as surveys and focus groups, are useless. In fact, traditional methods can be incredibly valuable in certain circumstances, such as understanding top-of-mind awareness, measuring attitudes over time, or gathering initial input on an idea. However, traditional market research methods lack reliability and validity and are poor predictors of future behavior. Because our decisions and behaviors are influenced by many factors that we are not consciously aware of, traditional methods cannot provide the kinds of rich insights needed for true innovation. To get to the hidden motivations and barriers affecting behavior, museums must devise a way to find out what audiences need without directly asking them.

Take a very common practice in marketing: a promotional offer for membership is sent out via email and then measured for effectiveness based on the number of clicks and coupon code redemptions. Success is judged based on the number of sales attributed to the membership promotion. In this scenario, marketers can even test various elements of the campaign, such as call to action, subject line, and button color. This approach makes a lot of sense when we are trying to answer the question "Why is this person doing this?" We can quickly see the cause-and-effect relationship between the email campaign and membership sales, so it is easy to feel satisfied with the outcome. Either the campaign worked (increase in membership sales), or it didn't (no significant change in membership sales). However, this type of evaluation does not get to the more important question of "Why isn't this person doing something?" To get the answer to that question, we need to deploy an entirely different approach to market research—one that involves building empathy and experimentation.

Museums must shift their focus away from the conventional marketing approach of asking "How can I get her to do it?" to asking instead "Why isn't she doing it already?" This simple reorientation will allow museum leaders to discover the barriers that are hindering behavior change.

The Five Whys

Developed by Taiichi Ohno, the originator of the Toyota Production System, the Five Whys is a deceptively simple interrogative technique designed to uncover the root cause of a problem. The process involves repeatedly asking "Why?" to drill down beyond the symptoms to get to the underlying cause of the problem. The method begins with the definition of a problem statement and then follows with a progressive sequence of five childlike "Whys?" until you have identified the source of the issue.

Ohno cites the following example of a welding robot that suddenly stopped working to demonstrate the technique:[10]

1. "Why did the robot stop?" Because the circuit was overloaded, causing a fuse to blow.
2. "Why was the circuit overloaded?" Because there was insufficient lubrication on the bearings.
3. "Why was there insufficient lubrication on the bearings?" Because the oil pump on the robot was not circulating sufficient oil.
4. "Why was the pump not circulating sufficient oil?" Because the pump intake was clogged with metal shavings.
5. "Why was the intake clogged with metal shavings?" Because there was no filter on the pump.

In the museum space, leaders can use the Five Whys technique to investigate common problems that arise in membership, such as an unexpected decline in the renewal rate:

1. Why is our membership renewal rate so low? *Because we had a low response rate on last month's renewal notice.*
2. Why was last month's response rate so low? *Because members were unable to renew online.*
3. Why were members not able to renew online? *Because the URL included on the renewal notice sent people to a broken link on the website.*
4. Why was the link broken? *Because there was a missing character in the URL.*
5. Why was there a missing character in the URL? *Because we didn't have time to proof the renewal notice before it went out.*

The Five Whys should not be used as a horizontal inquiry to explore all possible reasons for the problem or as a "gotcha" device to catch someone in a mistake. Rather, the technique is intended to go deep. The answer to each "Why?" serves as a breadcrumb, illuminating a trail with a new clue until the root cause of the issue is finally exposed.

In the renewal rate example, there is an indication that there is an issue with the renewal notice; however, it's unclear what has gone wrong until we arrive at the final "Why?" Guessing at what might have suppressed the renewal rate could lead to erroneous causes, such as the design of the envelope, the timing of the mailing, or the type or number of member events featured. However, using the Five Whys reveals that the problem was actually caused by a breakdown in the proofing process that led to a typo in the renewal notice. Without the Five Whys, most teams stop short at a superficial fix to a deeper problem or, worse, risk fixing something that's not broken.

The Five Whys technique is frequently used to understand what went wrong after something unexpected occurs; however, it is even more useful when trying to understand more complex challenges. Consider the following problem statement:

1. Why is our membership renewal rate so low? *Because we had a low response rate on last month's renewal notice.*
2. Why was last month's response rate so low? *Because last month's renewal list included a high percentage of first-year members who didn't renew.*
3. Why did we have such a large number of new members joining around this time last year? *Because they all joined during our spring membership acquisition campaign.*

4. Why did so many people join during the spring acquisition campaign? *Because we offered a 20 percent discount on membership.*
5. Why did we offer a discount on membership? *Because we needed to quickly increase year-end membership numbers to hit our projections.*

The above example illustrates the true power of the Five Whys. If the process had stopped at the first "Why?," it would be easy to assume that the reason for a low renewal rate was a fluke, a problem related to the renewal notice itself or some other inconsequential factor. The insight gleaned through root cause analysis using the Five Whys exposes that the low renewal rate was actually driven by a knee-jerk reaction to lagging membership numbers sometime last year. The use of a 20 percent discount to boost membership may have helped the department reach year-end projections, but the fallout from this seemingly innocuous decision created a ripple effect that resulted in a drop-off in the following year's renewal rate (and a subsequent financial loss) due to a large number of high-risk, first-time members.

The Five Whys technique is an invaluable tool that helps organizations fully explore and understand the underlying root of a problem. More often than not, the complications that show up on the surface are just symptoms of a much deeper issue. Stopping short at the first answer to any challenge is a band-aid approach. The persistent probing of the Five Whys forces teams to keep digging until the true source of the problem is uncovered.

ASKING BETTER QUESTIONS

Journalist and innovation expert Warren Berger developed an ingenious framework for tackling big, complex problems. Berger calls this approach Why-What If-How, and it is a three-part model that guides innovators through the stages of inquiry to unlock creativity and spark breakthrough ideas.[11] Why-What If-How aligns with modern theories in creative problem solving and design thinking by first framing the problem (Why), progressing to an ideation stage (What If), and eventually building upon those ideas to develop a solution (How).

By beginning with Why, the Why-What If-How framework provides questioners with a mechanism to identify the need or pain point and articulate a clear problem statement. In his book, *A More Beautiful Question*, Berger emphasizes the importance of using Why questions to "step back" and examine routines and assumptions. A good Why question is one that seeks true understanding. Why questions can be hyper focused on a narrow problem, for example, "Why aren't visitors becoming members?" Or they can be expansive and audacious, such as "Why is our museum not competitive with local craft breweries?" It is the Why question that grants us permission to begin thinking about things in a different way.

The next stage of the Why-What If-How model is the question What If—a blue sky moment where reality can be suspended and anything is possible. The purpose of asking What If is to remove all constraints to spur creativity and ideation. What If questions can, *and should*, be bold and improbable. The goal at this stage of inquiry is to push the boundaries of what's expected in order to get past assumptions and inspire innovation. What If questions explore the problem from all angles, such as "What if museums looked more like a start-up incubator?" or "What if we turned membership upside down and created a program that paid members to visit?" Using What If is an exhilarating and captivating exercise that can bring about the most inventive of ideas to solve a problem. During this phase of inquiry, it is critical not to dismiss or censor ideas. When asking What If, the greater the number and the crazier the ideas, the better. It also is necessary to allow time to fully explore many possibilities. The What If stage can span several hours to several months or even years, depending on the scope of the challenge. To allow the most creative ideas to bubble up, teams must ensure a safe space for unabashed imagination to ask What If.

The final stage, How, involves determining the first steps to bring a solution to reality, such as "How can we begin to test that idea?" or "How might we design a membership program that looks like that?" How is about beginning the process of designing ideas that can be tested in the real world. How is where abstract concepts must be formed into actionable strategies. Importantly, How is not about perfecting a concept and meticulously planning a rollout strategy. Rather, the How process should be nimble—focused on ideation, testing, and iteration. At this stage, the rougher the design, the better the feedback. Thus, teams must be courageous to let their ideas out into the world before they've been fully constructed.

Have museum leaders been getting the right answer to the wrong question? Humorist Mark Twain said, "It ain't what you don't know that gets you into trouble. It's what you know for sure that just ain't so." To reach new audiences and extend the museum's mission, leaders must be willing to challenge what they know for sure that just ain't so. By asking the right questions, museums will be able to unlock the opportunities that will help them thrive in uncertainty. Maybe what museums need is an opportunity to take a few chances and the courage to ask, What If?

NOTES

1. Evan Andrews, "The Mysterious Disappearance of Flight 19," *History.com*, updated September 1, 2018, https://www.history.com/news/the-mysterious-disappearance-of-flight-19.

2. Flight 19 disappeared in an area of the Atlantic Ocean triangulated by Puerto Rico, Florida, and Bermuda known as the Bermuda Triangle. While the Bermuda Triangle has been blamed for countless mysterious disappearances and unexplained phenomena, the National Oceanic and Atmospheric Administration (NOAA) states, "There is no evidence that mysterious disappearances occur with any greater frequency in the Bermuda Triangle than in any other large, well-traveled area of the ocean." For more information, visit https://oceanservice.noaa.gov/facts/bermudatri.html.

3. Jess Staufenberg, "Pilots 'Very Likely' to Misjudge Flying Conditions due to Irrational Decisions," *Independent*, May 17, 2016, https://www.independent.co.uk/news/science/pilots-very-likely-to-misjudge-flying-conditions-due-to-irrational-decisions-psychology-study-a7033481.html.

4. Kent E. Dove, *Conducting a Successful Capital Campaign*, 2nd ed. (San Francisco: Jossey-Bass, 2000), 510.

5. Uri Gneezy and John A. List, *The Why Axis* (New York: PublicAffairs, 2013), 182.

6. Colleen Dilenschneider, "Does Being Nonprofit Impact Perceptions of Cultural Organizations? (DATA)," *Know Your Own Bone*, September 27, 2017, https://www.colleendilen.com/2017/09/27/nonprofit-impacts-visitor-perceptions-cultural-organizations-data/.

7. Porter Novelli, "2018 Porter Novelli/Cone Purpose Premium Index," 7, https://static1.squarespace.com/static/56b4a7472b8dde3df5b7013f/t/5beb05738a922d56095b1a8f/1542129133082/2018+Cone+%2B+PN+Purpose+Index+Research.pdf.

8. Elizabeth Nix, "'Dewey Defeats Truman': The Election Upset behind the Photo," *History.com*, updated July 18, 2019, https://www.history.com/news/dewey-defeats-truman-election-headline-gaffe.

9. Philip S. Brenner and John DeLamater, "Lies, Damned Lies, and Survey Self-Reports? Identity as a Cause of Measurement Bias," *Social Psychology Quarterly* 79, no. 4 (December 2016): 333–54, doi:10.1177/0190272516628298.

10. Emi Osono, Norihiko Shimizu, and Hirotaka Takeuchi, *Extreme Toyota: Radical Contradictions That Drive Success at the World's Best Manufacturer* (Hoboken, NJ: John Wiley & Sons, 2008), 140.

11. Warren Berger, *A More Beautiful Question: The Power of Inquiry to Spark Breakthrough Ideas*, Electronic ed. (New York: Bloomsbury, 2014), 14–15.

Chapter Ten

Empathy, Emotion, and Experiences

People are alone and lonely. The number of adults living without a spouse or partner in the US has increased from 39 to 42 percent over the past 10 years.[1] A 2018 study found that 46 percent of Americans feel lonely sometimes or always and only 27 percent feel that they belong to a group of friends.[2] Loneliness is a public health crisis, posing greater risks than obesity and smoking.[3] Loneliness reduces your immunity, increases your risk of heart disease and other chronic health conditions, and contributes to high blood pressure, anxiety, and a variety of psychological health issues. Much of this sense of loneliness stems from social isolation and a lack of meaningful, in-person interactions on a daily basis. In particular, studies find that physical touch is missing from many people's lives. In the UK, 46 percent of people yearn for the simple act of hugging.[4] Is it any wonder, then, that there is a rapidly growing market for professional cuddling services?[5]

The benefits of touch are well documented, from the developmental importance of skin-to-skin contact for newborns to the improved circulation and immune-boosting power of massage therapy. However, unlike massage or physical therapy, cuddling addresses a deeper, more emotional need. Cuddling stimulates oxytocin, dopamine, and serotonin and lowers cortisol levels, which can help curb depression, reduce blood pressure, and boost your immune system. Cuddling can help you sleep better, relieves stress, and lowers your heart rate. So how much do you think people would be willing to pay for a professional cuddler? The answer might surprise you.

THE LONELINESS EPIDEMIC

When the first professional cuddling service was introduced, it was an entirely new product category without any preset consumer expectations, including price. This unique opportunity allowed professional cuddlers to define their service experience from scratch and to develop a pricing strategy that did not have a previously associated reference point. As the industry has become more established, prices for professional cuddling services have normalized across markets. Today, you can hire a professional cuddler for between $40 and $80 per hour or $700 for a strictly platonic sleepover.

While the idea of hiring a professional cuddler may seem absurd to some, the demand for such a service indicates a troubling reality in our society: people are starving for human connection. Considered by governments worldwide as a dire public health threat, loneliness can affect anyone at different times throughout their life—teenagers, seniors, young adults, new parents, empty nesters, caregivers, the bereaved, those with disabilities, refugees, expats, married people, divorced people, victims of crime, those who are unemployed or retired, military veterans, and the list goes on. In 2018, Prime Minister Theresa May appointed the UK's first ever government ministerial lead on loneliness. As part of a £20 million initiative to tackle the growing epidemic of loneliness, the UK's Department for Digital, Culture, Media and Sport published a comprehensive strategy that aims to increase participation in culture- and community-based activities to combat what has been called "one of the greatest public health challenges of our time."[6]

Much like the emotional and physical healing that professional cuddling seeks to provide, museums and the outdoors are now being prescribed as a therapeutic treatment to address the negative effects of loneliness. Between 2014 and 2017, researchers from University College London and Canterbury Christ Church University partnered with local museums to investigate the value of museums in combating isolation and loneliness among seniors. The study focused on the concept of "social prescribing" to link people with sources of community activity in an effort to improve their health and well-being. The participants, consisting of 115 people who were referred through local social and psychological services agencies, were enrolled in a 10-week museum-based set of programs involving creative and collaborative activities. The results of the program showed a significant impact on participants' quality of life, including a stronger sense of belonging, a renewed interest in learning and acquisition of new skills, having something to look forward to, and other healthy lifestyle changes.[7]

In Shetland, Scotland, doctors are prescribing time in nature to patients suffering from depression, anxiety, mental illness, diabetes, and heart disease.[8]

And the UK is not alone in its efforts to cure what ails us. Art, culture, and nature are now being prescribed by doctors around the world to combat the negative effects of isolation, stress, and disease. In Canada, the Montreal Museum of Fine Arts (MMFA) has invested in a range of therapy programs to promote well-being through art, including a partnership with the Médecins francophones du Canada, a professional physicians association, to allow doctors to prescribe 50 free museum visits a year for patients and caregivers.[9] In the US, the National Endowment for the Arts has convened a task force representing units from across the federal government, including the US Department of Health and Human Services, the National Institutes of Health, the National Science Foundation, and the US Department of Education, to encourage research into the role that art plays in improving health and educational outcomes.[10]

Nathalie Bondil, director general of the MMFA, predicts, "In the 21st century, culture will be what physical activity was for health in the 20th century."[11] Because loneliness and not having someone to go with are barriers to participation, museums should be proactively designing programs to address these issues, rather than waiting for doctors to prescribe culture and nature to patients.[12] Moreover, museums have an opportunity to build a sense of belonging and facilitate human connection.

While museums may not be in the business of hugs, the popularity of professional cuddling is a clear example of finding a need and filling it. People are seeking a community to belong to and a place where they can feel connected to others. Museums can be this place. However, getting the job of human connection done requires a reimagining of what membership can be.

BRIGHT SPOT: CELEBRATING THE ART OF FRIENDSHIP AT THE SAINT LOUIS ART MUSEUM

The Member Mornings program at the Saint Louis Art Museum is one of the most enjoyable perks of membership. A half hour before the Museum opens, several dates each month members are welcome to enjoy a complimentary coffee or beverage in the cafe prior to a docent-led tour. Much like an extra-early happy hour, the Member Morning is a great place to bring friends, as well as make new friends.

In fact, these mornings helped to create a group of friends who now loyally attend together once a month. Years ago, Ann Schmid spotted Noëlle Gunter sitting by herself. Also attending solo, Ann sat down and introduced herself. She mentioned her son living in Tokyo, and, coincidentally, Noëlle had previously lived there with her husband. Quickly bonding, they also over time became acquainted with Fran Schlapprizzi, another member who was bringing Mary Wojciechowski and Nancy Casey from her exercise class to Member Mornings. Soon rounding out the group was Katie Ward, Ann's friend from her church group.

Nowadays, rather than limiting the fun to just a morning, the women often make a day of it and enjoy lunch together afterward at Panorama. Scheduled by Fran, the group's official organizer, it was at one of these lunches that Noëlle was surprised when realizing how long they have been friends. When asked how long they've known each other, she at first answered "a few years." She then described how they watched the parking garage being built while enjoying their Member Morning coffee in the temporary cafe set up in Gallery 213. When told groundbreaking for the garage and new building was in 2010, Noëlle was reminded—like many of us often are—of how time flies.

Although they have different preferences in art—for example, Katie likes the abstract, such as Picasso, while Noëlle prefers the "whimsical," à la Magritte—they bond over learning something new about the Museum's collection each month, as well as gabbing about their unique life experiences.

"We all come with our own story," said Ann. "I've made some great friends." She then joked, "We probably see each other more than we see some of our own family members."

Courtesy of the Saint Louis Art Museum.

BUILDING A PRACTICE OF EMPATHY

Organizations that develop a true understanding of their customers' needs are able to unlock an immense capacity for innovation. Empathy, defined as "the action of understanding, being aware of, being sensitive to, and vicariously experiencing the feelings, thoughts, and experience of another," is vital to engaging audiences in a meaningful way.[13] Developing an empathic capability requires that museum leaders let go of their roles, experiences, opinions, and assumptions that stand in the way of being able to put themselves in another's shoes. Importantly, empathy is not a singular action but rather a continuous practice. Like building any other muscle, daily exercise is necessary to build institutional empathy and expand the boundaries of what's possible.

To understand how empathy can produce unexpected solutions, consider the extremely complex challenge of absenteeism in schools. In the US, chronic absenteeism, a measure of total accumulated missed school days, affects an estimated 5 to 7.5 million students.[14] Chronic absenteeism is associated with poor academic performance and lower scores on national standardized tests, exacerbating dropout rates, increasing achievement gaps, and eroding the promise of early education.[15] The most vulnerable students, including those living in poverty and from communities of color, are disproportionately affected by chronic absenteeism.[16]

To address the pressing challenge of chronic absenteeism, some schools have started installing washing machines. At first blush, a laundry machine may seem like an unlikely way to get kids to come to class more often. However, teachers realized that dirty clothes were keeping students from attending school. The principal of a Louisville, Kentucky, school where almost 70 percent of students qualify for subsidized or free lunches, observed that "If it's a choice between coming to school dirty, and have kids laugh at you or make fun of you, and staying home, they'll stay home."[17] This profound insight led that school and many others across the country to create laundry rooms where kids can wash their clothes for free. In one Kansas City, Missouri, school, attendance rates jumped 83 percent after a washing machine was installed.[18]

Without stepping outside of a traditional way of thinking and looking at the problem of school attendance through the perspective of a student, teachers and administrators would not have been able to understand how dirty clothes can affect students' self-confidence. Putting themselves in the shoes of students allowed school leaders to uncover a surprising, and incredibly simple, intervention to removing a critical barrier to attendance. This is the power of empathy. Finding a hidden barrier like self-confidence is an empowering insight that can lead to unconventional solutions to complex challenges. Sleuthing out these kinds of insights requires keen observation skills and an ability to investigate beyond the surface to understand the underlying drivers of behavior.

Innovation in museums cannot occur without a deeper understanding of the people they serve. To build their capacity for empathy, museum leaders can apply a wide range of methods to learn more about audience needs, motivations, and values. As a first step to developing empathy, museum leaders need to adopt "a beginner's mindset." The process of adopting a beginner's mindset starts with the mantra *question everything*—even if you think you know the answer. Questioning everything allows us to step back from our assumptions and helps us to not make judgments. When we approach a problem from a place of genuine curiosity, we can begin to understand the underlying motivations and barriers that are driving or restraining behavior.

A beginner's mindset allows for a fresh perspective to be applied to old problems. As Zen master Shunryu Suzuki wrote, "In the beginner's mind there are many possibilities, but in the expert's there are few."[19] Adopting a beginner's mindset involves pretending that you have no prior knowledge whatsoever about a particular topic. One of the most important aspects of adopting a beginner's mindset is listening—deep, active listening. Without listening, we cannot truly hear what our customer is saying, verbally or otherwise.

It is by asking questions and listening for what's underneath the answer that we are able to see problems from a new perspective. At the heart of a beginner's mindset is genuine curiosity for why things are the way they are, why things don't work, and why people behave the way they do. Empathy allows museum leaders to gain a deeper appreciation and understanding of audiences' emotional and physical needs and how they see, interpret, and interact with the world around them.

There are many approaches that museum leaders can use to build empathy with audiences. User studies, journals, in-depth interviews, analogous inspiration, bodystorming, and card sorting are all ways to practice listening and exercise our curiosity muscles. Because each technique has its own strengths and weaknesses, it is important to ensure that the approach or combination of methods is appropriate for answering the kinds of questions you want to understand.

EMPATHIC RESEARCH METHODS

User Studies. Observing audiences interacting with a product, experience, or marketing in real time can uncover important insights about how people think and feel about something. In many cases, user studies can help identify hidden motivations and barriers that participants themselves may not be aware of. For example, observing customers in the real world can reveal patterns in how people interact with signage, technology, or messaging. User experience testing can reveal unexpected habits, expectations, how customers interpret content, and what influences feelings of trust, first impressions, and decisions. Observing consumers in their daily lives allows a researcher to understand the nuance of context in a particular situation and to leverage this understanding for further discovery.

Journaling. A journal can be a powerful empathic research tool. Journaling is a nonthreatening method for collecting in-depth data about a person's experiences. Journals can take many forms, including photo, video, collage, or written. While participants will adapt their normal behavior somewhat with the knowledge that someone will be reviewing their journal entries, this technique is less invasive than observation in real time and can be a less intimidating way for customers to share their feelings. A journal can be a great way to go beyond an in-person interview to better understand the context in a person's life. Alternatively, a journal can provide a foundation in advance of an interview, allowing for a richer, more focused interview.

In-Depth Interviews. One-on-one in-depth interviews offer an opportunity to gain a better understanding of customers' perceptions, values, and aspirations. This type of research provides a deep understanding of how the unique circumstances of an individual's life differ from another person's life. The technique allows for a skilled researcher to obtain a rich context about the person's attitudes, behaviors, and mindset, which is crucial to revealing not just what they *say* they do but what they actually do and why. In-depth interviews are best conducted in-person so that the researcher is able to observe and respond to the participant's facial expressions, body language, and tone of voice. Unlike focus groups, where responses may be influenced by other participants, in-depth interviews provide the best opportunity to explore individual decision-making processes and to probe for context. This type of interview is best conducted by a trained researcher who is able to build rapport quickly, actively listen for insights, and adjust his or her language, posture, pace, and tone to empathize with the individual.

Analogous Inspiration. This technique is all about applying an out-of-context concept to solving a problem. By breaking down the key elements of a situation, experience, interaction, or process, it's possible to use an analogy as a launch pad to inspire a creative solution to a seemingly unrelated problem. Using an analogy is a simple and creative way to home in on the distinct activities, behaviors, and emotions involved with a particular challenge. Consider the following example: A museum team wants to explore how the museum might encourage new members to join its membership program. To get started, the museum team creates a list of parallel concepts that reflect the key elements of the problem needing to be solved. For instance, the emotional element of "being a member" might be reflected in the sense of belonging that comes from being part of a community of intensely passionate and likeminded people, such as cosplayers who attend Comic Con. The more unexpected the analogy, the better. For analogous inspiration to be effective, the museum team must *experience* the analogous research example in real life. Through experience, the museum team will be able to arrive at the insights that will inform the pain and pleasure points necessary for solution ideation.

Bodystorming. This technique involves physically experiencing a situation or product to derive new ideas. Through the use of props, impromptu role-play, and replicated spaces, bodystorming creates an opportunity for empathy by allowing researchers to experience how people interact with an environment or situation. Bodystorming is an immersive ideation method that puts your feet in the shoes of another (sometimes literally!). The process of bodystorming can open up a fresh viewpoint for understanding how others make sense of the world by interacting within a simulated scenario—complete with artifacts and people. Bodystorming may include constructing models, props, or structures to mimic a specific environment or situation. For example, researchers might wear water-filled goggles to experience what it feels like to cook with a vision impairment or reduce their height to the eye level of a five-year-old to experience the world as a child does. In a museum setting, bodystorming has infinite applications, from wayfinding and visitor experience management to membership product development and marketing. By acting out a scenario through bodystorming, we are able to focus more attention on understanding the problem, rather than jumping right to a solution.

Card Sorting. As a participatory research technique, card sorting allows a researcher to gain a deep understanding of the mental models and constructs that a person holds in his or her mind. Card sorting provides insight into how an individual makes sense of a subject or situation by illuminating how they categorize, prioritize, and label content. In a card sort, participants are given a deck of cards, each containing an image, word, or idea, and are asked to group items into categories. These categories may be concrete descriptions, such as "things to do with young kids," or more abstract concepts, such as "inspirational." In some cases, participants may be asked to create their own categories. Often, participants are asked to "think out loud" as they are sorting the cards so the researcher can follow along with their thought process. Such an exercise enables a deeper conversation about what someone values and why. For example, participants might be asked to organize cards, such as "puzzle," "painting class," and "picnic," into categories, such as "kids," "date night," and "health."

Practicing empathy is vital to understanding what lies beneath the actions, words, and expressions of others. People will inevitably withhold information for reasons such as fear of being judged, distrust, an inability to articulate their true feelings, or simply because they are unaware of what influences their behavior. This is why museum leaders must hone their empathic skills through research techniques that involve observation, emotional sensitivity, and immersion. To be able to make a meaningful difference in the lives of others, museums need to be able to unlock those insights that tell a deeper story. Empathy is the key.

SPARK: CREATING AN EMPATHY MAP

An "empathy map" is a valuable tool for synthesizing the insights uncovered through user studies, journals, in-depth interviews, analogous inspiration, bodystorming, and card sorting. Inspired by design firm IDEO, an empathy map comprises four quadrants that reflect your understanding of what a customer says, thinks, feels, and does (Figure 10.1).[1]

Empathy maps help teams to articulate what is known about a particular person, including his or her emotions, experiences, and behaviors. By extracting the insights gleaned from research in a visual format, an empathy map creates a shared understanding of a customer's motivations and values and aids in institutional decision-making. Empathy maps follow these six steps:

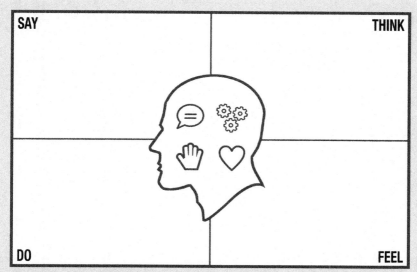

Figure 10.1. Empathy Map

STEP 1: Define the scope and purpose of the empathy map. For example, the goal of the empathy map might be to understand *why* someone is not a member. Importantly, a separate empathy map should be created for each customer segment that needs to be explored.

STEP 2: Gather materials and assemble the team. A whiteboard or a large flip chart can be used for a group setting, or a digital format can be used for individuals or virtual teams. Empathy mapping requires qualitative inputs from empathic research, such as user studies, journals, interviews, or card sorting.

STEP 3: Draw a map with four quadrants. Label the upper left-hand section with "Say," the lower left-hand section with "Do," the upper right-hand section with "Think," and the lower right-hand section with "Feel."

STEP 4: Combine and cluster insights. Begin populating the quadrants with verbatims, journal entries, observed body language, words, and other insights gleaned from the empathic research. It is helpful to color code items based on their tone or type. For example, items may be color coded based on positive/negative/neutral, motivation/barrier, or pain point/pleasure point.

STEP 5: Look at the map as a whole. Explore new insights or hypotheses based on the mapping. Is there anything new or surprising? Are there contradictions within or between quadrants? What outliers (or data points) did not fit into any quadrants? What themes were repeated across quadrants or exist in only one? Capture and synthesize your insights in a way that can be easily referenced and shared with the broader organization.

STEP 6: Determine next steps. Based on the insights revealed through the process of empathy mapping, make a decision about the next step for exploring the problem or developing a solution. Are there adaptations that could be made to existing products, marketing, or experiences that would address hidden customer needs or motivations? Can you ideate possible solutions to solve the problem(s)? Do you need to implement an intervention to address a barrier (e.g., a washing machine)? An empathy map can and should evolve over time based on new customer data or insights. Update and revise the empathy map as needed.

An empathy map reveals the underlying *why* behind a customer's actions, allowing an organization to proactively create products and marketing strategies that address real needs. Empathy maps can help identify pain points, friction, and barriers to participation. Once an empathy map is created, it should serve as a guiding document that continually reminds everyone on the team to make decisions with a customer-first focus.

NOTE

1. Tom Kelley and David Kelley, *Creative Confidence: Unleashing the Creative Potential within Us All* (New York: Crown Business, 2013), 222–24.

BRIGHT SPOT: STROLLER TOURS

It's difficult to imagine that parents could be lonely. Yet being a parent of a newborn or young child can leave little time for personal pursuits or socializing. Many parents of young children often feel disconnected from others. Stay-at-home parents and single parents are particularly susceptible to feeling isolated. A survey of parents found that 68 percent feel "cut off" from friends and family since having children.[1] Further, many parents have the perception that museums (unless it is a children's museum) are not an appropriate place for young kids. This perception is so common that the *Washington Post* published an article with the title "When Can I Take My Kid to a Museum?" to dispel the myths parents have about bringing young children and babies into an "adult" museum.[2]

Importantly, parents worry that bringing a baby into a museum will upset other visitors. In response to parents' nervousness about bothering other guests, several museums have introduced "stroller tours" to meet the needs of parents of newborns and pre-toddlers. The Clark Art Institute, Whitney Museum of American Art, and Toledo Museum of Art have all invested in stroller tours that are intentionally designed to offer a welcoming space for parents to socialize with other parents. Stroller tours are a beautiful example of empathic understanding. By taking a proactive approach to addressing the barriers to participation, these museums are now welcoming a previously underserved audience and facilitating relationship building among parents who have a shared interest—not to mention the opportunity to cultivate a new(born) generation of museum lovers.

NOTES

1. Sarah Knapton, "Parenthood Leaves Half of Mothers and Fathers Feeling Lonely," *The Telegraph*, November 6, 2017, https://www.telegraph.co.uk/science/2017/11/06/parenthood-leaves-half-mother-fathers-feeling-lonely/.
2. Jessica McFadden, "When Can I Take My Kid to a Museum?," *Washington Post*, August 1, 2014, https://www.washingtonpost.com/news/parenting/wp/2014/08/01/when-can-i-take-my-kid-to-a-museum/.

FROM TOUCHPOINTS TO JOURNEYS

Customer experience (CX) is defined as "how customers perceive their interactions with your company."[20] A measure of how customers feel about a brand overall, CX is the sum of all touchpoints that a customer has over his or her lifetime with an organization. According to the consulting firm Forrester, CX comprises a mix of quality and loyalty measures, including whether the experience delivers value, the ease of obtaining value, feeling good about the experience, the likelihood of continuing a relationship with the organization, the likelihood of buying additional products, and advocacy.[21] Thus, the entire organization must be involved in managing and delivering on the customer experience.

A core metric of CX is net promoter score (NPS), a benchmark that tracks how likely customers are to recommend an organization. NPS is based on the following scale:

- Promoters (score 9–10): Loyal enthusiasts who will keep buying and refer others.
- Passives (score 7–8): Satisfied but unenthusiastic customers who are vulnerable to attrition.
- Detractors (score 0–6): Unhappy customers who impede growth through negative word of mouth.

NPS is calculated by subtracting the percentage of "detractors" from the percentage of "promoters."[22] While an NPS survey can be deployed biannually, a continuous "drip" schedule provides a better pulse on customer sentiment in real time.

Inextricably tied to CX is customer satisfaction (CSAT), which is a measure of a customer's reaction to a specific interaction, product, or circumstance. CSAT also can include implicit metrics, such as online reviews, internal quality metrics, or mystery shopping scores.[23] While the drivers for customer satisfaction are unique to each organization, a CSAT survey generally seeks to gauge how satisfied a customer is with a recent experience. CSAT is a flexible and highly customizable metric that measures overall satisfaction based on those attributes that are most meaningful to customers.

As a component of CX, customer satisfaction is imperative for the long-term financial stability of museums because it leads to repeat visitation, contributes to membership growth and retention, and drives word-of-mouth referrals. There are many factors that contribute to CSAT; however, research shows that "entertainment" is a primary driver of visitor satisfaction at museums, even at memorial sites.[24] This is a critical finding because it illuminates the importance of ensuring that museum experiences are both educational *and* entertaining. Without experiences that engage audiences and create an emotional connection, museum content falls flat. And flat experiences aren't satisfying.

While measuring customer satisfaction based on individual touchpoints is a logical place to start, it is not enough to make customers happy with each separate interaction. Instead, organizations need to focus on improving the customer's end-to-end experience over the entire customer life cycle. Only then can museum leaders begin to understand the opportunities for making meaningful improvements that will positively impact customer value.

To obtain a holistic view of the entire customer experience, it is necessary to understand the complete set of touchpoints and interactions involved with a particular experience. Known as a customer "journey map," the process involves diagramming all of the steps that a customer goes through when engaging with the organization. As a visual interpretation of a customer's relationship with an organization, a journey map empowers teams to design solutions that better meet customer needs. Journey maps can take many forms, and there is no single right or wrong way to map a customer journey. For example, a journey map might focus on a specific aspect of the customer journey. At other times, the map may chart the customer journey from cradle to grave. Figure 10.2 shows an example of one variation of a journey map.

The process of journey mapping highlights opportunities to break down silos and create a shared vision of the customer experience. The most valuable aspect of a journey map is that it helps museum leaders to shift their perspec-

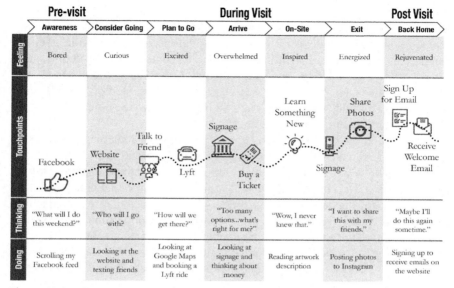

	Pre-visit			During Visit			Post Visit
	Awareness	Consider Going	Plan to Go	Arrive	On-Site	Exit	Back Home
Feeling	Bored	Curious	Excited	Overwhelmed	Inspired	Energized	Rejuvenated
Touchpoints	Facebook	Website	Talk to Friend / Lyft	Signage / Buy a Ticket	Learn Something New / Signage	Share Photos	Sign Up for Email / Receive Welcome Email
Thinking	"What will I do this weekend?"	"Who will I go with?"	"How will we get there?"	"Too many options...what's right for me?"	"Wow, I never knew that."	"I want to share this with my friends."	"Maybe I'll do this again sometime."
Doing	Scrolling my Facebook feed	Looking at the website and texting friends	Looking at Google Maps and booking a Lyft ride	Looking at signage and thinking about money	Reading artwork description	Posting photos to Instagram	Signing up to receive emails on the website

Figure 10.2. Customer Journey Map

tive from an inside-out viewpoint to one that is outside-in. Journey mapping is not simply a process of transcribing how things work today. It is an opportunity to imagine a future state. As a research-based tool, a journey map offers a new lens through which to view CX and allows an organization to ask "What if?" as a means of imagining the possibilities for new approaches. It is through the process of journey mapping that an organization is able to identify the *moments that matter*—those touchpoints and experiences along the journey that are most critical to the customer experience.

Journey maps should be exploratory and discovery based. A key goal of mapping is to unearth unknown problems in order to ideate possible solutions. However, journey mapping can be especially helpful when the problem is known but the solution is not. For example, if the membership program is in decline (the problem), a journey map offers a way to explore different possibilities to solve the problem without starting from a specific solution. In this way, journey mapping can help teams to conceptualize and visualize a day in the life of a customer to understand the larger context of how, when, and why decisions are made.

To be effective, a separate journey map must be created for each unique market segment, and it is helpful to imbue a market segment with a "persona" to bring the customer profile to life. A persona is a way to animate a static market segment by creating a fictionalized customer archetype that embodies the representative personality, values, and mindset of a segment. Through the use of memorable and engaging archetypal characteristics, personas can help to build empathy by painting a vivid picture of a customer. For example, personas should include aspects such as aspirations, social identities, behaviors, goals, pain points, and attitudes, as well as context-specific details, such as geography, influencers, and family status. Importantly, a persona should never include assumptions, falsified characterizations, stereotypes, or made up factoids. Instead, a persona should be based on the rich objective insights obtained through empathic research.

As technology becomes more cost effective and scalable, the abstract nature of personas will become more personalized and actionable. In the future, real-time behavioral data and user-defined inputs will enable personas to evolve into dynamic composites of individuals in the moment. While the promise of true personalization is still out of reach, advances in machine learning and predictive analytics are opening up new opportunities to capture data, interpret emotions, and extrapolate customer needs. Technologies such as marketing automation, dynamic content, social listening, voice and facial recognition, personal assistants, and wearables all have the potential to contribute to personalization that enhances the customer experience in a meaningful way. To prepare to capitalize on the opportunities of tomorrow, museums can begin today by investing in building empathy, mapping the customer journey, and developing interventions to improve the customer experience.

SPARK: CREATING A JOURNEY MAP

A journey map can range from very simple to intricate, depending on the goals of the project and the complexity of the customer life cycle. In its most basic form, a journey map includes a singular customer goal and path and a sequence of actions that are plotted along a timeline. A more complex journey map can include a wide range of touchpoints, motivations, decisions, emotions, and outcomes.

Refer to Figure 10.2, and use the following outline as a guide to create a journey map.

STEP 1: Define the scenario, business goals, and customer persona.
STEP 2: Break the journey into stages.
STEP 3: Plot the touchpoints that occur at each stage.
STEP 4: Capture the pain points, emotions, thoughts, and activities involved in each touchpoint.
STEP 5: Analyze and capture opportunities to leverage moments that matter.

CREATING AN EMOTIONAL CONNECTION

While customer satisfaction is a critical metric, CSAT and traditional value propositions are limiting when it comes to developing a deeper, more meaningful relationship with audiences. Museums must pursue opportunities to connect with audiences on an emotional level—their financial sustainability depends on it. Research shows that, when an organization satisfies an individual's emotional needs, both the customer and the museum benefit from the relationship. As customers advance through each stage of the "emotional connection pathway"—from (1) being unconnected to (2) being highly satisfied to (3) perceiving brand differentiation to (4) being fully emotionally connected—they become personally invested in the organization, which translates to a higher lifetime value for the museum.[25]

There are hundreds of hidden emotional motivators that drive behavior and lead to the fourth stage of being fully emotionally connected. Examples of such motivators include a desire to "stand out from the crowd," "enjoy a sense of well-being," "feel a sense of thrill," "feel a sense of belonging," "be the person I want to be," and "feel a sense of freedom." On a lifetime value basis, customers who are emotionally connected are more than twice as valuable as highly satisfied customers.[26] Moreover, emotionally connected customers are more loyal, visit more often, are less price sensitive, act on mission messaging, and advocate for the organization.

Emotional motivators will vary depending on a customer's position within their journey. For example, a desire to "feel a sense of thrill" may be a critical motivator when initially attracting a new visitor to the museum, whereas a motivation to "be the person I want to be" may be a more powerful driver as a visitor seeks to access this feeling by becoming a donor. Thus, emotional connectedness must be aligned with a customer's journey, including visiting, joining, renewing, upgrading, donating, and advocacy. Additionally, emotional motivators will differ by market segment, further emphasizing the need for more intentional product development, tailored marketing strategies, and experimentation in membership.

It is the customer experience that enables a museum to build emotional connection. However, audiences are often incapable of articulating which aspects of the customer experience resonate most with their emotional motivations. Indeed, in a study that mapped nearly 100 facets of the customer experience for a brokerage and investment firm, researchers found that those aspects of the experience that customers *said* were most important were not those that actually affected their emotional connections.[27] For example, while customers stated that assistance with transferring funds was highly important, analytics showed that this touchpoint had a minimal effect on emotional connection. Instead, experience touchpoints, such as a personal welcome note and educational videos about investing, were found to greatly affect key drivers of emotional connection, including the desire to stand out from the crowd and to bring order and structure to their lives.[28]

Importantly, it is not enough to indiscriminately stuff emotional language into marketing materials, make assumptions about what customers care about, or dictate to audiences why the mission should matter to them. Such approaches are inside-out focused, scattered, and ineffective. When museums behave in this way, they are not practicing empathy. Maximizing emotional connection with customers requires a two-step process: (1) identify and measure the emotional motivators that drive behavior, and (2) invest in those customer experience strategies that *actually* impact emotional connection. Doing so requires an investment in both empathic and behavioral research. Most organizations focus on those touchpoints in the customer journey that will quickly turn a dissatisfied customer into a satisfied customer; however, long-term sustainability is tied to a museum's ability to convert highly satisfied customers into emotionally connected ones. Notably, investing in *already* emotionally connected customers offers the greatest potential for profitability.

Identifying and quantifying emotional motivators is a complicated process because, remember, customers are often unaware of the motivations and values that influence their decisions. However, through the application of predictive analytics, empathic research, and statistical modeling of a museum's owned customer data, it is possible to uncover those unique emotional motivators that affect behavior. In some cases, key emotional motivators may reveal the potential for new products that can build an emotional connection in a way that a traditional membership program is not able to achieve. For example, a museum will be challenged to deliver on the emotional motivator of "enjoy a sense of well-being" through a transactional-based membership program, whereas a newly designed membership program that incorporates specific aspects of well-being, such as meditation, nutrition, and human connection, could be better positioned to access this emotional motivator.

Museums, perhaps more than any other industry, have the potential to build strong emotional connections with audiences. However, a more strategic approach is needed to uncover and leverage emotional motivators to attract and engage audiences. Armed with the meaningful insights that come from building empathic and behavioral data, museums will be able to tailor the marketing mix to resonate with those emotional motivators that drive behavior at each stage of the customer journey. Now is the time for museums to begin investing in data-informed strategies that will deliver a better customer experience and, in turn, lead to more predictable and profitable financial outcomes.

MEETING AUDIENCES WHERE THEY ARE

Museum audiences do not necessarily fit neatly into institutional categories or behave in expected ways. When museums attempt to impose institutional labels on visitors, members, and donors, they risk confusing audiences and alienating supporters. Customer journeys are not linear, and not everyone who is interested in supporting a museum's mission will visit, join, or give in a traditional manner. The key to becoming customer centric is making it easy for audiences to participate on *their* terms and inviting that participation into the museum. Adapting to meet audiences where they are will require a transformation in institutional mindset, processes, and technology.

One clear opportunity for museums to meet audiences where they are is via digital and mobile channels. The same technologies that are driving changes in consumer behavior, such as smartphones, social media, wearables, livestreaming, and machine learning, are also enabling museums to deliver more personalized and interactive experiences to their audiences. Examples of customer-centric technology in museums includes everything from customized mobile tours based on visitor interests to chatbots and near-field communication to augmented reality that brings objects and stories to life.

Technology can enhance learning and allow museums to connect with audiences in new ways. A customer journey may have numerous touchpoints that span geography, cross multiple devices, flow through several museum departments, and reflect evolving desires over time. Technology can be used to mitigate friction, resolve pain points, and enhance emotional connections with audiences.

BRIGHT SPOT: CULTURE SNACKERS
AT THE RIJKSMUSEUM[1]

In January 2018, the Rijksmuseum in Amsterdam launched a new state-of-the-art mobile app consisting of three main functionalities: (1) Rijksstudio, (2) multimedia tours, and (3) e-tickets. Through its interactive platform, Rijksstudio, the Rijksmuseum has made over 330,000 works of art available online that can be accessed by anyone, anywhere in the world, at any time. The Museum has registered 360,000 users, tracked more than 2,000,000 free image downloads, and shared 200,000 user-created digital collections.

Inspired by cocreation platforms, such as Pinterest, Rijksstudio delivers on the Rijksmuseum's mission to connect people, art, and history in a relevant and user-centric way. Through a partnership with the design platform Etsy,

Rijksmuseum also encourages users to take their collection as a starting point for their own craft and sell their creations through Etsy. With Rijksstudio, audiences can connect to art wherever they happen to be: at home, out with friends, or in the Museum taking a multimedia tour. This type of digital-first strategy has the power to transform an organization and capture the hearts and minds of customers. Another user-centered aspect of the mobile app is its automatic wayfinding system of 300 iBeacons, which is fully integrated with the multimedia tour, allowing the app to guide users to and from any location within the Museum.

Importantly, the Rijksmuseum's decision to implement a mobile app was not driven by technology for technology's sake. Instead, the development of the mobile app was the result of comprehensive user research and a journey-mapping process. The Rijksmuseum identified the Museum's "sweet spot" for leveraging a user-friendly technology that would deliver value to the customer in a way that only the Rijksmuseum could. Research showed that visitors often entered the numbers found on labels into the app to get more information on an artwork that interested them. This flexible functionality allowed the Rijksmuseum to meet the needs of what the Museum defined as "culture snackers," those who wanted to get small doses of information at certain times based on their own preferences and interests.

The Rijksmuseum's digital strategy has allowed the Museum to reach a wide range of diverse audiences, from passionate art lovers and history enthusiasts to professionals, students, and culture snackers. The Rijksmuseum recognized that exceptional content alone is not enough. It was more important for audiences to have an interactive environment that they could engage with in a personalized way. Moreover, by providing open access to the Museum's collection and empowering users' self-expression, the Rijksmuseum was able to connect with audiences at a deeper, more emotional level.

NOTE

1. Peter Gorgels, "Rijksmuseum Mobile First: Rijksstudio Redesign and the New Rijksmuseum App," MW18, published January 14, 2018, https://mw18.mwconf.org/paper/rijksmuseum-mobile-first-redesign-rijksstudio-the-new-rijksmuseum-app/.

REACHING NEW AUDIENCES THROUGH CROWDFUNDING

Digital technologies are opening up new opportunities for membership and fundraising. In particular, rewards-based crowdfunding platforms, such as Kickstarter and Indiegogo, offer an opportunity for museums to reach new audiences where they are and to cultivate support from people who may not think of themselves as traditional members or donors. Beyond the financial support that comes from a crowdfunding initiative, such a campaign enables the museum to involve audiences in bringing a project to life—giving them a sense of ownership and activating the endowment effect. Moreover, a crowdfunding campaign creates an opportunity to connect with an individual's emotional motivators, such as feeling a sense of thrill and feeling a sense of belonging.

Museums large and small have experimented with crowdfunding in recent years with varying degrees of success.[29] There are four types of crowdfunding models: (1) donation based, in which donations are given in support of a project without any compensation in return; (2) rewards based, in which nonfinancial incentives are given in exchange for a contribution; (3) lending based, in which repayment is expected; and (4) equity based, in which a share of the profits are returned to investors. All crowdfunding campaigns begin with a discrete project and a defined fundraising goal.

In a rewards-based model, funders, or backers as they are sometimes called, pledge based on a tiered rewards ladder that offers nonfinancial, exclusive project-themed goodies or experiences in exchange for a contribution of a certain amount. The fundraising goal must be met before a project can go forward. If the threshold is not reached by the specified deadline, the project is not funded, and all pledges are voided. The time limit for reaching the fundraising goal creates a sense of urgency, and funders often become evangelists working on behalf of the museum to ensure that the campaign succeeds.

Crowdfunding is a unique model—while not a traditional form of fundraising or membership, such campaigns are emerging as a way for museums to engage nontraditional audiences and open up new revenue streams in a more participatory and meaningful way. Crowdfunding attracts cause-based supporters, enthusiasts, and super fans who essentially become investors in the project. They are neither members nor donors (necessarily), yet funders are passionate advocates who want to be a part of the museum's mission.

While the effort to pull off a successful crowdfunding campaign can be considerable, the payoff can be immense. When the US Holocaust Memorial Museum launched its first Kickstarter campaign in 2017 to fund the translation and digitization of diaries from Holocaust victims and survivors, the campaign raised $380,000 ($65,000 more than its goal) from over 5,600 supporters, of whom 75 percent were new contributors to the museum.[30] The commitment funders have for the project creates a strong emotional connection, inspiring new audiences, who otherwise might not have contributed to the project, to give.

Historically, museums have included membership as part of the rewards to make the incentives as enticing as possible. However, doing so misses the broader opportunity—to develop a unique relationship with funders in a way that does not attempt to force them into a preexisting institutional mold.

Including membership as a reward undermines the distinctiveness of the campaign, makes assumptions about a funder's aspirations, and can devalue the concept of membership itself. Importantly, lumping funders into the category of membership eliminates the opportunity for the museum to tailor a discrete journey based on their unique needs and motivations. Instead of automatically folding funders into the standard membership model, museums should consider thinking about funders as a distinct market segment comprising individuals who think, feel, and behave differently than traditional members.

Crowdfunding has the potential to bring people together and unite them around a common cause. For museums, it is a greenfield opportunity that requires a new approach to audience development—one that is participatory and emotionally driven. As cultural innovator Jasper Visser observes, "the key to success in the 21st century is to make connections first, then involve them in value creating processes."[31] With the right project and strategy, crowdfunding can unlock an everlasting source for building a new base of passionate stakeholders.

BRIGHT SPOT: BUILDING A NEW COMMUNITY OF SUPPORTERS AT SPACE CENTER HOUSTON

"This was a place where amazing things happened," said William Harris, president and CEO of Space Center Houston, speaking about the Apollo Mission Control Center at NASA Johnson Space Center, the site where NASA's flight control team planned, trained, and executed a series of human spaceflight missions with a goal of landing a man on the moon and returning him safely to Earth. One of the most significant achievements in human history, Apollo 11 carried Commander Neil Armstrong, Command Module Pilot Michael Collins, and Lunar Module Pilot Edwin "Buzz" Aldrin to the moon, where, on July 20, 1969, Neil Armstrong took "one small step for a man, one giant leap for mankind." To commemorate the 50th anniversary of the Apollo 11 lunar landing, Space Center Houston, the official visitor center for NASA's Johnson Space Center, launched its own mission: a $5 million fundraising campaign to restore Historic Apollo Mission Control.

In 1985, Mission Control was named to the National Register of Historic Places; however, by 2015, the historic site was listed as "threatened" by the National Park Service due to deterioration caused by a high volume of visitors and a lack of preservation funding. To secure the funds needed to restore the site, Space Center Houston led a fundraising effort with the aim of creating a world-class visitor experience that would inspire future generations through this amazing story of technological and human achievement. In early 2017, the nearby City of Webster gave a lead gift of $3.1 million toward the campaign, along with a $400,000 challenge grant to assist Space Center Houston with its planned crowdfunding campaign for the project.

On July 20, 2017, Space Center Houston launched its first-ever crowdfunding campaign on Kickstarter. The campaign offered an array of exclusive perks to backers, from a digital download of a Michael Okuda–designed restoration project mission patch for $10 to a personal Mission Control tour with Gene Kranz, the retired NASA flight director who oversaw Apollo 11, for $10,000. Other rewards included a commemorative T-shirt, lunch with Apollo flight controllers, an autographed copy of Andy Weir's book *Artemis*, and 50th anniversary punch-out models of the Apollo 11 Command Module and the Saturn V rocket designed and produced by Space Center Houston specifically for the campaign (Figure 10.3).

The selection of Kickstarter over other crowdfunding platforms gave Space Center Houston a significant advantage. Kickstarter already had developed

Figure 10.3.   Kickstarter Campaign Exclusive Perks
Courtesy of Space Center Houston.

a strong community of space history fans through the Smithsonian's wildly successful "ReBoot the Suit" campaign for the preservation of Astronaut Neil Armstrong's suit the year before. Because of Space Center Houston's nonprofit status, Kickstarter assigned a designated liaison to the campaign to provide advice on design and implementation. Additionally, Kickstarter helped raise awareness of the campaign by featuring it as a "Project We Love," along with other outreach to the broader Kickstarter community.

The strategic marketing and communications plan for the Kickstarter campaign leveraged multiple platforms, including social media, earned media, email marketing, outdoor signage, and digital advertising. The strategy for all platforms centered around the objectives of motivating people to donate to the restoration project, increasing understanding and awareness of the significance of the Apollo Mission Control Center as a historic landmark, and communicating Space Center Houston's nonprofit status.

Space Center Houston elected to conduct the campaign over a 30-day period, beginning on the 49th anniversary of Apollo 11, and began communicating the campaign well ahead of the launch date. One month before launch, Space Center Houston started pitching story ideas to targeted news media. Approximately two weeks prior to launch, Space Center Houston published multiple assets, including website content, email communications, videos, and banners, and initiated a 10-day social media countdown. In addition, Space Center Houston launched a digital advertising campaign, including search engine marketing, social media, and digital display, timed to coincide with the launch date of the campaign.

Prior to launch, the content strategy for marketing highlighted specific Apollo mission milestones with historic imagery and retro graphics to generate nostalgia and raise visibility around the historic significance of the Apollo Mission Control Center. After the Kickstarter campaign launched, the content strategy shifted to keeping audiences engaged with the fundraising effort and encouraging action through Q&A opportunities, livestreams, high-quality videos and imagery, and stories from behind the scenes. On the Kickstarter platform itself, Space Center Houston's Development team crafted more than 30 updates on the campaign's progress and details of the restoration work to keep backers engaged and to encourage social sharing of the campaign.

The campaign was immensely successful, activating support from space enthusiasts around the world. Within 30 days, 4,251 backers from 25 countries pledged more than double the campaign's initial $250,000 Kickstarter goal, rocketing the campaign past the City of Webster's matching funds and ultimately raising nearly $507,000 in support of the restoration project. Further, the campaign produced nearly 300 news stories, garnering more than 400 million impressions and $1.8 million in equivalent advertising value. Social media content reached more than 200 million people organically, and paid advertising gained another 23 million impressions, including 16 million international impressions. On June 28, 2019, just in time for the 50th anniversary of the Apollo 11 lunar landing, NASA's Johnson Space Center held a ribbon-cutting ceremony marking the completion of the restoration and the start of the site's next big mission—welcoming daily public tours and preserving the legacy of the Apollo Program for future generations.

The Kickstarter campaign dovetailed with Space Center Houston's new membership messaging platform, which emphasizes philanthropic support. Consequently, Space Center Houston intentionally included membership as a backer perk and also promoted membership as a post-campaign add-on. Kim Parker, vice president of Development at Space Center Houston, noted that the campaign was a substantial undertaking for the institution, requiring a significant investment of staff time from both the Development and Communications teams for coordination, promotion, and fulfillment of the campaign.

Because more than half of the 4,251 backers had previously participated in another Kickstarter campaign, Space Center Houston was able to leverage the campaign to tap into an existing audience and build a new community of supporters. Importantly, the campaign allowed Space Center Houston to create a clear distinction between donating to the restoration project and being a member. Of the 4,251 backers, the museum was able to add 3,851 valid records to its database of donors. Of these supporters, just 36 (0.9 percent) were existing donors, and only 19 (0.5 percent) were existing members—demonstrating remarkable success in reaching an expanded audience. Further, 41 percent of the Kickstarter backers who received a membership as part of their rewards are still active members.

The campaign provided a unique opportunity to create a community of super fans that Space Center Houston plans to cultivate into long-term supporters over time. To that end, Space Center Houston has turned its attention to keeping these new enthusiastic backers engaged through continued communications on the Kickstarter platform. Next steps include exploration of a possible international level of membership, which could serve as a way to build an ongoing relationship with backers and others like them who are passionate about human spaceflight (i.e., cause-based supporters) but do not fit into the traditional membership model. Such a program would allow Space Center Houston to monetize its vast content collection and leverage its expertise to engage a broader audience worldwide.

Courtesy of Space Center Houston.

TAPPING INTO THE EXPERIENCE ECONOMY

A single Facebook post on July 15, 2017, announced the launch of its crowdfunding campaign on WeFunder. Forty-eight hours later, it was all over. The art collective Meow Wolf had shattered the record for an investment crowdfunding campaign, becoming the fastest company in history to raise $1 million from 480 nonaccredited investors—the maximum amount legally permitted under the US Securities and Exchange Commission rules.[32] The crowdfunding campaign, combined with subsequent fundraising efforts, has positioned Meow Wolf to expand into several major markets, including a $60 million project in Denver that will house more exhibit space than the Guggenheim; a three-story, 75,000-square-foot permanent exhibition in Washington, DC; a combined retail–entertainment–art installation in Las Vegas; and a 400-room immersive art hotel in Phoenix.[33]

The story of Meow Wolf's rise is incredibly nuanced. Meow Wolf is a for-profit public benefit corporation, and the crowdfunding campaign was for equity, entitling shareholders to a financial return on their investment. While reasonable minds can debate the merits of Meow Wolf's business model and the associated implications for the broader nonprofit cultural landscape, what is indisputable is that Meow Wolf is a game changer. As an arts and entertainment company, Meow Wolf has emerged as a leader in the booming "experience economy," creating immersive environments, such as a jungle gym, haunted house, children's museum, and vivid, selfie-friendly art installations, designed to attract the masses. In an Instagram-driven world, Meow Wolf has become a destination—offering people a reason to get out of the house, a way to participate in an experience with others, and lots of opportunities to share those experiences on social media.

And Meow Wolf is not alone. Across the world, museum-themed pop-up exhibits, puzzle rooms, and playful interactive installations are beguiling audiences young and old. There's the Museum of Ice Cream, with its infamous "sprinkle pool" filled with rainbow dots, the temporary Museum of Feelings, where various moods were "curated" to pair with Glade® fragrances, the Museum of Pizza, celebrating the history of its doughy namesake and featuring a cave of melted cheese, the wndr museum that "reimagines the traditional museum experience, inviting you to tap into the curiosity and playfulness that lives within and around all of us," and Cannabition, "the world's first immersive and interactive cannabis-themed art museum." All of these examples are encroaching on the traditional nonprofit museum's territory—taking away share of wallet, time, and attention.

While what was once a trend driven by millennials, people from every generation are choosing to spend their money on experiences over things. Research shows that 74 percent of Americans now prioritize experiences over products.[34] Experiential events, such as escape rooms and trivia nights, have grown exponentially in recent years. Escape rooms in the US have jumped from just 22 rooms in 2014 to an estimated 2,300 rooms in 2018.[35] And Geeks Who Drink hosts 469 weekly bar trivia nights across the US.[36] Airbnb now offers "one-of-a-kind activities hosted by locals" through its *Experiences* service.[37] And futurists are envisioning the mall of the future to be a "betterment zone," complete with a network of waterways, mindfulness workshops, and sensory gardens.[38]

These trends are indicative of a broader opportunity for museums to tap into the experience economy while strengthening their missions and connecting with audiences on an emotional level. Many museums already are implementing strategies to engage audiences in experiences through interactive exhibits, escape rooms, yoga classes, and trivia nights. However, the challenge museum leaders face is connecting the dots between one-off experiential offerings and a more strategic business model that allows for cultivation of a deeper relationship with audiences.

Without an empathic perspective, museums risk missing out on opportunities to better serve audiences. For instance, data show that the average visitor attends a cultural organization only once every 27 months.[39] This finding contradicts industry expectations that audiences will visit *at least* once a year. Because the majority of museum memberships are sold on an annual basis, either the traditional membership construct is falling short of meeting customer needs, or museums need to greatly improve audience engagement—likely both are true.

Visitation to museums is hindered by increasing competition for leisure time and dollars. To succeed, museum leaders must invest in building empathy to understand where they can leverage their strengths to better meet customer needs. As Larry Dubinski, president and CEO at the Franklin Institute, observes, "Cultural institutions across the country really fail when they give you their offering as opposed to saying, 'What do you want to see? What do you want to know more about?' . . . We just need to refine and look more closely at the newer generations, so we can go out and meet them where they're at."[40]

As museums strive to identify those moments that matter most in the customer journey, building a practice of empathy and uncovering customers' emotional motivators will be paramount. Moreover, as a "third place," museums are exceptionally positioned to proactively address loneliness and facilitate human connections. Innovation in membership holds promise for museums seeking to meet audiences where they are.

NOTES

1. Richard Fry, "The Share of Americans Living without a Partner Has Increased, Especially among Young Adults," Pew Research Center, October 11, 2017, https://www.pewresearch.org/fact-tank/2017/10/11/the-share-of-americans-living-without-a-partner-has-increased-especially-among-young-adults/.

2. Cigna, *2018 Cigna Loneliness Index*, 3, https://www.multivu.com/players/English/8294451-cigna-us-loneliness-survey/docs/IndexReport_1524069371598-173525450.pdf.

3. Sarvada Chandra Tiwari, "Loneliness: A Disease?," *Indian Journal of Psychiatry* 55, no. 4 (2013): 320–22, doi:10.4103/0019-5545.120536.

4. "Laughter Really Could Be the Best Medicine," Campaign to End Loneliness, accessed September 28, 2019, https://www.campaigntoendloneliness.org/laughter-really-could-be-the-best-medicine/.

5. Olga Oksman, "The Calm, Gentle Rise of Snugglers for Hire," *The Atlantic*, December 3, 2015, https://www.theatlantic.com/business/archive/2015/12/why-isnt-there-a-starbucks-for-hugs/418332/.

6. Department for Digital, Culture, Media and Sport, *A Connected Society: A Strategy for Tackling Loneliness*, October 2018, 2, https://assets.publishing.service.gov.uk/government/uploads/system/uploads/attachment_data/file/750909/6.4882_DCMS_Loneliness_Strategy_web_Update.pdf.

7. Dean Veall et al., "Museums on Prescription: A Guide to Working with Older People," 2017, 4, https://culturehealthresearch.files.wordpress.com/2017/10/mopguide.pdf.

8. Evan Fleischer, "Doctors in Scotland Can Now Prescribe Nature to Their Patients," Big Think, October 12, 2018, https://bigthink.com/personal-growth/doctors-in-shetland-can-now-prescribe-a-walk-in-nature.

9. Brendan Kelly, "Doctors Can Soon Prescribe Visits to Montreal Museum of Fine Arts," *Montreal Gazette*, updated October 11, 2018, https://montrealgazette.com/news/local-news/doctors-can-soon-prescribe-visits-to-montreal-museum-of-fine-arts.

10. "Arts & Human Development Task Force," National Initiatives, National Endowment for the Arts, accessed September 28, 2019, https://www.arts.gov/national-initiatives/task-force.

11. Kelly, "Doctors Can Soon Prescribe Visits to Montreal Museum of Fine Arts."

12. "What Share of Adults Who Were Interested, But Did Not Attend, Cited Lack of Someone to Go with as a Barrier?," Characteristics of Interested Non-Attendees of the Arts (2012), National Endowment for the Arts, accessed September 28, 2019, https://www.arts.gov/artistic-fields/research-analysis/arts-data-profiles/arts-data-profile-4/social.

13. "Empathy," *Merriam-Webster*, https://www.merriam-webster.com/dictionary/empathy.

14. Robert Balfanz and Vaughan Byrnes, *Chronic Absenteeism: Summarizing What We Know from Nationally Available Data* (Baltimore: Johns Hopkins University Center for Social Organization of Schools, 2012), 3, http://new.every1graduates.org/wp-content/uploads/2012/05/FINALChronicAbsenteeismReport_May16.pdf.

15. Alan Ginsburg, Phyllis Jordan, and Hedy Chang, "Absences Add Up: How School Attendance Influences Student Success," August 2014, https://www.attendanceworks.org/wp-content/uploads/2017/05/Absenses-Add-Up_September-3rd-2014.pdf.

16. "Chronic Absence," Attendance Works, accessed September 28, 2019, https://www.attendanceworks.org/chronic-absence/the-problem/.

17. Emily S. Rueb, "Schools Find a New Way to Combat Student Absences: Washing Machines," *New York Times*, March 13, 2019, https://www.nytimes.com/2019/03/13/us/schools-laundry-rooms.html.

18. Ibid.

19. Shunryu Suzuki, *Zen Mind, Beginner's Mind*, ed. Trudy Dixon (Boston: Shambhala Publications, 2006), 1.

20. Harley Manning, "Customer Experience Defined," *Forrester*, November 23, 2010, https://go.forrester.com/blogs/definition-of-customer-experience/.

21. "CX Index," Analytics, *Forrester*, accessed September 28, 2019, https://go.forrester.com/analytics/cx-index/.

22. "What Is Net Promoter?," NICE Satmetrix, accessed September 28, 2019, https://www.netpromoter.com/know/.

23. Susan Moore, "Present a Consolidated View of Customer Experience Metrics across the Organization to Achieve Consistency and Customer Experience Improvements," Gartner, May 28, 2019, https://www.gartner.com/smarterwithgartner/how-to-measure-customer-experience/.

24. Colleen Dilenschneider, "Cultural Organizations: 'Entertainment' Is Not a Dirty Word (DATA)," *Know Your Own Bone*, December 12, 2018, https://www.colleendilen.com/2018/12/12/cultural-organizations-entertainment-not-dirty-word-data/

25. Scott Magids, Alan Zorfas, and Daniel Leemon, "The New Science of Customer Emotions," *Harvard Business Review*, November 2015, https://hbr.org/2015/11/the-new-science-of-customer-emotions.

26. Ibid.

27. Alan Zorfas and Daniel Leemon, "An Emotional Connection Matters More than Customer Satisfaction," *Harvard Business Review*, August 29, 2016, https://hbr.org/2016/08/an-emotional-connection-matters-more-than-customer-satisfaction.

28. Magids et al., "The New Science of Customer Emotions."

29. Elizabeth Olson, "Soliciting Funds from the Crowd? Results Will Vary," *New York Times*, March 19, 2014, https://www.nytimes.com/2014/03/20/arts/artsspecial/soliciting-funds-from-the-crowd-results-will-vary.html.

30. Heather Joslyn, "More Nonprofits Are Running Their Own Crowdfunding Drives," *The Chronicle of Philanthropy*, September 26, 2017, https://www.philanthropy.com/article/More-Nonprofits-Are-Running/241291.

31. Jasper Visser, *The Museum of the Future*, February 2017, http://themuseumofthefuture.com/tmotf_live_12nu/wp-content/uploads/The-Museum-of-the-Future-Jasper-Visser.pdf.

32. Megan Bennett, "Meow Wolf Raises $1 Million in 2 Days," *Albuquerque Journal*, updated July 17, 2017, https://www.abqjournal.com/1034105/meow-wolf-raises-1-million-in-3-days.html.

33. Rachel Monroe, "Can an Art Collective Become the Disney of the Experience Economy?," *New York Times*, May 1, 2019, https://www.nytimes.com/interactive/2019/05/01/magazine/meow-wolf-art-experience-economy.html.

34. Expedia and The Center for Generational Kinetics, *Generations on the Move*, January 2018, 5.

35. Carly Mallenbaum, "Why Escape Rooms Have A Lock on the U.S.," *USA Today*, updated May 7, 2018, https://www.usatoday.com/story/life/people/2018/04/25/escape-rooms-trend-us/468181002/.

36. Jim Pagels, "The Economics of Trivia Night," Priceonomics, August 5, 2014, https://priceonomics.com/the-economics-of-trivia-night/.

37. "One-of-a-Kind Activities Hosted by Locals," Airbnb Experiences, Airbnb, accessed September 28, 2019, https://www.airbnb.com/s/experiences.

38. Blake Morgan, "A Vision of the Future Mall: Four Innovation Scenarios," *Forbes*, June 25, 2018, https://www.forbes.com/sites/blakemorgan/2018/06/25/a-vision-of-the-future-mall-four-innovation-scenarios/#69fbdc4c413a.

39. Colleen Dilenschneider, "How Often Do People Really Revisit Cultural Organizations? (DATA)," *Know Your Own Bone*, May 15, 2019, https://www.colleendilen.com/2019/05/15/how-often-do-people-really-visit-cultural-organizations-data/.

40. Bethany Ao, "To lure Dues-Paying Millennials, Philly Museums Tap onto 'Experiences,'" *Philadelphia Inquirer*, updated July 30, 2019, https://www.inquirer.com/life/museums-philadelphia-events-membership-after-hours-science-art-history-20190730.html.

Chapter Eleven

A Framework for Innovation

The average life span of a business model has fallen over the past 50 years from 15 years to less than 5 years.[1] A study of more than 30,000 public firms in the US found that companies are dying at an accelerated rate because "they are failing to adapt to the growing complexity of their environment."[2] Contributing to the shortened life span of a business model is a set of universal trends, including the accelerating speed of technology, declining product life cycles, increasing interindustry competition, and a shift toward customer experience as a differentiator.[3] Museums are not immune to this reality. Significant risk lies ahead for museums that apply existing business models to new markets, fail to invest in future-oriented growth areas, and continue to pursue strategies that were built in far more stable and predictable times.

The overarching business model of a museum is complex and unique to each organization. Most museums manage a "business model portfolio," operating a variety of interdependent business models at once. Multiple business models allow a museum to diversify its revenue streams and leverage its assets to serve distinct customer segments. For instance, a museum may create and monetize value through the discrete business models of admissions, membership, fundraising, programming, events, and other earned revenue activities, such as facility rental, food and beverage, gift shop, and ticketed attractions. Each of these functions represents a distinct business model—complete with its own customer segment(s), value proposition, and marketing mix.

To combat the forces that are fueling the decline in the average life span of a business model, museums must continuously reinvent themselves, and reinvention must include the creation of new business models for membership, fundraising, and audience engagement.

REINVENTING THE MEMBERSHIP BUSINESS MODEL

In 1994, Peter Drucker introduced a *theory of the business* that sought to explain why smart, successful organizations were failing. While he never mentions the term "business model," Drucker discusses the paradox of how organizations that were seemingly doing all the right things were struggling to keep up with changing market conditions. His conclusion? "The assumptions on which the organization has been built and is being run no longer fit reality."[4]

For many museums, the time has come to examine the fundamental assumptions on which the traditional membership business model is built. In particular, museums with established, successful membership programs have the greatest risk of dismissing or ignoring the early signs of trouble. In recent years, museums have invested in incremental improvements as membership programs have stalled or declined. Investment in short-term tactics, including blockbuster exhibitions, marketing campaigns, and pricing discounts, has resulted in a cycle of boom and bust. Moreover, membership revenue has not kept pace with increasing operating costs, and it is becoming more and more difficult for membership programs to increase profits and maintain, let alone grow, membership numbers. These results are clear indications that the product life cycle of membership is in decline.

Traditionally, membership has served more or less as a means to an end. That is, membership is essentially a *vehicle* by which visitors access programs, events, and other organizational assets in a discounted, expedited, or preferred manner. The existing membership business model is built on the assumption that all customers share the same needs and motivations. Conventional wisdom in the museum sector dictates that members will ascend predictably up the donor pyramid—becoming more involved and committed, delivering ever greater financial support to the organization over time. However, research is beginning to reveal that, more often than not, this is not the case.

Membership is an important source of revenue and a driver of audience engagement for museums. There is evidence that the traditional membership business model suffers from a lack of needs-based segmentation, unknown (and, therefore, unmet) customer needs, disconnected pricing strategies, mixed messaging, and an inconsistent customer experience. These challenges are limiting the opportunity for membership to create value for both customers and the museum. With a broad range of customer motivations and a rich blend of offerings, membership has immense potential to help museums become more customer centric and, in turn, more profitable.

Boston Consulting Group defines the practice of business model innovation as "the art of enhancing advantage and value creation by making simultaneous—and mutually supportive—changes both to an organization's value proposition to customers and to its underlying operating model."[5] Putting this practice to work for museums involves the development of nine core building blocks that comprise a new business model, including (1) customer segments, (2) value propositions, (3) channels, (4) customer relationships, (5) revenue streams, (6) key resources, (7) key activities, (8) key partners, and (9) cost structures.[6]

THE NINE BUILDING BLOCKS OF A BUSINESS MODEL

1. **Customer Segment(s).** These are the people you wish to serve and who will buy your product(s). Understanding the needs, motivations, and behaviors of each customer segment is critical to building a new business model. A key question in developing a business model is "Who is your most important customer?" Additionally, customer segments may also include audiences who do not produce revenue but are necessary for the business model to be viable. For example, users do not pay Google for search results; however, users are a critical aspect of Google's advertising model. Different customer segments require different value propositions, channels, and relationships. For a business model to be viable, the customer segment market size must be large enough to be profitable over time.

2. **Value Proposition(s):** This is the problem the product solves and the core value that the business model delivers to customers. The value proposition answers the question "What is the job that needs to be done?" for each customer segment. A value proposition must be differentiated from competition and tailored to each customer segment's unique needs.

3. **Channel(s):** The channels are the mechanisms for how an organization will communicate with and deliver the value proposition to customers. Channels often are divided into types and phases. For example, types of channels may include on-site sales, the museum website, and the gift shop, whereas channel phases may include awareness, evaluation, purchase, delivery, and post-purchase. Channels that support these phases may include digital advertising, a blogger, or search engine optimization. Thus, channels represent the marketing and sales strategies for communicating with and delivering value to customers.

4. **Customer Relationships:** Customer relationships are closely tied to channels. Customer relationships include management of the customer life cycle and may range from highly personalized to automated. Key questions in understanding the customer relationships dimension include "What type of interaction and service does the customer expect?" and "How do we get, keep, and grow customers?" Customer relationships are built on understanding of the customer journey and making decisions about how to deliver the customer experience. For example, customer relationships may

include dedicated personal assistance, self-service, automated services, or cocreation of products.

5. **Revenue Streams:** The various methods through which the organization will earn income from its offerings are the revenue streams. Revenue streams reflect the value customers are willing to pay for and how they will pay for it. Pricing psychology, consumption, and payment structures are involved in the dimension of revenue streams.

6. **Key Resources:** Key resources are the strategic assets (e.g., physical, intellectual, human, financial, etc.) that are required to execute on the business model. In many cases, the museum itself is a key resource. A museum's website or mobile app also may serve as a key resource. Similarly, resources might include services such as a concierge, docents, customer service, and technology, such as software that allows for advance ticket purchase. Intellectual property, people, and financial capital are also key resources.

7. **Key Activities:** The crucial processes that the organization needs to engage in to deliver on its value proposition are considered "key activities." Key activities include the touchpoints and methods for delivering value. For example, a behind-the-scenes tour or early access may be key activities for a membership business model.

8. **Key Partners:** The vendors, suppliers, strategic alliances, joint ventures, funders, and others who play an integral role in ensuring the museum can deliver on its value proposition are key partners.

9. **Cost Structure:** The infrastructure necessary to support the business model is known as the cost structure. The cost structure is inclusive of the expenses incurred by operating within the business model. Museums must include all tangible and intangible costs associated with delivering the value proposition, including people, physical, and out-of-pocket expenses.

Each of the nine building blocks contains a series of hypotheses about the new business model that, when validated through the lenses of desirability, viability, and feasibility, deliver long-term sustainability. Desirability considers whether audiences will want and value the product being envisioned. Viability evaluates the sustainability of the business model. And feasibility gauges how technologically, physically, or financially possible the concept is. Ultimately, a new business model's success is dependent on all three conditions being satisfied.

Complementing the nine building blocks is the "business model canvas," a tool that helps museums to visualize interdependencies and move beyond product-centric strategies toward more comprehensive business model design (Figure 11.1).[7]

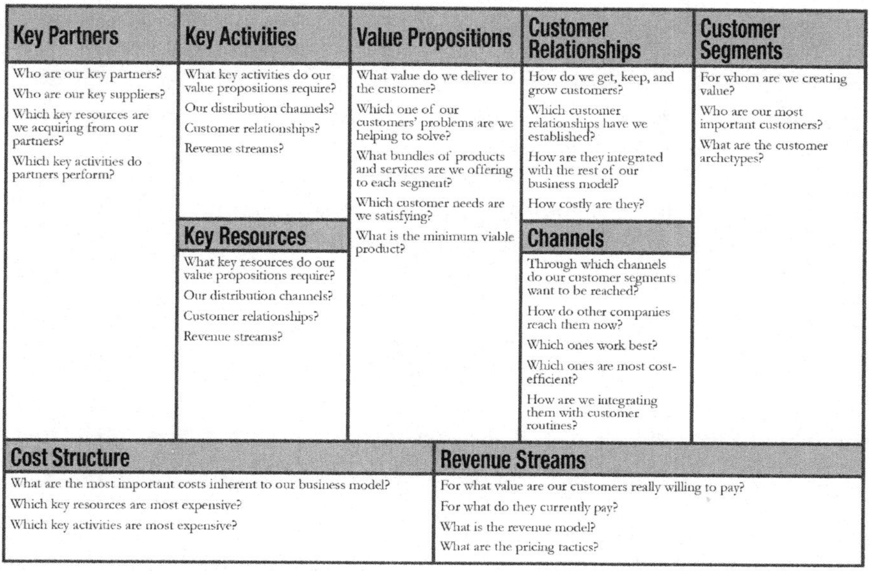
Key Partners
Who are our key partners?
Who are our key suppliers?
Which key resources are we acquiring from our partners?
Which key activities do partners perform?
Key Activities
What key activities do our value propositions require?
Our distribution channels?
Customer relationships?
Revenue streams?
Key Resources
What key resources do our value propositions require?
Our distribution channels?
Customer relationships?
Revenue streams?
Value Propositions
What value do we deliver to the customer?
Which one of our customers' problems are we helping to solve?
What bundles of products and services are we offering to each segment?
Which customer needs are we satisfying?
What is the minimum viable product?
Customer Relationships
How do we get, keep, and grow customers?
Which customer relationships have we established?
How are they integrated with the rest of our business model?
How costly are they?
Channels
Through which channels do our customer segments want to be reached?
How do other companies reach them now?
Which ones work best?
Which ones are most cost-efficient?
How are we integrating them with customer routines?
Customer Segments
For whom are we creating value?
Who are our most important customers?
What are the customer archetypes?
Cost Structure
What are the most important costs inherent to our business model?
Which key resources are most expensive?
Which key activities are most expensive?
Revenue Streams
For what value are our customers really willing to pay?
For what do they currently pay?
What is the revenue model?
What are the pricing tactics?

Figure 11.1. Business Model Canvas

Reprinted with permission from "A Better Way to Think About Your Business Model" by Alexander Osterwalder. May 2013, hbr.org. Copyright 2013 by Harvard Business Publishing; all rights reserved.

Developed by researcher Alexander Osterwalder, the three blocks on the left side of the canvas (key partners, key activities, and key resources) are associated with internal processes, efficiencies, and external relationships. The three blocks on the right side of the canvas (customer relationships, channels, and customer segments) are associated with customers and value. The value proposition is at the center, and the cost and revenue structures are at the bottom.

Used by leading global companies, such as GE, P&G, and Nestlé, the business model canvas is a tool that offers museum leaders a simple way to map out and visualize how a new business model can capture and deliver value to the market. Additionally, the canvas helps to identify dependencies, assumptions, and potential conflicts within a new business model. Development of new models for membership requires building empathy with customers and learning how the museum can best meet customers' needs to create value for both the customer and the business. Importantly, a separate business model canvas must be developed for each customer segment because the remaining eight building blocks are dependent on the business model fulfilling the needs of each unique customer.

Over time, business models naturally evolve to become less flexible and more resistant to change. As a result, business model innovation is mandatory for museums to remain resilient in the face of change. Investments aimed at improving and marketing the traditional membership business model may appear less risky than trying to create an entirely new business model; however, research shows that the greatest risk an organization can take is to decide *not* to create new business models that will decouple the institution's future from its existing business model.[8] Embracing a continual process of reinvention and investing in the development of new membership business models will transform the industry and secure the future of museums.

EXPERIMENTING WITH NEW MEMBERSHIP BUSINESS MODELS

Although controversial, one innovative membership business model that several museums are experimenting with is a "freemium" model, in which a free version of membership is offered with the goal of increasing participation by removing the barrier of cost. In a freemium model, premium versions are also available, allowing audiences to upgrade to a paid membership to receive enhanced benefits. LinkedIn, Spotify, the *New York Times* online, and YouTube are all examples of a freemium model. While not a revolutionary change to traditional museum membership, a freemium model does challenge the assumptions and value proposition of the existing membership business model.

Distinctly different from a free trial, the no-cost membership option in a freemium model is indefinite. Additionally, whereas a free trial typically includes access to the full-feature benefits of membership for a limited time, a freemium model offers no-cost members a restricted set of benefits. While a free trial can drive higher conversion rates to paid membership, a freemium model is better at generating engagement from a larger audience base.

Depending on the organization's goals, a freemium model can offer many benefits to the museum, including expanded participation from nontraditional audiences and a greater sense of belonging among members. For some, the traditional membership business model may be perceived as exclusive and promoting inequity. Thus, by removing the financial barrier to participation, a freemium model can serve as an important signal that the museum is welcoming to all. As the industry takes steps toward increasing diversity, improving inclusion, and challenging audience perceptions that a museum is "not for someone like me," new membership business models, such as the freemium model, that prioritize long-term involvement over short-term revenue are worthy of consideration.

SPARK: BUSINESS MODEL INNOVATION

Following Boston Consulting Group's guidance, the process of business model innovation begins with asking a series of questions to assess your museum's current situation, the needs of your customers, and the models of your competitors, including other possible leisure activities.[9] Take 30 to 45 minutes to think about and answer the following questions about your organization's membership model:

- What compromises does our current business model force customers to make?
- Why are nonusers or defectors dissatisfied with our offering?
- Do we offer customers a better value proposition than that of the competition?
- What alternative models are gaining share at the edges of our industry?
- If we were an industry outsider, what would we do to take advantage of the gaps or weaknesses in our business model?
- Do we have a plan for identifying potential business models, implementing them, and embedding business model innovation capabilities within the organization?
- What do we need to change in our organization and operations to implement a new business model?
- What information would we need to make a commitment to a new business model?
- How urgent is the perceived need for change in our organization?
- How should our ideas be championed?

Once you have answered these questions, review the business model canvas and begin sketching out possible scenarios for what a new membership business model might look like. Alone or with your team, invest the necessary time to develop several possible new business models for each customer segment. Designed to be a flexible way to explore different scenarios, the business model canvas can help museum leaders visualize various ways to meet a customer segment's needs. Figure 11.2 shows a simplified example of how the business model canvas can be used to map out a new membership business model that addresses the customer segment of "makers," individuals who are part of a movement that emphasizes learning by doing.

The example of a new membership business model shows how the business model canvas can be used to strategize how to meet the needs of a unique customer segment, makers. The value proposition, "learn by doing through an electronics project delivered to your door each month," promises to challenge members with projects that become more difficult over time. The channels for marketing, communication, and distribution include the website, social media, mail, and email. The customer relationship is a

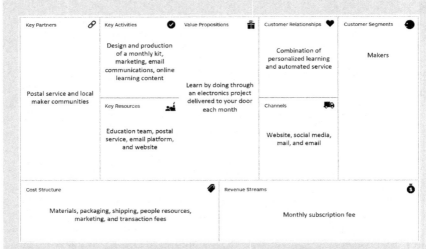

Figure 11.2.   Example of a Business Model Canvas for Membership

Source: The Business Model Canvas by Strategyzer.com made available under the Creative Commons Attribution-ShareAlike 3.0 Unported license (CC BY-SA 3.0) https://creativecommons.org/licenses/by-sa/3.0/.

combination of personalization and automation because the monthly maker kit is automatically delivered on a monthly basis; however, the companion online learning portal allows members to learn at their own pace. The revenue stream is a monthly subscription fee, and the key resources comprise the education team's knowledge to create the kit, the postal service for delivery of the kit, the museum's email platform, and the website that supports learning. Key activities include the design and production of the monthly kit, marketing, email communications with members, and management of online learning content. The postal service and local maker communities represent key partners, and the cost structure includes the hard costs for materials, packaging, and shipping as well as people resources, marketing, and transaction fees for monthly credit card processing.

BRIGHT SPOT: DEEPENING RELATIONSHIPS AT MIA

The Minneapolis Institute of Art (Mia) is a world-class art museum near downtown Minneapolis, Minnesota, housing over 90,000 works of art and representing more than 5,000 years of world art and culture. One of the first museums to offer free daily admission, Mia is committed to ensuring access to its collection, regardless of income. In 2012, the museum adopted a new strategic plan focused on moving Mia from an inward-looking museum to one that is audience centered. Mia's new strategic plan directed the museum to find new ways to attract and engage audiences and to rethink its business and operational models with a focus on providing an integrated approach to the customer experience.

Mia regularly dedicates considerable effort to tracking societal trends, consumer behavior, and changing demographics. In particular, Mia has identified several key trends that will have a significant impact on its long-term sustainability, including the rise in personalization ("show me you know me"), prevalence of cultural omnivores who maintain a much broader definition of arts and culture than ever before, and greater competition for leisure time, coupled with an increasing number of visitors who arrive feeling stressed.

Between 2012 and 2016, Mia saw a dramatic expansion of its audience, with annual attendance growing by 70 percent during this four-year period. However, despite this positive growth in visitation, membership remained flat. This challenge led Mia to ask some important questions about its membership program, including:

- In an era when fewer and fewer people are joining organizations, how will Mia engender allegiance in our audience?
- What does rabid fandom look like in the cultural sector?
- How might we maximize our investment in new technologies to ensure long-time loyalty?
- What forms might philanthropy take in the future, and how do we prepare for it?
- How do we begin to break the cycle of membership peaks and valleys that have been common in our sector in which "blockbuster" exhibitions produce a spike in membership numbers followed by high attrition?

To explore these questions, Mia set out to develop a road map for building and deepening relationships with its audiences. In developing the Museum's strategy for audience engagement, Mia drew inspiration from Daniel C. Funk and Jeff James's psychological continuum model, which characterizes an individual's psychological connection to sport, ranging from awareness to attraction to attachment to allegiance.[1] Mia's adapted model for cultivating audiences, from first-timer to loyalty, requires an understanding of audience

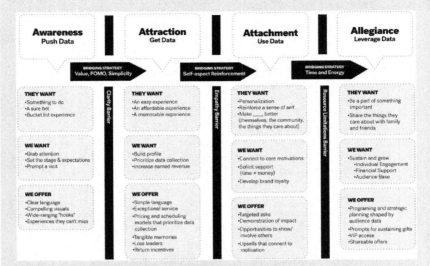

Figure 11.3.   Mia First-timer Journey to Loyalty
Courtesy of the Minneapolis Institute of Art.

needs, motivations, and the barriers to participation, as well as a deep under-standing of its own needs, capabilities, and assets (Figure 11.3).

In pursuing this audience engagement model, Mia realized that it needed to invest resources in fostering greater audience allegiance. Specifically, Mia made gathering and analyzing of meaningful data about its audiences an institutional priority. Next, Mia sought to answer a basic yet very powerful question: "Who is coming to Mia and why?" Mia then performed a market segmentation analysis to better understand how best to fulfill its customers' distinct needs. Based on this analysis, Mia identified four broad segments of customers, including "FOMO" (or Fear of Missing Out), Fan, Charitable, and Donor (Figure 11.4).

- **FOMO, or Fear of Missing Out:** Characterized by low engagement and low philanthropy support, this customer segment visits the museum very rarely or only once. For this audience, the motivation for visiting Mia is to see something they feel is a once-in-a-lifetime experience. Such an experience might be tickets to the groundbreaking exhibition *At Home with Monsters*, highlighting filmmaker Guillermo del Toro's creative process, or attending a Third Thursday happy hour–style event because all of their friends are going and they don't want to miss out on a fun night.
- **Fan:** This customer segment represents a high-engagement, low-philanthropy supporter who visits Mia often but does not provide much financial support to the Museum. These individuals might be free or contributing members, or they might not be members at all. Regardless of their financial status with

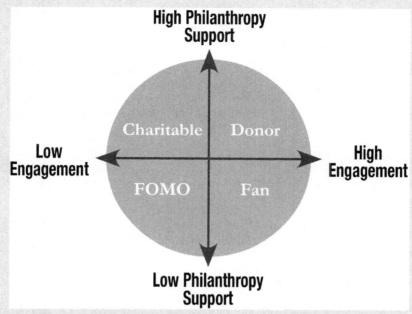

Figure 11.4. Philanthropy + Engagement = Level of Investment
Courtesy of the Minneapolis Institute of Art.

the organization, they are regularly participating in exhibitions, programs, and events.

- **Charitable:** Marked by low engagement and high philanthropy, this customer segment supports the Museum financially at a high level but does not typically attend exhibitions or participate in programs and events. This may be because Mia is one of many organizations they support, or perhaps they do not have time to visit the Museum as much as they would like.
- **Donor:** This customer segment is characterized by high engagement *and* high philanthropy. Donors are similar to Fans in their enthusiasm for exhibitions and programming; however, they also support Mia at a high financial level.

By recognizing an individual's unique interests and preferences, Mia has been able to craft personalized content and experiences that meet each customer segment wherever they happen to be in the audience journey. In turn, Mia hopes that such a strategy will generate a cycle of ongoing engagement, greater participation, and philanthropy. Kristin Prestegaard, Mia's chief engagement officer, noted, "We always have an eye on consumer trends and changing demographics. We believe in the power of art to transform communities. And to do so, we need to evolve with what our audiences are looking for to be relevant to them."

Mia also is investigating the questions "What is *membership*?" and "What is *our* definition of loyalty?" Moreover, Mia has begun to dig deeper into the purpose and design of its membership program to explore how the idea of membership might be expanded, modified, or redefined to become more relevant in its audiences' lives. Like many cultural organizations, Mia's traditional audience has been declining, eroding its membership base. At the same time, Mia recognized that the traditional model of membership (e.g., planning in advance, purchasing a package of predetermined benefits, paying up front, taking a big risk without a trial, etc.) has less appeal to new and younger audiences.

Mia had an aha moment when the Museum realized that some audiences considered themselves as being loyal to Mia; however, they were not interested in becoming members. This insight prompted Mia to explore how it might get new audiences to raise their hand and tell the Museum that they were interested in being involved—even if they were not likely to become a contributing member. This prompted the team at Mia to ask themselves, "What if we eliminated the financial barrier to participation?" From this question, Mia introduced My Mia, a new membership model that starts at no cost. The only requirement for participation is an email address.

My Mia offers a sliding scale of financial contribution ranging from $0–$149 for Contributor level access, $150–$499 for the Investor level, $500–$2,499 for the Partner level, and $2,500–$4,999 for its Patron level. A key distinction between My Mia and other museum membership programs is how the model shifts control to the customer. For example, an individual may choose to contribute nothing and will still receive ticketing privileges, discounts, communications, and event invitations. Alternatively, an individual may select from a suggested donation range or contribute at any amount. This "pay-what-you-wish" (PWYW) pricing structure empowers audiences to choose how they would like to contribute on their own terms (Figure 11.5).

The program is demonstrating strong adoption. While the Museum is paying attention to traditional membership metrics, total household count is no longer Mia's primary way of measuring involvement. Instead, Mia is interested in learning how its various audiences move fluidly between being a free member, a participant, and a contributor. As Prestegaard explained, "Since we introduced the new membership model, we've doubled the membership total number, but we need to explore a long-term revenue model that balances traditional month-to-month metrics with members' lifetime customer value."

Mia's audience engagement model has allowed for flexibility in the relationship between museum and individual. Audiences are no longer forced into a specific box as defined by the Museum. The intent behind this new model is to offer audiences the opportunity to demonstrate their level of engagement however and whenever they want. This is a radically different approach to the traditional concept of the donor pyramid, which assumes that an individual will follow along a predictable continuum from visitor to paid member to donor. Importantly, Mia's audience engagement model,

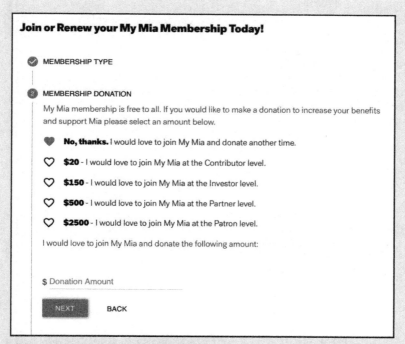

Figure 11.5. My Mia Levels of Access
Courtesy of the Minneapolis Institute of Art.

including My Mia, is championed by its chief engagement officer, head of advancement, and head of technology—a partnership that establishes shared goals and distributed ownership of the customer experience. Without this alignment and collaboration across departments, Mia acknowledges that the strategy would not be successful.

Institutionally, Mia has a long history of innovation, risk taking, and empathy building. The Museum has invested in "innovation grants" (internal pots of money earmarked for creative initiatives) and conducted thoughtful experiments to explore where opportunities for innovation may exist. For example, Mia team members used an innovation grant to attend Comic Con to observe what rabid fandom looks like in action. In another case, Mia prototyped a rewards-based loyalty model that was tested with a sample of about 300 visitors. Through this real-world experiment, Mia found that the idea of rewards was not a compelling motivator for its audiences.

Mia has now turned its attention toward building a long-term data strategy. The Museum has built its own in-house analytics team and is making strides toward centralizing its data, analytics, and marketing strategies. As Mia strives to become a data-informed organization, the Museum is working toward developing a model for measuring customer lifetime value and is exploring audience motivations in greater depth. In particular, Mia will be investigating why people choose to unsubscribe (opt out of free membership) and why long-standing free members stay engaged.

Mia's next big initiative will be investing in data mining to search for anomalies, patterns, and correlations that will help inform future decisions, including segmenting audiences into "microclusters" and the development of highly personalized journeys. It's all part of Mia's focus on building greater audience allegiance. Armed with data and emboldened by a clear vision to deepen the Museum's relationship with its audiences, one thing is certain: as its customers' needs, expectations, and behaviors change over time, Mia intends to be ready.

NOTE

1. Daniel C. Funk and Jeff James, "The Psychological Continuum Model: A Conceptual Framework for Understanding an Individual's Psychological Connection to Sport," *Sport Management Review* 4 (2001): 119–50.

Courtesy of the Minneapolis Institute of Art.

THE EMERGING FIELD OF SERVICE DESIGN

If the membership business model represents the "what" of a customer-centric organization, the emerging discipline of service design focuses on "whom" the organization serves. Service design "helps to choreograph the processes, technologies and interactions driving the delivery of services, using a human-centered perspective."[10] Essential to a museum's ability to proactively respond to customer needs, deliver value, and improve profitability, the practice of service design enables the holistic management of the end-to-end customer experience.

Once a new business model is developed, service design follows as an intentional strategy to create a distinct experience with a specific customer segment in mind. Authors Andy Polaine, Lavrans Løvlie, and Ben Reason observe in their book *Service Design: From Insight to Implementation*, "It is because many services are almost invisible that nobody takes care to design them."[11] Yet it is the various intangible touchpoints a customer has with an organization that comprise the customer experience; therefore, they must be identified and intentionally designed. Such touchpoints include the people and systems involved in delivering the service, such as the museum's website, mobile app, and admissions desk, as well as engagement strategies and wraparound services, such as email marketing, events, social media, and member services.

In recent years, the customer experience has become a critical driver of sustained growth for organizations, making understanding the customer journey, putting customers' needs first, and focusing on moments that matter a business imperative for museums. As a practice, service design focuses on the customers' unique goals by identifying new and meaningful ways to meet their needs, rather than simply improving upon existing processes and systems. Moreover, the scope of service design allows an organization to create experiences that will deepen engagement and break down barriers to participation. Ultimately, service design embodies the fundamental basis of value exchange within a business model.

In the service designer's toolkit are empathic research, customer journey maps, storyboards, and personas, as well as the "service blueprint," which serves as an extension of a customer journey map, connecting the front stage (those people and processes that have direct contact with customers) and backstage (those people and processes that are invisible to the customer) with the customer experience. By mapping all of the interactions a customer has (or will have) with an organization, a service blueprint gives the organization visibility into the people, processes, physical evidence, and systems involved at each specific touchpoint. For example, on a typical visit, a member may interact with numerous systems, artifacts, and departments, such as the website, e-commerce software, facilities, visitor services, wayfinding signage, interpretation, and the gift shop. Before or after the visit, the member may interact with a different set of people and processes, such as email, member services, and direct mail. The service blueprint shines a light on all of this otherwise hidden or disconnected activity by documenting the complex, internal workings of the organization to provide a comprehensive picture of the complete customer experience. Without this surface-to-core view, an organization cannot leverage moments that matter and make meaningful changes to the customer experience.

In 2017, Forrester published its report *Predictions: Dynamics That Will Shape the Future in the Age of the Customer*, noting that the trend of customers' "adventurous, experimental, and downright fickle behavior—once thought of as 'Millennials being Millennials'—has gone mainstream," predicting that more than one-third of organizations will begin restructuring to operationalize empathy and become "customer-obsessed operations."[12] These emerging trends require organizations to shift from functional silos to a structure that better supports an exceptional customer experience. For museums, service design must follow the development of new membership business models to ensure that the customer experience is meticulously crafted with the customer in mind. Gone are the days when customers were willing to muddle through a less-than-ideal experience in an attempt to achieve their goals. Modern consumers have high expectations and will quickly abandon a product or organization that does not prioritize their needs. Accordingly, the practice of service design is necessary for museums to be able to intentionally affect the customer experience in a way that cultivates more and better audience engagement.

THINKING LIKE A DESIGNER

Technology designers and product designers have always focused on the end user through methods such as user experience and ergonomics. In recent years, organizations of all kinds have started to take a more audience-centric approach to serving their customers better. In particular, the practices and philosophy of "design thinking" have been introduced to the disciplines of service design and marketing.

Renowned systems philosopher, Buckminster Fuller is credited with developing the initial tenets of design thinking when he began applying the scientific method to design while teaching Comprehensive Anticipatory Design Science at MIT's Creative Engineering Laboratory in 1956.[13] However, it wasn't until 1969 that design was first described as a "way of thinking" by cognitive psychologist Herbert Simon, who defined the process of design as a science.[14] Emerging from the theory and practice of a wide range of disciplines, the contemporary concept of design thinking is both an ideology and a methodology. At its core, modern design thinking is fundamentally about developing solutions that are human centered. It is this obsessive focus on approaching problems from the perspective of the individual that sets the philosophy of design thinking apart—and it is how museums will be able to create new membership business models that fulfill unmet customer needs.

The design thinking methodology comprises five distinct process modules: (1) empathize, (2) define, (3) ideate, (4) prototype, and (5) test. After initial empathic research has been conducted, the process proceeds to the second step of defining the problem. Once these first two steps have been completed, the process becomes more flexible, and teams may move fluidly between the remaining three modules of ideation, prototyping, and testing. Let's explore how the design thinking methodology unfolds.

The Five Modules of Design Thinking

Module 1: Empathize

A foundational principle of design thinking is building empathy. Through empathic research, organizations are able to understand their audiences on a psychological and emotional level. The goal of empathizing is to set aside assumptions in order to gather real insights about customers from their perspective. Adopting a beginner's mindset enables an organization to uncover customers' hidden needs, motivations, and barriers. By looking for patterns and exploring what audiences think, feel, do, and see, museums can find the clues that will lead them to discover their customers' unmet needs.

Module 2: Define

Defining the problem is a critical step in the design thinking process. Developing a well-defined problem statement involves consolidating and analyzing all of the research and data to draw out the insights that will help articulate the problem from a customer perspective, as opposed to focusing on the goals of the organization. "We need more members" is a poorly defined problem statement because it is framed from an institutional perspective rather than from the perspective of the customer. In the absence of a well-articulated problem statement, it is impossible to develop an effective customer-focused solution. Often, defining the problem starts with asking the question "How might we . . .?" followed by a specific customer pain point, barrier, or need. For example, "How might we design an experience that helps parents visit more often?"

A best practice for ensuring that the organization has zeroed in on the problem is to check in with customers and ask them whether it is, in fact, the *right* problem. When it comes to defining the problem, identifying the *right* problem is the difference between breakthrough innovation and incremental improvement. In defining the problem, there is a risk of jumping to an answer prematurely by focusing on technology, marketing strategies, or product features. A good problem statement does not suggest a solution. Rather, it should leave room for a wide range of ideas and creative solutions. Consider the difference in the number of ideas that might be explored based on the following two problem statements:

- "How might we give members more choice in customizing their benefits?"
- "How might we empower audiences to define their own experience at the museum?"

While both questions seek to solve the challenge of giving audiences more control, the first problem statement is too narrow because it begins with the premise of the existing model of membership. In contrast, the second problem statement is a greenfield, where new and innovative solutions can be imagined without the constraints of the existing model of membership.

Module 3: Ideate

Ideation marks the transition point from discovering problems to exploring solutions. Once the problem has been clearly scoped, an organization needs to turn its attention to brainstorming possible products, interventions, and strategies that can solve the challenge. At this stage, it is important to prioritize breadth over depth. During ideation, it is best to go wide first to identify many divergent possibilities. The more ideas the better. As Nobel Prize–winning scientist Linus Pauling observed, "The best way to have a good idea is to have lots of ideas."[15]

When ideating, museum leaders must push themselves to go beyond solutions for incremental improvements. Ideation is crucial to challenging the norm and breaking out of the status quo. At the ideation stage, teams should feel empowered to dream up novel, unconventional, and even implausible ideas. The goal of ideation is to push past expected solutions into uncharted territory to find creative possibilities that will unlock true innovation.

There are many types of ideation techniques that museum leaders can use to generate a high volume of fresh ideas. Regardless of the technique(s) employed, for ideation to be successful, it is important to change the physical space and create a relaxed environment that introduces new stimuli. This can be accomplished by meeting away from the typical business setting of a boardroom or even the museum itself. Use of tactile and ambient stimuli, such as toys, images, sketches, music, lighting, colored pens, and sticky notes, can help to get the team's creative juices flowing. Further, inviting outside voices and end users into the ideation process leads to more nuanced and inventive solutions.

Ideation is at the heart of the design thinking methodology, and it is important not to shortcut this step. Be bold and courageous in your ideation. Most importantly, have fun! Giving yourself and your team a safe space to be daring is how to get the most innovative ideas to bubble up. Begin with divergent thinking to stretch outside of the box to generate as many ideas as possible, then apply convergent thinking to identify the most interesting and actionable possibilities. Once a set of possible solutions has been identified, move quickly to develop a prototype.

Module 4: Prototype

Prototyping is all about experimentation. A prototype can be described as a scaled-down or simulated version of the solution that enables the team to test the idea with real audiences *before* investing significant resources in developing the full product or intervention. During the prototype stage, the solution may be accepted, improved, redesigned, or rejected based on the results of the testing.

The process of prototyping allows an organization to obtain feedback from individuals for whom the solution is intended to serve. Prototypes can be created for services, physical goods, virtual interfaces, processes, interactions, or experiences. As an experimental design tool, a prototype allows an idea to be tested quickly and inexpensively with the objective of validating the concept before moving forward. Prototypes can take many forms, such as a storyboard, a landing page, a low-fidelity mockup, signage, or an ad. Experiences can even be prototyped using a combination of role-playing or simulated services. The goal is to *show*, not tell. Any representation of the proposed solution is fair game as long as it allows the organization to learn from customer feedback what does and does not work. Once a prototype has been developed, it is time to test it with real audiences to understand whether the proposed solution is, in fact, the right one.

Module 5: Test

The Stanford d.School encourages design thinking practitioners to "prototype as if you know you're right, but test as if you know you're wrong." Using the prototype as a conversation starter, museum leaders can explore how the proposed solution might solve for the customers' needs. Through the process of testing, customer feedback helps to highlight any constraints, flaws, or assumptions in the prototype—or the problem statement.

Unlike a pilot program, which is intended to go to market fully formed, the goal of testing is to design an experiment that will allow the museum to learn quickly about what does, and does not, work. With each new learning, revisions are made to the prototype to inform development of a final solution. Testing with real audiences allows for a cycle of iteration in order to fine-tune the concept. The results of the testing phase often will lead an organization back to a previous step based on new insights that reveal gaps in understanding, help to refine the original problem statement, or generate new possible solutions.

By design, experiments are expected to have a high rate of failure. Organizations must be prepared to start over if it is discovered that the prototype does not adequately address the problem. While it can be intimidating, launching an idea into the world before it is "ready" provides the opportunity for invaluable learning. Once a version of the proposed solution has been validated through testing, it is time to scale up and invest in implementation. As a continuous process, adaptations should occur even after a final product or intervention goes to market as the organization continues to learn from audience feedback.

Ultimately, the design thinking methodology helps organizations to uncover unmet needs, reduce the risk associated with bringing new ideas to market, and design solutions that are revolutionary, not just incremental. Every business model eventually will run out of gas. Because each discrete business model is tied to a unique customer segment, the model must be adapted or refreshed as consumer habits, preferences, needs, and behaviors change. If an organization has not been incubating and experimenting with new ideas that will provide new sources of growth, it will inevitably find itself in crisis.

SPARK: CREATING A MIND MAP

While there are myriad tools to help spur ideation, one ingenious aid for brainstorming is a mind map. Mind mapping is a visual practice that stimulates creativity by using keywords and sketches to trigger associations and quickly generate lots of ideas. Mind maps can be created alone or in a small group.

A mind map begins with a blank page and a central theme or problem captured in the center. From the center, lines are drawn to highlight connections to related ideas and thoughts like branches growing out from a tree trunk. Colors, doodles, and shapes can be used to help link or group ideas together. By encouraging exploration of different pathways and connecting concepts around a central theme or problem, a mind map introduces spontaneity and creativity to improve problem solving.

Drawing upon the research and concepts introduced in chapter 10, I'd like to invite you to take 30 to 60 minutes to create a mind map that envisions a membership concept with the explicit goal of addressing loneliness. For the purposes of this exercise, do not restrict your ideas to the traditional model of membership. Instead, use this opportunity to explore an entirely new offering, completely separate and distinct from your current membership program. Stretch your thinking to imagine a new concept with its own perfect marketing mix.

As you explore this new membership concept, consider the following questions: What types of events, programs, experiences, or services might this new membership concept include, and how would they be different than your current membership program? What might you call this new membership concept and why? How would you market this new offering? What specific job will this new membership concept get done?

If you're struggling to get started, I've sketched a mind map in Figure 11.6 with some ideas for a new membership concept to address the challenge of loneliness. Feel free to build on these ideas, or create your own mind map from scratch following the steps outlined below.

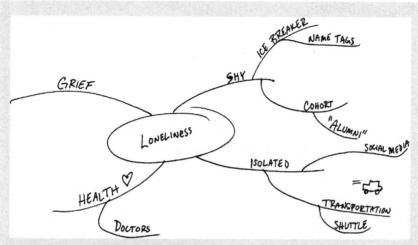

Figure 11.6. Example of a Mind Map

STEP 1: Take out a large sheet of paper and place it horizontally in front of you.

STEP 2: Write or sketch the theme or problem you want to explore in the center of the page (e.g., addressing loneliness). Keep the topic or problem statement as short and simple as possible to allow for a greater number of associations and sub-ideas.

STEP 3: Add at least four main branches radiating outward from the central topic. Write keywords connected to each branch that represent the big ideas related to the topic you are mapping.

STEP 4: Create secondary and tertiary branches that build on associations and topics.

STEP 5: Be bold. Challenge yourself to push past expected solutions and generic concepts. Explore ideas until the entire page is filled or you run out of ideas. If you have lots of ideas, your mind map may overflow onto additional pages.

DESIGNING ON THE EDGE

In statistics, a normal distribution has a symmetrical bell-shaped density curve (a bell curve) with a single peak in the center (representing the mean) and two "tails" that extend outward on the left and right sides. The majority of data points are clustered around the center, while those values that are less likely to occur appear farther away from the center—on the edges of the graph. Most often, organizations invest time and money in serving the majority—those in

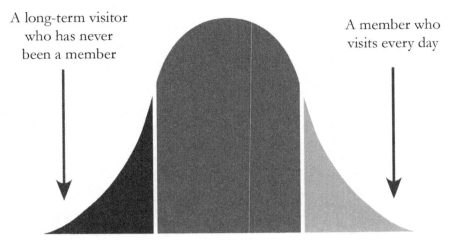

A long-term visitor
who has never
been a member

A member who
visits every day

Figure 11.7.   Example of Extremes on the Edges

the center of the bell curve. However, important insights can be gleaned from talking to people who are not in the majority.

In design thinking, the term *extremes* refers to individuals who fall on the edges of the bell curve. Extremes always come in pairs of either "super users" (e.g., brand fanatics, experts, and early adopters) or "nonusers" (e.g., cynics, abstainers, or laggards). For example, consider the following pair of extremes shown in Figure 11.7: (1) a long-term visitor who has never been a member (behavior on the far-left edge of the curve) and (2) a member who visits every day (behavior on the far-right edge of the curve).

Extremes are people who feel a particular customer need most acutely or not at all. By understanding the perspective of extremes, organizations can sharpen the value proposition of existing and/or new products. For instance, if a museum wants to gain insight into why members join, the pair of extremes to understand may be (1) a member who buys bundles of gift memberships to give away as gifts to friends and family (a "fanatic") and (2) an individual who has never been a member of any museum (an "abstainer"). Understanding an extreme nonuser helps to amplify the problem statement, whereas engaging with a super user helps to highlight those features and aspects of a product that are the most valuable.

Seeking out individuals with extreme points of view, surprising habits, and unique circumstances can be a rich source of creative inspiration. Moreover, customers on the super-user edge tend to be influencers. These extremes are the early technology adopters, the brand enthusiasts, and the trendsetters. They hack products to unlock hidden value, unbox the latest must-have tech, and proactively search out inventive solutions to meet their needs. The super user's behavior often exposes unexpected use cases for a product and points in the direction that the mainstream will be moving. In contrast, nonusers also can reveal trends of things to come by indicating broader barriers and societal shifts that are difficult to see from within a museum's walls.

As museum professionals, we tend to live in a bubble surrounded by people who think, feel, and act like us. This limits our ability to empathize with others who do not share our worldview, experiences, or industry knowledge. By engaging with extremes, museum leaders can connect with nontraditional audiences and gain a deeper understanding of what their broader communities value.

When asked, "Who is membership for?" the most common answer given by museum leaders is "Everyone." However, when museums design for "everyone," they end up designing for no one. To illustrate the point, consider the story of how the US Air Force identified the root cause of a rash of pilot deaths in the 1950s. Even though the Air Force had improved technology and training, flight performance was declining with devastating results. The high death rate remained a mystery until the Air Force finally realized that the cockpit was to blame.

Based on the physical dimensions of an average male pilot, the cockpit was designed to be a standard size. However, when a young Harvard graduate named Gilbert S. Daniels was asked to measure thousands of airmen on a set of 10 physical dimensions, he found that not a single pilot met the average across the 10 dimensions.[16] That is, by designing for every pilot, the Air Force had designed a cockpit that didn't fit a single one and, sadly, at a great cost.

It is a myth that there is such a thing as an average visitor, a typical member, or a normal donor. We are all unique individuals with different needs, life experiences, and motivations. Yet museums design marketing, products, and experiences for the average visitor, member, and donor. While such an approach allows museums to operationalize processes, streamline workflows, and gain efficiency, it also codifies a one-size-fits-none approach to membership and fundraising.

Designing for the average has never produced innovation. Just as technology and product designers have learned that designing for the few is the best way to design for the many, museums, too, must begin to develop a more personalized approach to engaging audiences. Understanding how extremes think and move through their lives will open up a new perspective from which museum leaders can see the world. Moreover, leveraging the design thinking methodology will allow museums to build empathy with customers and uncover innovative solutions to address customers' needs. Ultimately, the future-proofing of museums requires the development of new membership business models and thoughtful service design to create more relevant and meaningful customer experiences.

NOTES

1. "Business Model Innovation," Strategy, Boston Consulting Group, accessed September 28, 2019, https://www.bcg.com/en-us/capabilities/strategy/business -model-innovation.aspx.

2. Martin Reeves, Simon Levin, and Daichi Ueda, "The Biology of Corporate Survival," *Harvard Business Review*, January-February 2016, https://hbr.org/2016/01/ the-biology-of-corporate-survival.

3. Sarah Cliffe, "When Your Business Model Is in Trouble," *Harvard Business Review*, January-February 2011, https://hbr.org/2011/01/when-your-business-model -is-in-trouble.

4. Peter F. Drucker, "The Theory of the Business," *Harvard Business Review*, September–October 1994, https://hbr.org/1994/09/the-theory-of-the-business.

5. "Business Model Innovation," Strategy, Boston Consulting Group, accessed September 28, 2019, https://www.bcg.com/en-us/capabilities/strategy/business -model-innovation.aspx.

6. Alexander Osterwalder, "A Better Way to Think about Your Business Model," *Harvard Business Review*, May 6, 2013, https://hbr.org/2013/05/a-better-way-to -think-about-yo.

7. Ibid.

8. Clayton M. Christensen, Thomas Bartman, and Derek van Bever, "The Hard Truth about Business Model Innovation," *MITSloan Management Review*, September 13, 2016, https://sloanreview.mit.edu/article/the-hard-truth-about-business -model-innovation/.

9. Zhenya Lindgardt, Martin Reeves, George Stalk, and Michael S. Deimler, "Business Model Innovation: When the Game Gets Tough, Change the Game," Boston Consulting Group, December 2009, https://www.bcg.com/documents/file36456.pdf.

10. "What Is Service Design?," Service Design Network, accessed September 28, 2019, https://www.service-design-network.org/about-service-design.

11. Andy Polaine, Lavrans Løvlie, and Ben Reason, *Service Design: From Insight to Inspiration* (New York: Rosenfeld Media, 2013), 31.

12. Forrester, *2017 Predictions: Dynamics That Will Shape the Future in the Age of the Customer*, 2–5.

13. Jo Szczepanska, "Design Thinking Origin Story Plus Some of the People Who Made It All Happen," *Medium*, January 3, 2017, https://medium.com/@szcz panks/design-thinking-where-it-came-from-and-the-type-of-people-who-made-it-all -happen-dc3a05411e53.

14. Rikke Dam and Teo Siang, "Design Thinking: Get a Quick Overview of the History," Interaction Design Foundation, accessed September 28, 2019, https://www .interaction-design.org/literature/article/design-thinking-get-a-quick-overview-of -the-history.

15. Robert Wallace Olson, "The Art of Creative Thinking," *Everyday Handbooks* 508 (May 14, 2009): 69.

16. Lory Hough, "Beyond Average," *Harvard Ed. Magazine*, Fall 2015, https:// www.gse.harvard.edu/news/ed/15/08/beyond-average.

Chapter Twelve

Innovation as a Core Competency

Grace Murray Hopper, US Naval officer and pioneering computer scientist, once famously remarked, "Humans are allergic to change. They love to say, 'We've always done it this way.'"[1] A bold innovator, Hopper hung a counterclockwise clock in her office to remind herself and others that just because something has been done a certain way in the past is no reason it can't be done a better way in the future. Museum leaders often fall into the trap of "We've Always Done It This Way," not challenging the status quo or questioning long-standing assumptions that risk missing an opportunity to find a better way.

In the spirit of finding a better way, museums must prioritize experimentation in innovation initiatives for audience development. Doing so is the only way to combat the forces afflicting the traditional membership business model and unlock new opportunities to connect with audiences in a meaningful way. Museums are entering a period of significant challenges. Increasing operating costs, evidence that the traditional business model of membership is in decline, and an ever-increasing competitive landscape for leisure activities indicate that the industry has reached a critical juncture where what worked in the past will not serve museums going forward. Thus, change is required for museums to keep ahead of the curve and remain relevant. The future of the museum sector is dependent upon its ability to understand customers' needs and take steps to address those needs. Moreover, engaging nontraditional audiences and deepening relationships with existing ones requires building empathy, removing barriers to participation, intentionally designing interventions, and enhancing the customer experience.

For museums to avoid becoming obsolete, innovation is an imperative. The challenge is determining how to invest in innovation while supporting existing customers and maintaining the museum's current membership revenue model. To ensure long-term sustainability, museums must simultaneously advance their capabilities in making impactful improvements to the existing membership program *and* invest in new membership business models. Accomplishing these concurrent goals requires significant attention in four critical areas: (1) tuning the "Performance Engine" of membership, (2) measuring what matters, (3) implementing validated learning, and (4) developing an innovation practice.

TUNING THE PERFORMANCE ENGINE OF MEMBERSHIP

In their influential book *The Other Side of Innovation*, authors Vijay Govindarajan and Chris Trimble describe an organization's ongoing revenue-generating operations as a "Performance Engine."[2] A traditional membership program fits the definition of a Performance Engine well: It has an explicit goal of achieving steady, predictable growth through a variety of repeatable activities while maximizing return on investment (ROI). Thanks to the efforts of dedicated museum membership managers everywhere, the membership Performance Engine has matured into a long-standing and successful business model for museums. Striving for greater efficacy year over year, the owners of a museum's membership Performance Engine prioritize consistency and profitability and focus attention on improving efficiency in acquiring, retaining, and servicing members. Measured on its ability to produce results based on past performance, the membership Performance Engine is a well-oiled machine.

Unfortunately, the very activities that have enabled the membership Performance Engine to become an established business model (e.g., servicing customers, improving productivity, maximizing ROI, etc.) are the same practices that are contributing to its decline. This is not a failing of museum leadership. It is simply the unavoidable pattern of a business model life cycle. Why is this? It is because the predictability and repeatability that has allowed the membership Performance Engine to scale and evolve into a mature business model is fundamentally incompatible with innovation. Therefore, as the traditional business model of membership has become more efficient and profitable over time, it also has become less and less innovative.

Thankfully, all is not lost. Through thoughtful and intentional change, it is possible to revitalize the membership Performance Engine to yield optimal results. In much the same way that a car's engine can be modified to achieve maximum horsepower, adjustments can be made to the existing membership business model to maximize performance. Unlike the necessary maintenance activities required to keep the membership Performance Engine running, such as basic acquisition campaigns and routine retention strategies, *tuning* the Performance Engine involves deeper and more holistic changes to the underlying business model.

The activities involved in tuning the membership Performance Engine are distinctly different than the process of maintaining the ongoing operations of a membership program. Tuning requires significant adjustments to the choice architecture, testing of behavioral interventions, and substantial changes to the marketing mix. Tuning activities are not simply more of the same, such as more frequent renewal notices or additional on-site signage to promote membership, nor are they increased investment in standard approaches, such as direct mail campaigns or other marketing tactics. Rather, tuning requires rethinking the nine building blocks of the current membership business model and introducing intentional nudges to improve the efficacy of the membership Performance Engine. Examples of tuning include:

- Reframing the value proposition of membership
- Activating social identities
- Implementing a default opt out
- Leveraging the endowment effect
- Applying anchoring or other pricing strategies
- Emphasizing the warm glow of giving
- Priming for generosity
- Modifying the choice set
- Using social norms or social proof to influence decisions
- Tailoring the customer experience for a specific customer segment

Tuning the membership Performance Engine entails a rigorous process of experimentation to validate assumptions and requires the crucial task of building empathy to understand customers' needs, motivations, and values. By purposefully tuning the membership Performance Engine, museum leaders will be able to proactively enhance the existing membership program to meet the needs of existing and new audiences.

MEASURING WHAT MATTERS

The rise of big data and easy access to copious analytics have ushered in an era where data is king. Across the museum sector, museum leaders (as well as their consultants and advertising agencies) are under increasing pressure to translate voluminous datasets into tangible value. Paradoxically, while many museums are becoming more data driven, few are data informed. The difference is not merely semantic. In a data-driven museum, data *guides* decision-making, whereas in a data-informed museum, data *verifies* intuition. This distinction involves striking a balance between collecting data to guide decisions about current operations versus leveraging data to inform future directions.

Because data collected from current operations are a reflection of the existing membership business model in action, they are inherently limited. Based on the traditional membership program and how current audiences behave, the majority of data available to museum leaders are generated from a snapshot of the past. Therefore, they are systemically biased. The way data are collected and interpreted can greatly affect their value and validity. Low-quality, inaccurate, or incomplete data can result in the cherry-picking of data and misinformed decisions. Becoming a data-informed organization requires a more agile approach to using data that involves articulating and validating a hypothesis. Without improved data literacy and a more enlightened view of the role of data, museum leaders can end up wading in a shallow data pool that limits their ability to see beyond their past and current market conditions.

The availability of more and better data has led to an insidious practice in membership and marketing. The ability to measure nearly anything has resulted in a prevalence of spurious correlations. Abundance of data has made it easy to show a correlation between two variables, even when that correlation is utterly irrelevant. The perceived need to justify a return on investment or demonstrate progress leads many to interpret data in a way that shows results in a positive light. Too often, museum leaders and their trusted advisors use correlation as a way to explain how a particular action translates to an outcome.

Simply, correlation is a way of measuring the relationship between two variables. However, in some cases, such a relationship can be sheer coincidence. When provided with enough data, it is possible to find variables that correlate even when they should not. For example, Figure 12.1 shows that

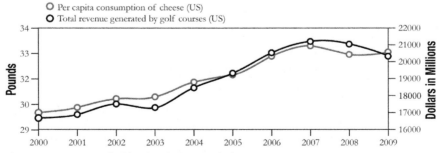

Figure 12.1.   Example of a Spurious Correlation

Spurious Correlation made possible by Tyler Vigen via tylervigen.com and available under Creative Commons Attribution 4.0 International license (CC BY 4.0) http://creativecommons.org/licenses/by/4.0/.

per capita consumption of cheese in the US correlates with total revenue generated by US golf courses.

This example of a spurious correlation between cheese consumption and golf course revenue stems from the practice of "data dredging," which allows for two unrelated variables to be correlated by comparing datasets. Although it is laughable to think that the consumption of cheese has anything to do with golf course revenue, spurious correlations also can be made in situations where it is expected that two variables *should* correspond. For example, a museum would expect an advertising campaign to drive an increase in membership sales; however, attributing a lift in membership numbers to a marketing effort risks making a potentially specious conclusion. It is important to note, while correlation indicates that a relationship *might* exist, causation demonstrates clear cause and effect.

Museums that strive to be data driven are at risk of placing value on "vanity metrics," which can suggest seemingly positive results yet do not substantiate genuine trends or clear cause and effect. For example, traditional marketing and membership performance metrics, such as matchback analysis, renewal rate, social media followers, and website traffic, may show positive results in the short-term while concealing an underlying problem. Additionally, many metrics represent a single data point that does not tell the full story. Consider the following scenario: A museum invests in a direct mail campaign to promote membership. The matchback analysis shows that a certain percentage of people who received the direct mail campaign ultimately joined, thereby correlating increased membership sales with the campaign. However, this metric is a dead end because it does not provide verifiable information about who joined and why or deliver any actionable insights to inform strategic direction about what to do next to cultivate these new members. Thus, it is "true but useless."

Museums largely use metrics in an obligatory manner—checking the box to demonstrate due diligence on a marketing effort or to distribute status reports, such as membership totals, renewal rate, cost per acquisition, conversion rate, click-through rate, and return on investment. Thus, the majority of metrics are tactical in nature, measuring activities that have little to no impact on long-term goal attainment. Moreover, such metrics are superficial and tend to be retrospective, measuring participation and return on investment from past activities.

Metrics are good, but key performance indicators (KPIs) are better. A KPI is a uniquely robust measure designed to objectively validate intuition and guide strategy. To be meaningful, a KPI must be a quantifiable measure that demonstrates whether the museum is achieving its stated long-range goals, and it must help museum leaders to make decisions about what to do next.

Unfortunately, most museums have not identified those KPIs that are actual drivers of change. Instead, museums tend to use short-term metrics as a stand-in for true KPIs. For example, many museums often look to the short-term metric of cumulative membership household count as a proxy for audience engagement. Similarly, renewal rate is often ascribed as an indicator of loyalty. Yet such metrics do not authoritatively demonstrate the attainment of either engagement or loyalty (concepts that each museum will likely define differently for their own institution). But because these metrics are easy to measure, they are measured. Consequently, the vast majority of metrics that museums track today do not rise to the level of being a true KPI.

Just because something is easy to measure, doesn't mean that it should be. Tactical, rearview metrics do nothing to help museum leaders understand the long-term impact of specific actions or unveil future opportunities. A commitment to developing meaningful KPIs will reposition data-driven museums to be more data informed. Leading organizations already are using a distinctly different approach to KPIs that provides a deeper understanding of customers in a more holistic, integrated way.[3] For instance, more meaningful KPIs include customer lifetime value, member involvement, emotional connection, and Net Promoter Score (NPS). Once an institution has identified those growth-oriented KPIs that truly move the needle on long-term goal attainment, a more sophisticated approach to measurement is required. Implementation of two simple techniques can help museum leaders obtain a better view of KPIs and become more data informed: (1) process behavior charts and (2) cohort analysis.

Process Behavior Charts

Museum leaders tend to use metrics as binary (e.g., hit or miss) performance measures. However, two data points do not make a trend. Additionally, linear trend lines can be manipulated to show an upward or downward trend, depending on the timeframe that is being measured. Taking a more growth-oriented approach to KPIs demands that museum leaders stop comparing and making decisions based on "before and after" data points, such as actual versus projected membership numbers, this year's versus last year's performance, and month-to-month renewal rates.

In membership, performance metrics can fluctuate greatly based on a number of factors, such as seasonality, exhibitions, marketing, pricing discounts, weather, and more. Such fluctuations are often just "noise" that do not repre-

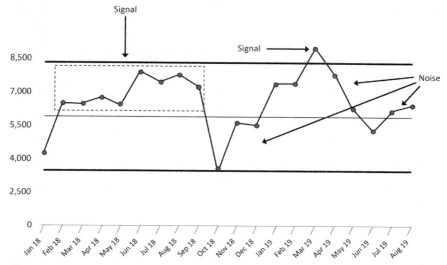

Figure 12.2.   Example of a Process Behavior Chart

sent a statistically significant change in the overall level of performance of a program. Adoption of a *systems perspective* as a way to view data empowers museum leaders to see through the noise present in every metric and focus on those activities that effect meaningful change. By providing context regarding the stability of a specific KPI, a systems perspective enables museum leaders to take a step back and examine the big picture.

A "process behavior chart," or "control chart," is an elegantly simple tool that provides museum leaders with a way to visualize meaningful performance measures from a systems perspective (Figure 12.2). Rather than reporting on retrospective hit or miss metrics, a process behavior chart provides objective insight into which activities *actually* affect overall performance in real time, helping museum leaders filter out the noise and see whether a fluctuation within a given metric is statistically significant. In this way, data points that do not indicate a genuine trend or "signal" can be safely ignored as noise.

The first step in creating a process behavior chart is to "plot the dots" by generating a run chart (a line graph of data plotted over time) of the baseline data. Next, three elements are calculated: (1) the average, (2) a lower natural process limit, and (3) an upper natural process limit. It is critical that the lower and upper natural process limits are *calculated*—they are not goals or invented boundaries.

THREE RULES THAT GOVERN SIGNALS

Signals are governed by three rules that teach museums how to spot the cause and effect of a strategic decision:[1]

- Rule 1: Any data point above or below the lower and upper limits.
- Rule 2: Eight consecutive data points that are either above or below the baseline average.
- Rule 3: A cluster of three out of four data points that are closer to the lower or upper limits than they are to the baseline average.

NOTE

1. Mark Graban, *Measures of Success: React Less, Lead Better, Improve More* (Colleyville, Texas: Constancy, Inc., 2019), 30.

Once plotted, the baseline data points will fluctuate within the bounds of the lower and upper limits, and a prediction can be made that any future data points are likely to fall within these limits. With this foundation in place, museum leaders can objectively observe how specific strategies, marketing investments, or changes to the membership program affect a given KPI. It is this foundational systems perspective that uniquely enables a museum to begin focusing attention and resources on those strategies that demonstrate meaningful impact.

Cohort Analysis

Museum leaders can gain better insight into KPIs by conducting a "cohort analysis," which translates complex datasets into observable human-scale behaviors. The gold standard for innovation-oriented measurement, this technique is useful when trying to understand how customers flow through the organization. Rather than tracking cumulative totals or gross numbers, such as membership revenue or total membership households, a cohort analysis groups customers that share a common characteristic together so that their behaviors can be measured over a period of time.

Museums can leverage a cohort analysis to uncover trends that would otherwise be hidden when viewing the data in the aggregate. To illustrate the power of cohort analysis, consider the following scenario: A museum designs an experiment to test a new membership concept by running an A/B split test in which two versions of the prototype are offered to customers at the same time. Customers in the experiment are grouped into two cohorts based on their purchase of either version A or version B of the prototype. Over time, the museum will be able to measure how engagement in one cohort is performing compared to the other. Thus, cohort analysis enables a more critical examination of how strategic decisions affect KPIs based on real insight into audience behaviors.

The current industry standard is to measure membership program efficacy using cumulative metrics (e.g., renewal rates, totals by membership category, overall membership household count, etc.). Observing customer data at the individual behavioral level through cohort analysis is a more evidence-based approach that can reveal an unexpected problem or hint at a growth opportunity. Moreover, cohort analysis is the only way to understand how a strategy or change affects long-term goal attainment.

Too often, museums make full-scale changes to a program without evidence to prove out the long-term effects of such decisions. This approach puts museum leaders at a severe disadvantage to be able to course correct in the moment because there is no clear way to tease apart which aspect of the strategy is working or failing. Before museums invest significant resources on wholesale change, they need access to data that informs decision-making. In this way a cohort analysis acts as a gut check, helping museum leaders prioritize and direct investment to those efforts that actually move the needle on long-term goals.

IMPLEMENTING VALIDATED LEARNING

There is a movement under way that is profoundly changing the way organizations innovate. Developed by entrepreneur Eric Ries, the "lean startup" is a transformative methodology that advocates for experimentation, rapid prototyping, and validated learning to accelerate product design and business model innovation. Although it originated with the Silicon Valley tech startup in mind, the lean startup methodology is an exceptionally valuable innovation practice for any organization.

Established on a deeply profound insight, the lean startup advocates for *immediate* measurement and response to an action. It is this singular principle that demonstrates the potential to create real and lasting change in an organization. Using the scientific method as a foundation, the lean startup requires a defined hypothesis to be articulated, tested, and validated through a process

BUILD-MEASURE-LEARN FEEDBACK LOOP

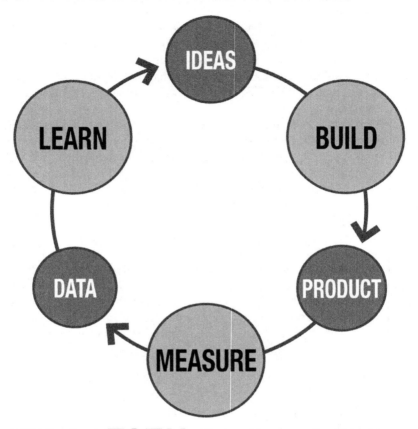

Minimize *TOTAL* time through the loop

Figure 12.3. Build-Measure-Learn Feedback Loop

Source: The Lean Startup/Hadel Studio. I have made considerable effort to find and contact the copyright owner of Figure 12.3 featuring the Build-Measure-Learn Feedback Loop. Should the rightful owners come forth, I shall obtain proper permission and include the appropriate credit line in future printings of this book.

of experimentation that follows a cycle of building a prototype, measuring results, and learning from customer feedback. This "build-measure-learn feedback loop" ensures rigor in experimentation and demands that museum leaders learn quickly to improve upon initial ideas (Figure 12.3).[4]

In the lean startup approach, the build phase of the feedback loop involves the creation of a prototype based on a clearly articulated hypothesis that establishes a prediction about what will happen when customers engage with the prototype. Next, an experiment is designed to test the hypothesis. Finally, customer feedback is derived from the experiment and used to improve the prototype, and the cycle begins again. With an emphasis on nimbleness and speed, the lean startup eliminates waste (both time and money) by developing a prototype that represents a minimum viable product (MVP). The MVP is used to extract input from real customers as quickly as possible. Unlike traditional product development, which delays launch until the product is perfected, the goal of the MVP is to accelerate the learning process by testing the fundamental hypothesis of the new business model before going to market with a fully formed product.

It is not only okay, but encouraged, that the MVP be rough around the edges, a bit messy, and incomplete. In fact, an MVP does not even need to be an *actual* product to be able to serve the purpose of testing a hypothesis. To illustrate the concept of an MVP, consider the origin story of the popular file-syncing software company, Dropbox. With a market valuation of more than $12 billion, Dropbox has honed a very complex product through more than a decade of development and hundreds of millions of dollars of investment to overcome significant technical hurdles.[5] However, the company did not begin with the polished, seamless product now used by more than 500 million users worldwide.[6] Instead, founder Drew Houston recorded a simple three-minute video that demonstrated the concept of its yet-to-be-developed file-sharing software by simulating how the software would work.[7] This video was the MVP used to test the hypothesis that file syncing was an unmet customer need. With this visually explanatory video, prospective customers did not need to physically use the actual product to immediately see the value that Dropbox offered. Shortly after the video's release, Dropbox signed up 75,000 people to its waitlist.[8] The lesson of Dropbox's simulated software emphasizes the power of *minimum* in MVP and demonstrates that the biggest risk an organization faces is investing resources in building something no one wants.

The lean startup is a coherent end-to-end methodology for business model innovation that museums can implement to test ideas with the aim of solving unmet customer needs. After mapping out a new membership business model using the business model canvas, a lean startup approach translates the static concept into a dynamic hypothesis-testing machine. With its focus on validated learning, the build-measure-learn feedback loop informs objective decision-making incrementally, thereby reducing the risk associated with investing in new ideas.

Validated learning is, in essence, the proactive discovery of a new business model. In *The Lean Startup*, Ries advocates for rapid iteration to unearth growth opportunities. Based on the results of each cycle through the feedback loop, museum leaders should feel empowered to make data-informed decisions about what to do to advance their idea to the next level.

The lean startup holds promise for revolutionizing the museum membership business model. As Michel Gelobter writes in his book *Lean Startups for Social Change*, the biggest shift nonprofits must make in adopting the lean startup methodology is to switch from a plan-fund-do approach to a build-measure-learn approach.[9] Museum leaders place a premium on strategic planning, generating multiyear plans that detail a variety of tactics, resource allocations, and expected outcomes. While planning is important, it also is inherently risk averse and discourages experimentation. A traditional strategic planning approach works well when the future is fairly predictable and there are explicit, demonstrated ways to solve clear problems. However, the challenges facing today's museums are not predictable, nor do they have proven solutions. By turning the traditional strategic planning process on its head, the lean startup methodology promotes an entrepreneurial mindset and helps an organization become more data informed. Rather than spending precious time and budget executing on a new, untested concept that may ultimately turn out to be flawed, a validated learning approach enables museums to innovate smarter and faster to unlock ideas that have the potential to generate sustainable, long-term funding streams.

BRIGHT SPOT: THE SUMMER ADVENTURE AT CARNEGIE MUSEUMS OF PITTSBURGH

There's no cultural organization in the world quite like Carnegie Museums of Pittsburgh. With a legacy of discovery dating back to 1895, Carnegie Museums is a family of four diverse museums, including Carnegie Museum of Art, Carnegie Museum of Natural History, Carnegie Science Center, and The Andy Warhol Museum. In 2011, the Carnegie Museums' membership team launched a pilot program dubbed the *Summer Adventure* as a way to enhance the member experience on-site during the summer. The program included a text-based scavenger hunt at each of the four museums, which encouraged members to text a keyword during their visit to initiate the scavenger hunt and receive clues via their mobile devices.

The text-based scavenger hunt had a total of 24 participants. However, the membership team found that this type of scavenger hunt was a less-than-seamless experience for members. With this learning, Carnegie Museums took a different approach the following summer by capitalizing on the ever-growing rise of social media. For the 2012 *Summer Adventure*, the membership team developed a scavenger hunt that included a series of clues encouraging members to take photos in specific locations and a landing page where they could upload and tag their photos to be entered into a contest. At the end of the season, members were invited to vote to select winners from the 20 entries. While the photo scavenger hunt was engaging, the process required images to be uploaded via desktop, making it difficult for mobile users to participate.

After the 2012 *Summer Adventure* fell flat, the membership team had a better understanding of what did—and did not—work. Carnegie Museums recognized that providing multiple avenues for people to connect with the museums would be important for improving participation. Moreover, up to this point, the summer offerings did not have a cohesive visual identity. Cari Maslow, associate vice president of Engagement at Carnegie Museums of Pittsburgh, dreamed of creating a summer filled with events united under the umbrella of a branded member experience. From this idea, Carnegie Museums' *Summer Adventure* was born.

In 2013, the membership team designed a small, wallet-sized map that contained descriptions of each of the summer events with spaces where members could earn a stamp for each visit. As members collected stamps, they would boost their chances of winning at the "End-of-Summer Celebration" drawing in August. And the text-based scavenger hunt was updated and reintroduced in 2013. The goals of the refined *Summer Adventure* program were to:

- Raise the visibility of all four museums included with a Carnegie Museums' membership, as members often believed that they were a member of only one or two museums.
- Offer compelling reasons to visit and—down the road—renew their membership.
- Provide a strong visual identity to promote member events during the summer.
- Heighten the perceived value of membership by showcasing a full summer package of events available to members.

With over 400 people in attendance at the End-of-Summer Celebration and strong turnout for the summer events, Carnegie Museums believed they had designed a concept that could scale. Ms. Maslow noted, "The look of the adventure in 2013 wasn't as cohesive as we'd hoped, but it was a step in the right direction."

In 2014, Carnegie Museums partnered with a local illustrator to design a branded map that mirrored the Pittsburgh landscape (with a few creative liberties) and a bold, retro logo for the *Summer Adventure*, along with bright, whimsical illustrations that transformed the museums from staid to light-hearted. The following year, Carnegie Museums drafted formal contest rules that would satisfy Pennsylvania legislation around small games of chance and could be used in subsequent years.

Through the membership team's process of learning and iteration, Carnegie Museums identified several distinct challenges of the *Summer Adventure*.

First, the program was contingent on the admissions team distributing the maps to members when they visited, which was not ideal. The membership team realized that they needed to create an experience that museum admissions desks did not have to facilitate. Second, Carnegie Museums lacked a comprehensive way to gauge participation in the *Summer Adventure*. Third, the *Summer Adventure* in its existing format required a member to be on-site to collect stamps or participate in the scavenger hunt, limiting the ability of Carnegie Museums to connect with members off-site.

Understanding that digital engagement would be key to engaging new audiences and retaining existing ones, Carnegie Museums' Innovation Studio presented a concept to create a chatbot for the *Summer Adventure* that would be funded by a grant from the Knight Foundation. The chatbot would be an animated representation of the founder himself, Andrew Carnegie. Andy CarnegieBot, as it was aptly named, would guide museumgoers through trivia, a scavenger hunt, polls, and event reminders using simulated conversation via the Facebook Messenger app.

In January 2018, work began on the digital infrastructure, on-site imagery, and graphics for the chatbot, including Andy CarnegieBot's various likenesses. Simultaneously, the membership team partnered with marketing and education to develop the scavenger hunt, coordinate marketing and signage efforts, and create trivia, polls, and event content (Figure 12.4).

Figure 12.4. Summer Adventure Visual Identity
Courtesy of Carnegie Museums of Pittsburgh.

In 2018, the digital platform for the Summer Adventure allowed the museums to open the experience to all visitors, with special prizes reserved exclusively for members. During the first two months, nearly 250 people participated in the scavenger hunt. Because there was no set starting point for the scavenger hunt, users could join the hunt at any point, making participation much easier. However, Carnegie Museums quickly discovered several opportunities for improvement. For example, on-site staff needed to be provided with the clues and exact locations of all scavenger hunt items to help members in their quest, scan codes went missing or were difficult to scan, larger signs were needed to combat lighting and location issues, and a certain hard-to-find badger clue was leaving audiences stumped. After addressing these issues, Carnegie Museums saw scavenger hunt completion rates rise from 25 to 43 percent. As Ms. Maslow observed, "The popularity of the scavenger hunt points to the ongoing importance of providing engagement opportunities to supplement the onsite experience." Overall, 814 people engaged with Andy CarnegieBot during the 2018 *Summer Adventure*, with women accounting for 60 percent of users, suggesting that the chatbot may appeal to one of Carnegie Museums' largest existing audiences: mothers with young children.

The 2019 *Summer Adventure* saw a higher adoption rate than expected, with 1,038 users participating. After reviewing usage data from the previous summer, Carnegie Museums decided to eliminate the polls and rewards and streamlined the trivia. Additionally, a list of helpful hints was provided to in-gallery and frontline staff, and the scavenger hunt clues were crafted to be more straightforward to reduce confusion—scavenger hunt participation increased 136 percent over 2018. The June kickoff for *Summer Adventure* included prominent Andy CarnegieBot signage and staff demonstrations to show visitors how to use the chatbot, scan stamps, and join the scavenger hunt.

The success story of Carnegie Museums' *Summer Adventure* is a testament to its culture of innovation. Had the membership team abandoned its concept for *Summer Adventure* after lackluster results in 2011, the vision for this imaginative audience engagement program would not have come to fruition. Moreover, it was Carnegie Museums' commitment to persistent iteration—nine years in the making—that led to the unexpected innovation opportunity to introduce Andy CarnegieBot to its *Summer Adventure*. Ultimately, without the membership team's systematic experimentation, Carnegie Museums would not have been able to build upon critical learnings over the years. Now, with a solid foundation and new technology in place, Carnegie Museums is ready to take on its next adventure . . . summer 2020.

Courtesy of Carnegie Museums of Pittsburgh.

DEVELOPING AN INNOVATION PRACTICE

Decades of research reveals important differences between organizations that innovate and those that do not.[10] First, nimble organizations do not treat the practice of innovation as something "special" or as a singular event. Instead, they view the practice of innovation as an ongoing activity to be cultivated alongside other core competencies. Such organizations *systematically* create an innovation strategy that guides the creation and capture of value. Second, growth-oriented organizations link innovation initiatives to broader financial, people, and technology resources. Without prioritization of such resources, an innovation initiative cannot thrive. Lastly, innovative organizations foster a culture that nurtures creativity, including a tolerance for failure, a willingness to experiment, and a climate of psychological safety.

The membership Performance Engine is a reliable and vital source of revenue for museums. Therefore, an innovation practice must be developed without disrupting the ongoing operations of the existing membership program. Specifically, museums need to find a way of conducting institution-wide experiments that do not risk interrupting or threatening the current membership business model. Although it may appear that investing in improving an existing product is less risky and more profitable than searching for a new one, a well-designed innovation strategy will help museum leaders evaluate the trade-offs between short-term results and long-term outcomes and align resources around common priorities.

One way to develop an innovation practice without disrupting the membership Performance Engine is to adopt an incubator approach to innovation initiatives. An incubator approach leverages a "dedicated team" that is custom built for each specific innovation initiative to include subject matter experts from across the organization, as well as external expertise to support empathic research, market research, design thinking, and strategy.[11] Outside experts can provide invaluable perspective to the dedicated team and are able to recognize and challenge organizational sacred cows and institutional biases that can hold an innovation initiative back. The skill set within the dedicated team must include the ability to be creative, adopt a beginner's mindset, ask the right questions, build empathy with customers, and be comfortable with uncertainty and ambiguity. It is important that members of the dedicated team embrace their role with an optimistic view and approach the initiative as different from their daily activities. A best practice for encouraging a fresh perspective is to have each member of the dedicated team write his or her own job description for the project, including new and unique titles that reflect the role of the individual as part of the dedicated team.

While the membership Performance Engine's owners are focused on enhancing and evolving the current membership business model, the dedicated team's attention is focused on uncovering unmet customer needs and experimenting with new membership business models. So, whereas the membership Performance Engine's mandate is to make meaningful modifications to the existing business model that generates a positive ROI, the dedicated team's mandate is to learn about customer needs as quickly and inexpensively as possible. Therefore, both teams must develop innovation as a core competency by employing the build-measure-learn feedback loop.

A museum's capacity for innovation is determined by how it manages its interdependent resources. Healthy innovation systems require information, input, and significant integration of effort from a diverse array of contributors. Thus, collaboration is paramount to developing an innovation practice. The dedicated team must rely on shared resources from the membership Performance Engine and other functional areas of the organization, such as marketing, education, visitor services, and technology. Without access to such resources, the dedicated team's efforts will be stifled, and the innovation initiative will die on the vine. Success of the dedicated team is dependent upon the owners of the membership Performance Engine and other organizational resources being given explicit permission *and* direction to partner with them.

Developing an innovation practice requires a willingness to embrace uncertainty and ambiguity. Above all, an organization's culture shapes the way its people think and behave, and the shared values that an organization holds must be accepting of experimentation and risk taking for it to develop innovation as a core competency. For an innovation practice to take root, there must be a tolerance for "productive failure." It is imperative that museum leaders create a psychologically safe climate for teams to speak openly and honestly about problems. Productive failure involves understanding that unexpected and, sometimes, undesirable outcomes are an essential part of innovation. In fact, the most innovative of organizations *intentionally* seek to generate productive failure for the express purpose of learning because, without it, the valuable insights that could help them uncover risks and future growth opportunities are lost. Therefore, museum leaders must work diligently to create the conditions necessary to encourage and sustain innovation.

TRY SOMETHING

For decades, museums have worked diligently to improve efficiencies, maximize return on investment from marketing efforts, increase renewal rates, and establish a stable revenue stream through the traditional membership business model. This strategy has worked well, enabling museums to serve and extend their missions to millions of people around the world. However, making incremental improvements to the existing membership model is no longer enough. The trends are clear: to ensure their survival, museums must invent new business models for audience engagement. Staying the course is not an option.

Museum leaders and their teams often feel frustrated by the limited amount of time they have to work on new ideas. In fact, 58 percent of employees report being so busy with day-to-day tasks that innovation is put on the back burner.[12] Yet carving out time for innovation is crucial. By prioritizing investment in innovation as a core competency, it is possible for a museum to become more entrepreneurial, nimble, and customer centric. The first step is to tune the Performance Engine to optimize the existing membership business model. Next, museums must invest in developing an innovation practice by institutionalizing the methodologies of design thinking, service design, and the lean startup.

Reimagining membership requires an intense focus on the customer experience and a relentless commitment to validated learning. To understand what customers really need—not what they *say* they want or what museums think they *should* want—requires that museums become data-informed organizations by building empathy, asking the right questions, and collecting empirical data from experiments with real customers. Ultimately, the key to museum future-proofing lies in understanding customers' hidden motivations and unmet needs, removing the barriers to participation, filtering out the noise, and investing in new products that will get the job done.

Tomorrow's success stories will come from museum leaders who invest today in innovation. Their museums will be the exemplars having unlocked opportunities to connect more deeply with audiences by building nimbleness, productive failure, and flexibility into their institutional planning.

Innovation, by definition, has no precedent. The way forward may require a refinement, a reboot, or a reinvention of membership as we know it. In the immortal words of Franklin D. Roosevelt, "It is common sense to take a method and try it: If it fails, admit it frankly and try another. But above all, try something."[13]

PARTING THOUGHTS

There is momentum building within the museum sector as institutions adapt to meet changing customer expectations. As the bright spots featured in this book demonstrate, the path to audience engagement involves an outside-in focus, a proactive approach to meeting audiences where they are, and the courage to ask, What If?

This book is a beginning. Studies to understand member motivations are under way, MVPs and new membership models are being tested, and cross-organizational working sessions on design thinking and the lean startup methodology are in progress.

As I write these final words, I find myself more energized now than when I began by the immense potential we have to advance the field of membership. I am inspired by the promise of innovation in membership to create a positive impact on our museums and the communities they serve, and I hope you are too.

I set out writing this book to start a dialogue. I invite you to join a growing community of choice architects and share your story at membershipinnovation.com. Let's keep the conversation going. Here's to making the future!

NOTES

1. "Grace Murray Hopper Name of Yale Undergraduate College," Graduate School of Arts and Sciences, Yale University, accessed September 28, 2019, https:// gsas.yale.edu/grace-murray-hopper.

2. Vijay Govindarajan and Chris Trimble, *The Other Side of Innovation: Solving the Execution Challenge* (Boston, MA: Harvard Business School Publishing, 2010), 10.

3. Michael Schrage and David Kiron, "Leading with Next-Generation Key Performance Indicators," *MITSloan Management Review*, June 26, 2018, https://sloan review.mit.edu/projects/leading-with-next-generation-key-performance-indicators/.

4. Eric Ries, *The Lean Startup* (New York: Crown Business, 2011), 75.

5. Alex Barinka, "Dropbox Tops Private Valuation as Shares Soar in Market Debut," *Bloomberg*, updated on March 23, 2018, https://www.bloomberg.com/news/arti cles/2018-03-22/dropbox-could-prove-to-its-peers-a-down-round-is-nothing-to-fear.

6. Trefis Team, "Dropbox Is Doing Well, But Looks Rich in the Face of Industry Headwinds," *Forbes*, May 21, 2018, https://www.forbes.com/sites/greatspecu lations/2018/05/21/dropbox-is-doing-well-but-looks-rich-in-the-face-of-industry -headwinds/#49f17f3036ed.

7. Eric Ries, "How Dropbox Started as a Minimal Viable Product," *TechCrunch*, October 19, 2011, https://techcrunch.com/2011/10/19/dropbox-minimal-viable -product/.

8. Sean Wise, "Want to Build a Billion-Dollar Business? Learn These Lessons from Dropbox," *Inc.*, March 27, 2018, https://www.inc.com/sean-wise/how-to-make -20b-in-10-years.html.

9. Michel Gelobter, *Lean Startups for Social Change: The Revolutionary Path to Big Impact* (Oakland, CA: Berrett-Koehler Publishers), 26.

10. Gary P. Pisano, *Creative Construction: The DNA of Sustained Innovation* (New York: Hachette Book Group, 2019), 16.

11. Govindarajan and Trimble, *The Other Side of Innovation*, 58.

12. Macy Bayern, "The Death of Innovation: 58% of US Workers Too Overwhelmed with Daily Tasks," *TechRepublic*, September 17, 2018, https://www.techre public.com/article/the-death-of-innovation-58-of-us-workers-too-overwhelmed -with-daily-tasks/.

13. Franklin D. Roosevelt, "Oglethorpe University Address," The New Deal Franklin D. Roosevelt Speeches, Pepperdine University, accessed September 28, 2019, https://publicpolicy.pepperdine.edu/academics/research/faculty-research/new -deal/roosevelt-speeches/fr052232.htm.

Index

Note: Page references in *italics* refer to figures.

National Center for Arts Research
(NCAR), xxiv, 5
National Endowment for the Arts
(NEA), 3–4, 12–13, 153
National Oceanic and Atmospheric
Administration (NOAA), 149n2
National Portrait Gallery, 6–7
National Public Radio, 128
needs analysis and fulfillment, 151–154
"negative substitution" effect, 4
NerdWallet, 108
Netflix, xv–xvi
net promoter score (NPS), 161
Newfields (Indianapolis Museum of
Art), 40–45, *42, 44*
new product lines, 111
new-to-the-world products, 110
nonprofit cultural organizations,
awareness of, 139
nudges
choice architecture for, 59–61
ethics of, 76

O
"Octopus Initiative" (Museum of
Contemporary Art Denver), 129
Ohno, Taiichi, 145–147
one-for-one business model, 95–97, *96*
Osterwalder, Alexander, 182
Other Side of Innovation, The
(Govindarajan and Trimble), 204
Owens, Sarah, 51–53
owners and ownership
endowment effect, 61–69, *67*
ownership shift, 26
Oxford University, 50

P
pain of paying, *123,* 123–125, *125*
paradox of choice, 71–73
Patagonia, 88–89
pay-what-you-wish (PWYW) pricing
structure, 190
Pension Protection Act of 2006, 70
Performance Engine, 204–205, 218–219

persona, 163–164
philanthropy
buy-to-give concept, 95–97, *97*
disconnect of loyalty, philanthropy,
and, 23
membership *vs.,* 82, *90,* 90–95, *93,*
104n19
member's motivation to join and,
97–98
See also donors and donations
Pinacoteca di Brera, 22
pivotal generation, demographic trends
and, 11–13
Pixar, 60
place (4 Ps), 108–110, *109,* 131n9
"Plan Ahead Pricing" (Children's
Museum of Indianapolis), 120–
122, *121*
Polaine, Andy, 193
positioning, of products, 113, *113*
Predictions (Forrester), 193
Prego (Campbell Soup), 29–30
prescriptions, 88
present bias, 143–144
Prestegaard, Kristin, 189, 190
price
4 Ps (product, place, price,
promotion), defined, 108–110,
109, 131n9
lower-priced products, 111
pay-what-you-wish (PWYW) pricing
structure, 190
pricing psychology, 117–130
admissions models and, 119–122,
121
anchors for, 122–123
applying strategy for, 117
free concept for, 127–128, 129–130
market value method, actual cost
method, and program cost method
for, 117–118
pain of paying and, *123,* 123–125,
125
quality perception and, 125–127
subscription programs, 128–129

About the Author

Science that sparks curiosity, art that broadens perspectives, zoos and gardens that bring joy, and history that provides a deeper context for how the world works—these are the experiences that compelled Rosie Siemer to focus her life's work on museums.

In 2009, her passion for nonprofit marketing inspired her to launch FIVESEED, a research and strategy partner to arts, culture, and conservation organizations worldwide. Under Rosie's leadership, FIVESEED has guided dozens of museums in the development and execution of data-informed strategies that deepen audience engagement and build long-term financial sustainability. She has provided consulting services to a number of internationally respected cultural organizations, including the Louvre Abu Dhabi, Museum of Science Boston, Saint Louis Art Museum, Desert Botanical Garden, Space Center Houston, Smithsonian's National Zoo, History Colorado, Mt. Cuba Center, and the Murphy Arts District.

Sharing her expertise to help museums thrive, Rosie frequently facilitates workshops on audience development and speaks on the topics of building empathy, choice architecture, and the future of membership. She also enjoys sharing her time with professional, cultural, and community organizations and has served on a number of boards, including the Denver Police Museum, World Trade Center Denver, and the American Marketing Association. Rosie is a graduate of Metropolitan State University of Denver where she earned dual degrees in Marketing and Business Management.

Museum Membership Innovation: Unlocking Ideas for Audience Engagement and Sustainable Revenue is the culmination of nearly a decade of research and field experience. Rosie also co-authored a comprehensive resource guide for cultural membership professionals, *Membership Marketing in the Digital Age*. She has visited more than 90 museums in 12 countries (and counting!)—many of them on her own time and her own dime—for the sheer enjoyment of it. When she's not researching, writing, or museum hopping, Rosie enjoys Scotch-tasting and watching sci-fi movies.